By describing the historical and social framework within which these schools developed during the last fifty years, the author contributes towards an understanding of the way in which modern ideas in education are emerging in London and in the country as a whole.

This is a book that will appeal to the perplexed parent who wants to do the best for his child, as well as to the professional educationist.

Member of a well-known Irish literary family, Dr. Flann Campbell was educated at Trinity College, Dublin, where he took an honours degree in economics. Later, he studied under Professor David Glass at the London School of Economics and Political Science, and received a Doctorate of Sociology in 1953.

Dr. Campbell has had more than ten years' varied teaching experience in private preparatory and grammar schools, college of commerce, and evening institute. He is at present teaching economics in a large comprehensive school in London, and also lecturing in sociology for both the Extra-Mural Department and the Institute of Education of the University of London.

Dr. Campbell's main interests lie in educational _____ field of study neglect___ that he believes is n___ to take its proper pla___ education. He is a f___ tributor to the specia___ topical educational problems.

ELEVEN-PLUS
AND ALL THAT

THE GRAMMAR SCHOOL
IN A CHANGING SOCIETY

Flann Campbell M.A., Ph.D.

C.A. WATTS & Co
40 Drury Lane London W.C.2

First published in 1956
by C. A. Watts and Company, Limited
40 Drury Lane, London W.C.2
Printed in Great Britain
in Times New Roman
by The Alcuin Press
Welwyn Garden City
Herts

TO MY WIFE

Contents

Acknowledgments

THE writer wishes to acknowledge the large number of individuals and organizations who have assisted in various ways with the preparation of this book.

Thanks are due first to the Education Committee and Education Officer of the London County Council, who gave the writer a term's leave of absence from his teaching duties to enable him to complete his research; and secondly to the Leverhulme Grants Committee and the Central Grants Committee of the University of London, who gave financial aid. The London County Council has kindly given permission to quote from a number of official documents. However, it must be understood that the opinions expressed in this book are the writer's, and that the Council does not accept responsibility for them.

This book is a substantially revised version of a thesis, "The Changing Environment of the London Grammar School 1900–1950", for which the author was awarded the degree of Ph.D. in the University of London in 1953.

Acknowledgments are also made to past (and in some cases, present) headmasters of Holloway, Highbury, Owen's, and William Ellis Schools; to the headmistresses of North London Collegiate, Highbury Hill, and Mary Datchelor Schools; to the former L.C.C. District Education Officers for Islington, Miss G. Davis and Dr. Copley; to Miss C. Avent of the L.C.C. Youth Employment Service; to the Secretaries of the Incorporated Association of Headmasters and the Girls' Public Day Schools Trust; and to the Librarians of the L.C.C., National Union of Teachers, and Finsbury Public Libraries, for their cooperation and assistance.

The writer would like to express his thanks to the following authors, publishers, and editors who have kindly accorded him permission to include excerpts from their works: Dr. Cyril Bibby, Professor Cyril Burt, Mrs. Jean Floud, Professor D. V. Glass, and Miss Lynda Grier; George G. Harrap and Company Limited, Macmillan and Company Limited, The Oxford University Press, and Routledge and Kegan Paul Limited; and the Editors of *The New Statesman and Nation* and *The Times Educational Supplement*.

Acknowledgments

The writing of this work owes much to Mr. H. L. Beales of the London School of Economics and Political Science, who first encouraged the writer to begin his research into the history of the London grammar schools, and to Professor D. V. Glass, also of L.S.E., who at every stage gave invaluable help and advice. Lastly, a special debt of gratitude is owed to the staff and boys of Holloway School, who have taught the writer more, perhaps, than they realized.

In a work of this kind, covering a wide historical field and containing much statistical material collected together for the first time, it is possible that there will be some factual mistakes. If any such inaccuracies exist, the writer apologizes for them in advance, and hopes that they will be pointed out to him.

Introduction

LONDON provides an immensely rich field for the educational sociologist to explore. There have been large movements of population and changes in class-structure during the last fifty years. Within a comparatively small area it is possible to find wide differences in social status, housing conditions, cultural background, political and religious beliefs. Town-planning and other problems relating to building sites, playing space, and transport of pupils are of special importance in such a large urban area where land is scarce and expensive. There is a wide variety of occupational choice available for school-leavers in industrial as well as Government, commercial, and other "white-collar" jobs. London, as the capital city, naturally provides a wider range of leisure-time facilities than are normally found in provincial towns. Politically, the London County Council offers the unusual spectacle of having been for over twenty years continuously controlled by the Labour Party with a large majority; this Council spends over £30,000,000 annually on education, which is more than the national education budget of some governments.

There are large numbers of secondary schools—some old-established foundations dating back to Elizabethan times, others comparatively modern schools maintained by the Council. Several famous and flourishing public schools, firmly established and financially secure, are situated within the County boundary, in contrast to the numerous smaller private schools, which are squeezed remorselessly by rising costs and falling revenues. There are unreorganized elementary schools containing pupils of all ages from five to fifteen, modern secondary schools, central schools, and technical schools in great variety and profusion. Indeed, there is a richness and complexity of social life, combined with a diversity of educational organization, that is perhaps unrivalled in any other part of Britain.

The seventy-nine grammar schools controlled by the London County Council are of special interest in this connection, not only because they offer a particularly illuminating example of the interplay of social and educational ideas, but also because they have reached a turning point in their history. The year 1954 marked the tenth anniversary of

Introduction

the 1944 Education Act, and the fiftieth anniversary of the taking over by the Council of the endowed grammar schools in London. It also marked the beginning of large-scale experiments with comprehensive high schools, which are intended ultimately to replace the present tripartite system of grammar, modern, and technical schools. The mid-twentieth century, in fact, records the end of one important era and the beginning of another in the story of London secondary education.

London County Council Achievements

The London County Council in many respects can look back with pride and satisfaction on its grammar school achievements during the last fifty years. It has opened twenty-seven new maintained schools, and given substantial financial aid to fifty-two old ones, enabling the latter to improve their amenities in a way that would have been impossible solely through the medium of charity or private enterprise. It has increased the number of grammar-school places from under 15,000 to over 35,000 and provided many fine new buildings and playing fields. Tens of thousands of working-class boys and girls, who might otherwise have been forced to leave school at fourteen or fifteen, have been enabled by means of scholarships to have a good secondary schooling, and in many cases to go on to a university. Every year between the two World Wars, the London County Council spent an average of nearly one million pounds on its grammar schools, with the result that they had a reputation in staffing, teaching, and examination results that was among the best in the country.

During the last ten or fifteen years, however, the difficulties confronting the schools, which were already accumulating before the Second World War, have become more acute. In the first instance, the problem of selection has not been solved. It had been hoped by the pioneers of school reform that once the scholarship scheme was sufficiently developed the question of selection would prove comparatively simple. It was expected that all fees would ultimately be abolished, and that entry to the grammar schools would be determined solely on intellectual merit. An aristocracy of talent would replace an aristocracy of birth and money. By claiming that innate, as distinct from acquired, mental ability could be measured by intelligence tests some psychologists implied that it would be possible to devise scientifically accurate and reliable methods of selection for the different types of secondary school.

Experience, however, has proved these hopes to be false. On general philosophical and social grounds, there have emerged strong objections to the attempts made to divide the child population at an early age into "successes" and "failures", those who have passed the common entrance examination, and those who have not. On practical grounds it has been made clear by the psychologists themselves that intelligence tests—while proving an expedient diagnostic device for administrators —do not, in fact, measure inborn intelligence. Experiments have shown that I.Qs. may be varied by deliberate coaching by as much as ten or fifteen points, thus casting even further doubt on their validity as an accurate measuring-rod of mental ability.

Moreover, the child population of London has fluctuated so seriously during the last two or three decades as to throw doubt upon the claims that were made about the scientific basis of the actual selection of the "grammar-school type". In theory, intelligent children for whom advanced academic work is considered most suitable comprise only a small and fairly stable proportion of the total child population. In practice, the percentage of eleven-year-olds chosen for grammar schools varies widely from place to place, and from time to time. London, for example, accepted proportionately nearly three times as many boys and girls of the age-group eleven to fifteen years into its grammar schools in 1945 as it did in 1930.

Secondly, under the tripartite system of secondary education the curriculum has proved peculiarly inflexible and unadaptable to modern needs. The bookish, academic syllabus, which was so characteristic of grammar schools in the nineteenth century, has not been greatly modified, although many more pupils are now admitted to the grammar schools. The requirements of the General Certificate of Education and of university entrance examinations continue to dominate the time-table, in spite of the fact that at least one-third of all entrants never sit for (or alternatively fail) the Certificate examination, and only about one in twenty go on to the universities. Technical education has made practically no headway in these schools, although industrialists emphasize the vital importance of the technologist and applied scientist in the nation's economy.

Thirdly, a disturbingly large number of pupils continues to leave school before reaching the age of sixteen years, thus hindering the development of the grammar-school course, which has been designed with a five- or seven-year syllabus in view. This premature leaving results in a waste of public money, frustration of teachers, and the disillusionment of the pupils themselves. Furthermore, even among those pupils who stay at school until their course is completed too large a proportion flock into the "white-collar" and minor professional occupations, although from the point of view of the country as a whole, as well as of the pupils themselves, they might be better suited in manual or technical jobs.

Lastly, the schools are affected to a special degree by their predominantly urban and working-class environment. All grammar schools in big cities have to face this problem, but those in London particularly, because of its immense size and the special nature of its population movements, have been affected more than most. Commerce and industry have continued to spread in the central area. The population as a whole has fallen considerably, and because of the migration of the middle classes to the suburbs it has also become more markedly working class in social composition. The violent fluctuations in child population have created many problems in staffing and accommodation, and the exceptionally high cost of land and lack of space for building and playing fields have made it very difficult to find suitable sites for new schools.

Sociological Factors in Education

The approach to education in this survey is historical and sociological rather than psychological, not because the latter aspect is considered unimportant, but because, in the writer's opinion, the environmental factors have been too long neglected in the study of English education.[1] During the last forty or fifty years there has been a large

---

[1] Published material relating to the sociology of education is not very extensive in Britain. Reference is made in later footnotes to various sources from which information relating to sociological factors in education may be obtained. Apart from these references, useful data concerning secondary schools in London may be found in the following:

"A Sociological Study of a Grammar School in a Working-class Community", by Morven S. Brown, Ph.D. thesis. (London Univ., 1950.)

"The Influence of the Socio-cultural Environment upon the Educational Progress of Children at the Secondary School Level", by W. J. Campbell, Ph.D. thesis. (London Univ., 1951.)

"The Views of Adolescents on some Aspects of the Social Class Structure", by H. T. Himmelweit, A. H. Halsey, and A. N. Oppenheim. (*The British Journal of Sociology*, Vol. III, No. 2, June 1952.)

"Selection for Secondary Education and Achievement in Four Grammar Schools", by A. H. Halsey and L. Gardner. (*The British Journal of Sociology*, Vol. IV, No. 1, March, 1953.)

amount of time and money devoted to the problems of educational psychology and the study of individual children. Considerable advances have been made in teaching methods and examination techniques, and a great deal learnt about processes of mental development.

The sociology of education, on the other hand, is a subject that in this country is still in its most elementary stages. The number of students studying sociology in training colleges and university education departments is very small, and very little fundamental research has so far been done on the relation of schools to their social environment. Yet, in a world in which vast changes are occurring in national and international relationships, social structure, technology, family life, religious beliefs, and opportunities for leisure and entertainment, it is becoming increasingly clear that the study of education must be broadened to embrace many more aspects of life than were formerly regarded by traditional educationists as strictly relevant. Social and economic influences press ever more powerfully upon our schools, moulding and shaping them in so many important and significant ways, that any attempt to ignore them must inevitably lead to mistakes in educational theory as well as to stagnation in practice. In London especially it is impossible to understand the current controversy about the comprehensive high school without an appreciation of the various historical and social trends affecting secondary schools during the last two or three generations.

No attempt is made in this book to try to describe the possible changes that may have occurred in the intelligence of London children. The exclusion of this most controversial aspect of education is deliberate: first, on the practical grounds that the data available is not sufficient in quantity to enable firm conclusions to be drawn from it, and secondly because, in the writer's view, it is doubtful whether the measurement of "intelligence" can ever become an exact science. The old issue between Nature and Nurture has not been resolved, and is not likely to be resolved for a long time. It is necessary only to study the history of intelligence testing over the last forty years and the many changes in authoritative opinion that have occurred, to see what errors have been made, and to realize what a barren and fruitless task has been the search for pure intelligence as distinct from acquired ability. A further discussion of this most tantalizing topic (aptly described by an American writer as "an Elysian field for the tired mind in a dogmatic mood"), with particular regard to the way in which official opinion has altered under the pressure of events, is given in the chapter on Scholarships.

On the other hand, in contrast to the lack of precise information about the way in which innate intelligence is distributed among different social classes, occupational groups, or geographical areas, there is a good deal of convincing data available showing the relationship existing between environment and *achievement* at school. Teachers have long known of the influence of "good" and "bad" homes upon the progress of their pupils, and what this day-to-day experience has taught them is amply confirmed by many other sources. For instance, if the history of the Junior County Scholarship examination is studied over a long period it will be found that the more prosperous London boroughs won proportionately at least five times as many awards as the poorer boroughs. Similarly, the school-leaving age, which directly affects such matters as the Certificate examination results and university entry, is closely related to economic conditions in the local school catchment-area. Standards of entry to the grammar schools are affected by changes in the birth-rate; pupils' attitude to work is influenced by living conditions at home; willingness to stay at school beyond the statutory leaving age is partly determined by the state of the juvenile employment market; opportunity to remain in the sixth form may be largely conditioned by the size of parental income, and so forth.

Whether in the last resort success at school depends mainly upon heredity or environment we have no means (at least, so far) of deciding. Indeed, it would seem a waste of effort, in our present state of knowledge, to spend too much time arguing as to the precise importance of one or the other factor. The fact remains—and even the most extreme partisan of the importance of genetic factors will hardly deny it—that environmental conditions are of the greatest significance in determining the rate of children's progress, not only in intellectual matters, but also in moral standards and emotional stability.

It is one of the main purposes of this book to give an account of some of these environmental conditions, and by so doing to throw fresh light on contemporary problems facing the London grammar schools. By describing the historical and social framework in which these schools developed during the last fifty years it is hoped that certain vexed questions of secondary-school organization and psychology may be seen in their proper perspective.

Are London's Educational Problems Unique?

The question naturally arises whether the special attributes of London —its vast size, its varied social developments, its ancient grammar schools, its Labour-controlled Council, and so forth—do not mean that its secondary-school[1] problems are unique; that we cannot, in fact, generalize from the lessons of London's educational history. It is true that the experience of the London grammar schools cannot be exactly paralleled in other parts of the country, just as it is clear that each region of Britain has its own special local problems in education. A small rural grammar school, for instance, situated in a predominantly farming area and accepting 10 per cent. of the local eleven-year-olds is not faced with exactly the same difficulties as a large school situated in an industrial area and taking 30 per cent. of the secondary age-group. A socially and academically highly selective grammar school in a well-to-do residential area of, for example, Surrey, is confronted with a somewhat different situation from that facing a grammar school full of working-class pupils in the East End of London.

Nevertheless, it would appear that the great majority of aided and maintained grammar schools (the direct-grant schools being in rather a different category) are affected by much the same kinds of problem in England and Wales. Broadly similar political, social, and technological developments in recent years have raised issues with which all grammar schools, irrespective of their traditions, size, or locality, are faced—among the most pressing being stricter Ministry and local authority control, the abolition of fees, an increased number of working-class entrants, the undesirably large percentage of premature leavers and failures in Certificate examinations, the need for more technical facilities for pupils entering industry, and the demand for closer liaison with other types of secondary school. London may be exceptional, and its environmental conditions unusual, but its educational problems are not very different in kind—even if larger in scale—from those of any other large urban area in this country.

---

[1] The reader is advised to be clear as to the nomenclature used in this book. The word "secondary" is used in its pre-1944 sense—it applies to grammar and independent, but not to central or modern secondary, schools. Similarly, when the word "London" is used without qualification, it applies to the County of London.

I grant much of your meaning herein as needful in a commonwealth; but yet utterly to exclude the ploughman's son, and the poor man's son from the benefits of learning . . . is as much to say, as that Almighty God should not be at liberty to bestow His great gifts of grace upon any person, nor nowhere else, but as we and other men shall appoint them to be employed, according to our fancy and not according to His most Godly Will and pleasure, Who giveth His gifts both of learning, and other perfections in all sciences, unto all kinds and states of people indifferently . . . wherefore, if the gentleman's son be apt of learning, let him be admitted; if not apt, let the poor man's child that is apt, enter his room.

Archbishop Cranmer, 1541

Chapter 1

LONDON GRAMMAR SCHOOLS, 1904–10

... the great majority of the boys attending the secondary schools of London are of the middle and lower middle class, with a fringe of sons of professional men, and (in endowed schools) a sprinkling of the children of working men.—Charles Booth[1]

By the latter half of the nineteenth century new social needs were demanding a better-educated working and lower middle class. The elementary schools were not sufficient to supply the educational demands of industry. Many old fee-paying grammar schools were modernized to provide expanding demand for black-coated workers.—Henry Hamilton[2]

SECONDARY education was in a stage of transition when the London County Council took over responsibility for the London grammar schools in 1904. Powerful new forces were gathering beneath the apparently placid surface of Edwardian society to shake the centuries-old structure of the grammar schools, as of other ancient institutions. Britain no longer had a monopoly of the world's manufacture and commerce, and there was a lack of skilled technicians and administrators able to hold their own with the highly trained products of the German schools. The working class were beginning to feel their strength, and were not as a matter of course content to be debarred from the privileges of secondary schooling. Women were insisting on admission to professional life as an alternative to perpetual housework and motherhood. Politically, the period was marked by the foundation of the Labour Party and the growing power of the trade unions. Economically, it was the end of full-blooded *laisser-faire* capitalism and the beginning of that moderate degree of Government control that is called the Welfare State.

[1] *Life and Labour of the People in London,* by Charles Booth, Vol. III, p. 261 (Macmillan, 1904).
[2] *History of the Homeland,* by Henry Hamilton, p. 537 (Allen and Unwin, 1947).

1

Several outstanding individuals took part in the movement for reform. Fabians such as Sidney Webb and Graham Wallas agitated in the London County Council for an extension of the scholarship system. Far-sighted administrators such as Morant and Sadler, perceiving that the old financial base of the grammar schools was crumbling, that the existing secondary system was undemocratic, and that curricula were often narrow and biased, advocated State intervention on a substantial scale. Organizationally, they wanted a system that would preserve what was best in the traditional schools, while at the same time introducing new sources of income and a wider range of pupils; so far as curricula were concerned, they looked for subjects that would meet the needs of the rapidly increasing body of "white-collar" and professional workers. In London there were other factors that made for stress and strain, particularly the changes in the size and class-structure of the population as the birth-rate began to fall and the middle class moved into the suburbs.

The various types of secondary school reacted in different ways to the new social and educational trends. The London public schools, such as St. Paul's, Merchant Taylors', and Mercers', being secure in their finances and prestige, were not much affected by the movements for reform. Their pupils being mostly children of the rich, they needed no financial assistance from the State and were not prepared to sacrifice their independence. Moreover, they had no doubts about their function in society of creating an educational and social *élite*. Traditionally, they considered it to be their duty to train people for leadership in the Church, law, medicine, Army, Civil Service, industry, and commerce. Subsequent economic and political developments have not fundamentally changed that role. The teaching of English and foreign languages (particularly the classics) and some mathematics, encouragement of corporate (or team) spirit, and the inculcation of such moral standards and manners as befit an English gentleman were their dedicated mission, and neither their most ardent supporters nor their most bitter opponents would have denied this. Stability of social status, and consequently a firm belief in the correctness of their policy, were among their most marked characteristics. The only social change to which they appeared susceptible at this time was that of the gradual encroachment of London's population upon their buildings; and as the city spread, they moved away to new sites where the vulgar influences of commerce or slums would not contaminate them.

But the lesser endowed schools, which were to become the backbone of the future State-aided grammar-school system in London, were in a less happy position. Many of them were old established with venerable customs and traditions, but towards the end of the nineteenth century it was already apparent that they must change radically and quickly if they were to survive. The new economic and political pressures were undermining their social basis, and compelling a re-examination of old ideas and values.

Even before the end of Queen Victoria's reign they had been forced by financial pressure to introduce more science teaching and to take more scholarship pupils. As expenditure increased owing to higher salaries for teachers and improved buildings and equipment required by the Board of Education, so they had to look around for new sources of income. But more important than the financial question, urgent though it was, were the new vocational demands being made by society upon the endowed and proprietary schools. For generations these schools had jogged along more or less successfully carrying out their accepted function of providing a liberal education for the sons (and to a lesser extent, daughters) of shopkeepers, small businessmen, lesser professional people, and other members of the middle and lower middle classes. In the 1880s and 1890s they had been persuaded to increase science teaching to meet the growing demands of industry. However, under the new dispensation envisaged in the 1902 Education Act they were required to educate a vastly increased number of children, from poor as well as more prosperous homes, for a greatly expanded range of occupations. Their now more clearly defined function was to train boys and girls to take their place in that rapidly growing body of "white-collar" workers that would be intermediate between the upper class for whom the public schools catered, and the working class for whom elementary education was considered sufficient.

It was perceived by more far-sighted educationists such as Morant and Webb that private enterprise combined with charity, which had been the old basis of secondary education, was inadequate to carry out this task, and therefore the State had to step in. Twenty years previously, Matthew Arnold, in one of his most brilliant excursions into the relation of education to society, had pointed out how necessary it was for the State to provide secondary schools as they had provided elementary schools. "What is really needed is to follow the precedent of the Elementary Education Act, by requiring the provision throughout the country of a proper supply of secondary schools; with proper buildings and accommodations, at a proper fee, and with proper guarantees given by the teachers either of a university degree or of a special certificate for secondary instruction", he wrote.[1]

But despite the ideas of Arnold and other reformers, little was done by the State during the last quarter of the nineteenth century to reform the secondary schools, except for the reorganization of certain charitable foundations and the encouragement of science teaching. *Laisser-faire* ideas remained strong, and for the Government to intervene was considered new and revolutionary. As late as 1908–9 Morant wrote:

> That the State has any concern with secondary education is a comparatively modern idea in England. Since the date of the great educational foundations of the sixteenth century it was left pretty much to private effort and the operation of the law of supply and demand until a generation ago. Even now it has not attained to a sufficient degree of organization, though immense progress has been made in this direction in the last seven years . . . the term "secondary" has been left in the air; and this is a sort of symbol of the way in which secondary education itself was long neglected . . . This isolation and consequent neglect of secondary education over so long a period is at the root of the difficulties which have had to be faced in the last few years in all grades of education in England.[2]

Problems Facing the London County Council

Broadly speaking, there were three main difficulties confronting the London County Council when it drew up plans for reorganizing the grammar schools in the ten years before the First World War.

First, there was the question of the total number of children for whom secondary-school accommodation should be provided. This was a straightforward enough problem in so far as it involved a study of the birth-rate and population trends (much useful experience in this connection had been gained by the old London School Board, which, at the time of its demise, had nearly 1,000 elementary schools, with approximately 750,000 children under its control); but it was complicated by the fact that, whereas the elementary schools were comprehensive, the secondary schools were selective in their choice of pupils. It was comparatively simple for the Council to decide that more places were

[1] *Mixed Essays*, by Matthew Arnold, p. 172 (Smith Elder and Co., 1903).
[2] Report of Board of Education, pp. 31–32, 1908–9.

needed in girls' schools, and that the provision of grammar-school places was very unevenly distributed between the different metropolitan boroughs, but it was far more difficult for the Council to make up its mind as to what proportion of the child population should ultimately stay at school beyond the elementary stage.

The second problem, which arose out of the first, concerned the basis on which selection should be made. Children had mainly been chosen for grammar schools on their ability to pay fees, and to a lesser extent on their ability to win scholarships. Thus, the question of social class was deeply involved, for the grammar schools had grown up chiefly as middle-class institutions dependent upon fee-paying pupils and accustomed to think in middle-class terms. This concept of the middle-class nature of the grammar school meant that the Council could not plan its selection methods purely on the basis of intellectual merit—it had to take social factors into account as well. Hence, neighbourhoods scheduled for the expansion of grammar-school places had to be studied carefully in terms of relative wealth or poverty, the number of local inhabitants engaged in professional or industrial occupations, and other economic aspects. One borough might have two or three times as many children of secondary-school age living within its boundaries as that of a neighbouring borough, but its grammar-school needs might not be considered so great because of its relative poverty, overcrowding, or high proportion of unskilled inhabitants. The development of a centrally organized and large-scale system of scholarships was, of course, an important aspect of this social question.

The third problem was that of administration, involving the co-ordination and integration of schools that had previously been independent of State control or semi-autonomous, and the introduction of new methods for granting financial aid to such schools.

Child Population and Secondary-School Accommodation

The number of children for whom secondary education should be provided was the most intractable problem facing the authorities, and in fact it has continued to vex the Council up to the present day. The difficulty of deciding what percentage of children should stay at school after the age of eleven or twelve was further complicated by the continuous fluctuation of the child population.

The population of London had grown rapidly in the nineteenth century from 959,310 in 1801, to 4,536,267 in 1901. This fivefold increase was due to the decrease in the death-rate, and the consistently high birth-rate, which reached a peak of nearly 37 per 1,000 in 1867, and began to fall slowly only in the mid-1870s.[1] The death-rate, which had risen to the exceptionally high figure of over 30 per 1,000 in the cholera epidemic of 1849, began to fall fairly steadily from the mid-1860s, influenced by many of the new medical discoveries and the sanitary reforms of men like Edwin Chadwick. In the sixty-odd years between 1841 and 1904 it averaged 22.2 per 1,000, and by the 1890s it had dropped to just under 20 per 1,000.

The increase in population was not spread evenly over the whole of the County of London. As early as 1861 the peak was reached in the central area comprising the City, Westminster, St. Marylebone, Holborn, Finsbury, Shoreditch, Bethnal Green, Stepney, Southwark, Bermondsey, Lambeth (north of Kennington Lane), St. Pancras (south of Euston Road); but the outer boroughs continued to grow until London as a whole reached its maximum between 1901 and 1911. The density of population varied greatly from borough to borough, with thickly concentrated areas of population and bad overcrowding mainly in the old-established centre and east centre, and with wider dispersion and less overcrowding nearer the County boundaries. For example, Lewisham and Wandsworth to the south of the river, and Hampstead to the north, had a population density less than half that of the east central boroughs of Finsbury and Shoreditch in Edwardian times.

During the nineteenth century, because of the continually growing population and consistently high birth-rate, there were ever increasing numbers of children to be educated.

In 1870, when the London School Board assumed responsibility for elementary education, there were approximately 112,000 children born each year in London (incidentally, about one in six of these died before reaching one year of age). Thirty years later the average number of children born was approximately 130,000 annually. There were about 750,000 children enrolled at the Board's schools, mainly aged 5–12, but including some in 3–5 and 12–14 age-groups. In 1901, there were 504,072 children aged 10–15 (roughly speaking, the secondary age-group) living in London.

The poorer boroughs, despite a higher infantile death-rate, contained considerably more children per head of adult population than the richer districts. There was also a slight excess of girls over boys in all age-

[1] The mean birth-rate was 32·9 per 1,000 between 1851 and 1904.

6

groups above the age of six (more boys were born than girls but they tended to die earlier in infancy). These factors had to be considered when new school-building was contemplated.

Secondary-School Accommodation, 1904–10

To meet the needs of the half million children of secondary-school age who were living in London at the beginning of this century there were about eighty schools, with accommodation for approximately 25,000 children.

It is not possible to give more precise figures for this period because of the lack of accurate statistics, and the meagre nature of official sources. The total number of secondary schools, their names, finances, and number of pupils, were not recorded in systematic form by the London County Council or the Board of Education until 1909—the explanation of this lack of information being that the old London School Board's sole concern was with elementary education, and the Council's responsibility for secondary schools dated only from 1904. Another cause of confusion was that it was often difficult to discover the exact status of a school; or, if the status was known, then the terminology for describing it was obscure and liable to variation. Thus it was frequently difficult to distinguish between "public" and "private" schools, and it was sometimes the case that schools classified as "secondary" contained a large proportion—occasionally more than half—of children under eleven years of age. The biggest gap in our knowledge is about the private schools, which numbered several hundreds in Edwardian times, but about which very little is known.

However, sufficient suitable and reliable data are available in Charles Booth's sociological survey of London in 1890, in special memoranda prepared by Sidney Webb, and in the Minutes, Annual Reports, London Statistics, and other official London County Council documents, to make it possible to reconstruct a reasonably clear picture of London secondary education at the beginning of this century.

Charles Booth reckoned that in 1890 there were in London between sixty and seventy secondary schools more or less public in character, with approximately 22,000 pupils in attendance.[1] A similar estimate was made by Llewellyn Smith in his special survey of London technical

---

[1] *Life and Labour of the People in London,* by Charles Booth, pp. 247–306, First series, "Poverty" (3), (Macmillan, 1904).

education in 1892.[1] In his report, Smith listed thirty-nine boys' schools with a total attendance of 11,118, and thirty-two girls' schools with an attendance of 7,579; but this list excluded the Roman Catholic schools and also several important schools that did not come within his definition of "publicly controlled". Eleven years later, Sidney Webb wrote:

> London has to-day certainly no less than 25,000 boys and girls between seven and nineteen in its secondary schools. . . . The publicly managed schools number no fewer than eighty-five, well dispersed over the whole county.[2]

A year after the London County Council took responsibility for secondary-school education, Webb had to admit, however, that the authorities were still in the dark as to exactly how many secondary-school places existed in London. He wrote:

> No complete survey or examination has ever been made of the London secondary schools. The Technical Education Board regularly inspected those aided by the Council, and for these (unfortunately little more than half) complete statistical information is in our possession. Those in receipt of Government grants are inspected by the Board of Education, which has from time to time allowed access to its reports: but these schools are, in the main, those aided by the Council. Neither the Board of Education, nor the Council has any authority to inspect the rest, except by invitation of the governing body in each case; but in connection with the Council's scholars and otherwise much information has been obtained concerning nearly all of them, which cannot be presented in statistical form. . . . Without counting the higher elementary, or higher grade departments of the public elementary schools on the one hand, or the pupil teacher centres on the other, the eighty-eight secondary schools which are regarded as public in character, to which the Council's scholars are sent, have accommodation for 30,000 scholars . . . no statistics exist as to (a) the extent to which these schools are used by boys and girls resident outside London; (b) the far greater extent to which London boys and girls are sent away from London for their schooling; and (c) the total number and accommodation of the private venture schools within the County, or the number of their scholars.

[1] Report to the Special Committee on Technical Education for the L.C.C., by H. Llewellyn Smith, pp. 169–170, 1892.
[2] *London Education*, by Sidney Webb, pp. 28–9, 1903.

In addition to these 88 schools there are a score of others (such as Queen's College, Harley Street; the King Alfred School, Hampstead; and various Roman Catholic girls' schools) which are apparently equally public in character, but as they have never applied for aid, and do not publish statistics, no information about them is at present available.[1]

The first comprehensive survey of secondary-school accommodation in London was made by the Council in 1909, by which time it had opened nineteen maintained grammar schools in different parts of London.[2]

The survey stated the conclusion that there were secondary-school places for 43,984 children, or 9·35 per 1,000 of the population. However, these figures included 8,995 places at private schools. The latter figure (which was admittedly incomplete as the total number of places in private schools was estimated at between 20,000 and 30,000), included 58 per cent. of children under twelve years of age. A better over-all figure was that of 30,543 in attendance at 108 schools of a "public or semi-public" character. Out of this 30,543, no figures were given for those under eleven years of age, but judging by the 1905 figures these probably amounted to 12 to 15 per cent.[3] Included in the total were approximately 3,500 attending such famous public schools as St. Paul's, Westminster, Merchant Taylors', and the City of London. Nearly 4,000 pupils lived outside the County boundary, but came into London for their education—879 from Essex, 1,716 from Middlesex, 507 from Surrey, 438 from Kent, and 454 from other counties.

From these various figures, with allowances made for such complicating factors as the number of children under secondary-school age, children aged 10–15 attending efficient private schools, and out-county pupils, there emerges a total of approximately 25,000 London boys and girls of the appropriate age-groups receiving fairly satisfactory secondary education. The inadequacy of this figure in terms of potential

[1] Memorandum on Public Secondary Schools in London for the Education Committee of the L.C.C., by Sidney Webb, 1905.
[2] Report of the L.C.C. Education Officer upon Secondary School Accommodation in London, Parts I–II, 1909. In 1906 the L.C.C. Education Officer had reported (to the Council's Higher Education and Scholarship Sub-Committee, Jan. 10, 1906) that there were 51 schools—26 boys', 19 girls', 6 mixed or dual—aided by the Council, and attended by 15,023 pupils, of whom 2,167 were under 11, and 1,087 over 16 years of age. The previous year the figure had been 14,713 pupils.
[3] According to Llewellyn Smith's survey of 1892, 24 per cent. of the boys and 28 per cent. of the girls attending 71 London Secondary schools were under twelve years of age.

secondary-school population will be appreciated when it is realized that in 1901 there were over 500,000, and in 1911 over 480,000, in the 10–15 age-group. In other words, only about one child in twenty in London was getting efficient secondary schooling in the first decade of this century.[1]

Boys and Girls

The old tradition that the female sex did not require higher education died hard and was responsible for the inadequate supply of places in girls' post-primary schools. Only towards the end of the century, when the suffragette movement was beginning to gather momentum, and such pioneers of women's education as Miss Buss and Miss Beale had forcibly impressed upon public opinion the need for more girls' secondary schools, did such organizations as the Girls' Public Day Schools Trust come into existence.

They provided, however, proprietary schools charging fairly high fees, and, corresponding as they did in this way to the boys' public schools, they were not available to the majority of people. Therefore, at this time there was a serious shortage in the number of girls' grammar schools available for the lower middle class, and even more so for the working class. In 1906, the ratio of boys to girls attending less expensive endowed schools was about ten to six, and this was at a time when there was a tremendous demand for girls to go into the elementary teaching profession.

Geographical Distribution of Schools

The geographical distribution of secondary schools was also very uneven in London at the turn of the century. There was an acute shortage of places in some districts, and a surplus in others. Commercial districts like the City, and poorer mixed industrial-residential boroughs like Finsbury and Stepney, were more than adequately served with grammar schools considering their local needs, whereas large expanding boroughs like Wandsworth and Lewisham, where the

[1] "The annual output of the Public Elementary Schools in England, i.e. the number leaving them every year, is now about 600,000. Of these 1 in 22 proceeds to a secondary school, and 1 in 46 receives free education there." (Report of Board of Education, 1911–12.)

population was rapidly growing, had hardly any suitable secondary-school places at all. Charles Booth published a table showing this lack of balance in 1890:[1]

School Board District	Secondary-School Accommodation	Accommodation per 1,000 population
City	2,250	53·5
Westminster	2,030	9·8
Chelsea	1,450	3·3
Marylebone	2,180	3·7
Finsbury	1,660	3·2
Hackney	1,220	2·8
Tower Hamlets	1,500	3·4
Southwark	500	2·2
West Lambeth	880	1·5
East Lambeth	1,530	4·3
Greenwich	1,770	4·5

Fifteen years later the position was worse, for the centrifugal movement of population had continued, but few new school places had been provided. In 1900, the great majority of the endowed schools were concentrated in central or east-central London, and all the famous boys' public schools, with the exception of Dulwich College were, or had recently been, situated within a stone's throw of St. Paul's.[2]

Admittedly, the proprietary schools were more widely distributed (only five out of twenty-eight were in the central area); but as they catered almost exclusively for fee-payers this meant that thousands of poorer children had no local facilities at all for secondary education.

On the other hand, it is clear from existing information that the proportionate attendance was far higher in the newer outer boroughs than in the older central areas. For example, in 1909 (by which time the London County Council had opened nineteen new grammar schools and thus helped to restore the balance) Wandsworth, Battersea, Deptford, Camberwell, Woolwich, Lewisham, Greenwich, Stoke Newington, Hackney, Hampstead, and Hammersmith had an average of more than five children per thousand in attendance at secondary schools, whereas, Southwark, Bermondsey, Poplar, Bethnal Green, Stepney, Shoreditch, Finsbury, and St. Marylebone had less than four

[1] *Life and Labour of the People in London*, by Charles Booth, pp. 247–306, First series, "Poverty" (3), (Macmillan 1904).

[2] Thirty out of forty-five of the lesser endowed schools were situated in the central area, and of the other fifteen most were situated nearer to the centre than they were to the County boundary.

per thousand.[1] This paradox—that the areas having most schools needed them least, and the areas having least schools needed them most—has an historical explanation. The old endowed schools were built in or near the City. In the course of time the metropolis spread in all directions, engulfing the open fields and swallowing what had once been separate villages. The old central area around St. Paul's and Westminster had become less residential, or if it remained residential, was occupied by a poorer population. In contrast, the "outer ring", including such places as North Islington, Hampstead, Lewisham, Streatham, Hammersmith, and other districts near the County boundary, had grown mainly in the nineteenth century and had become inhabited by a more middle-class population.

Thus, on the one hand, the development of commerce and industry, overcrowding, and the impoverishment of the area surrounding the City reduced the local demand for secondary schools, whereas, on the other hand, the new middle and lower middle classes of the suburbs wanted secondary schooling, but found local provision insufficient.

That the Council was aware of the urgent need for new secondary schools in what were then the suburbs of London was shown by the repeated references in early reports to the need for accommodation in certain areas. For example, in 1905, it was reported of Fulham that:

> There is no public secondary school of any sort in the whole of the large and rapidly growing division . . . which has a population now reaching 160,000.

It was pointed out that Woolwich, with a population of over 125,000, had only the Polytechnic available, and Wandsworth was similarly lacking in secondary-school facilities.

> There is a serious deficiency in girls' secondary schools in several of the seven county divisions which made up the old School Board division of Hackney . . . Though the greater part of this district has been too poor to maintain girls' secondary schools, it is, we are glad to say, not too poor to furnish a good quota of Junior County Scholars and probationers. For a population reaching half a million, the only girls' secondary schools of a public character are the Skinners' Company School at the extreme north of North Hackney, and the Lady Holles School in South Hackney.[2]

[1] Report of the L.C.C. Education Officer upon Secondary School Accommodation in London, Parts I–II, 1909.
[2] Report of the L.C.C. Education Committee, 1905.

Out of the twenty-eight proprietary schools that existed in London in 1900 (of which twenty-four were opened between 1850 and 1900, three between 1800 and 1850, and one before 1800), the more widely dispersed of them, situated in such expanding districts as Hampstead, North St. Pancras, Blackheath, Clapham, Sydenham, Putney, Wimbledon, Dulwich, Streatham, Stoke Newington, and Hammersmith, were not sufficient to meet all local needs. Parents were accustomed to sending their children long distances to what they regarded as suitable secondary schools—this policy of going to non-local schools had long been traditional among wealthy children—but judging from the figures for the "catchment-areas" of the less expensive endowed schools at this time in London, it was customary also for middle- and lower-middle-class boys and girls to travel a considerable distance each day to school.

Class Bias

Another serious defect in the provision of secondary-school places in London was the marked social bias that existed in the schools. These schools were by no means uniform in their economic background, but they were all decidedly middle class in their social composition.[1]

This middle-class status was taken for granted in official reports, and generally accepted by public opinion.

> The words "secondary" and "middle class" came to be thought of as meaning the same or nearly the same thing. The idea that elementary and secondary schools represent not successive stages of education but alternative kinds of education meant for different social classes is deeply rooted, and may be said to have dominated practice until recently,

wrote Robert Morant.[2]

[1] The Schools Inquiry Commission of 1868 had actually gone further in their social analysis, dividing secondary schools into three grades according to the occupations of their pupils' parents. In the first category were schools used by "men with considerable incomes independent of their own exertions" and "the great body of professional men, especially the clergy, medical men and lawyers". In the second category were schools used by children who must leave about sixteen, and go into the "army, all but the highest branches of the medical and legal professions, civil engineering and so on". In the third category were schools for the children of "smaller tenant farmers, the smaller tradesmen, the superior artisan". (See Report of the Schools Inquiry Commission, 1868, Vol. I, p. 20.)

[2] Report of the Board of Education, pp. 31–2, 1908–9.

13

Secondary or higher schools in England and Wales . . . were at the time of their origin, and even down to a comparatively recent date, to a considerable extent institutions for the education of children, chiefly boys, either belonging to the more prosperous classes or selected for their ability,

said the Spens Report.[1]

When a survey was made on a fairly wide scale of the occupations of parents of children attending certain secondary schools in 1897, it was found that about two-fifths of the parents were middle class in their social background, nearly half were lower middle class, and less than one-tenth working class. Llewellyn Smith in his survey of London secondary education in 1892 reported:

A great proportion of the parents whose sons attend secondary schools are fairly well off, as is shown by the following estimate of the proportion of pupils drawn from various social strata in the existing secondary schools of London, based on returns from twenty-nine schools:

	Percentage
Professional, trading and middle class:	85
Artisans and labourers:	15
Total:	100

Secondary schools . . . are doing a most valuable work for girls' education in London . . . they mainly provide for the middle classes.[2]

Charles Booth even emphasized the fine social distinctions that existed between the old endowed and the newer proprietary schools:

The majority of the professional class who attend . . . the endowed schools are the sons of clergymen, doctors, accountants, and school-masters; while licensed victuallers are prominent among the parents of the middle class besides, of course, clerks, shopkeepers, managers,

[1] Report of the Consultative Committee on Secondary Education, p.1, H.M.S.O., 1938.
[2] Report to the Special Committee on Technical Education for the London County Council, by H. Llewellyn Smith, pp. 66–68, 1892.

agents and officials. The working-class contribution to the pupils of secondary schools is drawn almost purely from the upper stratum. . . . Proprietary schools draw their pupils purely from the professional middle class, as is only to be expected, since they must charge a self-supporting fee. In such a school in north-west London the composition is as follows: Professional 29 per cent., middle class 71 per cent. Thus the great majority of the boys attending the secondary schools of London are of the middle and lower middle class, with a fringe of sons of professional men and (in endowed schools) a sprinkling of children of working men.[1]

Some years later, when the new scholarship scheme had been in operation for a period, a larger proportion of children from skilled working-class homes was finding its way into the London grammar schools. However, as late as 1905–10 two-thirds or more of the grammar-school entrants were still coming from the more prosperous sections of the community.[2] The very names of some of the London secondary schools during this period suggests their *bourgeois* origin, viz. the "Burlington Middle Class School for Girls", "Mayo Middle Class School" (now Highbury Hill School for Girls), and the "Corporation of Middle Class Education in the Metropolis and Suburbs Thereof" (now the Central Foundation School for Boys).

Types of School

There were in London at the beginning of the century three main types of secondary school, corresponding broadly to the various social strata of the upper, middle, and lower middle classes. These were the public, proprietary, and lesser endowed schools.

The public schools were characterized by the fact that they were old established; taking no financial aid from the State or local authority, they usually possessed rich endowments and almost invariably charged high fees. They sometimes took boarders as well as day pupils, but even if they were exclusively day schools, their catchment-areas remained fairly wide. There were eight such schools in London in 1909, with a total attendance of 3,478 pupils, namely:

[1] *Life and Labour of the People in London*, by Charles Booth, Vol. 3, pp. 260–1, (Macmillan, 1904).
[2] See Chapter 3 "The Changing Social Structure of the Grammar Schools".

LONDON PUBLIC SCHOOLS IN 1909

School		Founded[1]	Borough	Pupils	Annual Fees £ s.
St. Paul's	(B)	1509	Hammersmith	583	24 9
St. Paul's	(G)	1904	,,	241	21 0
Merchant Taylors'	(B)	1561	Finsbury	500	12 12 to 14 14
Westminster	(B)	1561	Westminster	270	31 10
Dulwich	(B)	1619	Camberwell	700	24 10
City of London	(B)	1837	City	717	15 15
City of London	(G)	1894	,,	259	12 12
Mercers'	(B)	1542	,,	208	10 10

The second group of schools were the so-called proprietary schools, which were usually owned by limited companies, had no endowments or State aid, but were not run primarily for profit. As they had no other financial resources, they generally charged comparatively high fees. Average fees for girls' proprietary schools were about £15 per annum compared with the endowed-school average of about £6–£8. The fees for boys' schools ranged from £9 for the less well known, to thirty guineas for the better known, such as University College School. The most representative of these schools were those organized by the Girls' Public Day Schools Trust between 1870 and 1890. They served a social stratum somewhere between the rich families who sent their children to such schools as St. Paul's, and the middle and lower middle class who sent their children to the lesser endowed schools. There were in 1909 twenty-eight such proprietary schools with a total attendance of 697 boys, and 6,357 girls.

PROPRIETARY SCHOOLS, 1909: BOYS

School	Founded	Borough	Number of Pupils	Annual Fees £ s.
University College School	1833	St. Pancras (later Hampstead)	360	31 10
Philological (Marylebone Grammar)	1792	Marylebone	80	10 10
Brockley (West Kent Grammar)	1887	Lewisham	117	9 14
St. Clement's (Holborn Estate)	1862	Westminster	140	4 10

[1] There is not always agreement among authorities as to the exact date on which a particular school was founded. For some schools the date of the original foundation or charitable bequest is given, for others the date of reorganization or of the actual opening of the school to pupils. For example, the original bequest for the City of London School for Boys was in 1442, but the school was not actually proposed by the City Corporation until 1834, and it was opened in 1837.

PROPRIETARY SCHOOLS, 1909: GIRLS

School	Founded	Borough	Number of Pupils	Annual Fees
				£ s.
North London Collegiate	1850	St. Pancras	412	17 17 to 22 1
Notting Hill and Bayswater High	1873	Kensington	209	10 10 to 16 10
Paddington and Maida Vale	1878	Paddington	181	10 10 to 16 10
Highbury and Islington	1878	Islington	142	16 10
Kensington	1880	Kensington	186	16 10
South Hampstead	1876	Hampstead	424	11 11 to 12 12
Dulwich	1878	Lambeth	232	10 10 to 16 10
Blackheath	1880	Lewisham	431	11 5 to 17 5
Clapham	1882	Wandsworth	471	10 10 to 16 10
Sydenham	1887	Lewisham	282	16 10
Francis Holland, Baker Street	1878	Marylebone	170	25 4 to 31 10
Francis Holland, Graham Street	1881	Westminster	128	31 10
Mary Datchelor	1877	Camberwell	497	10 10
Whitelands College	1841	Chelsea	197	6 6 to 9 9
Skinners'	1890	Hackney	355	7 7 to 10 10
Godolphin and Latymer	1905	Hammersmith	406	7 10
Kensington Park	?	Kensington	132	6 6 to 12 12
St. Clement's, Holborn Estate	1862	Westminster	124	4 10
East Putney	1893	Wandsworth	209	10 10 to 16 10
Streatham and Brixton	1887	Wandsworth	336	16 10
Lady Holles	1711	Hackney	383	5 10 to 9 9
St. Mary's College	1872	Paddington	84	10 10 to 19 10
Kennington	?	Lambeth	174	6 6
Streatham College	1886	Wandsworth	192	9 9 to 15 15

The thirty-seven lesser endowed schools were the most important group of secondary schools in London. With their 9,181 boys and 3,797 girls, they were later to become the backbone of the grammar-school system under the status of "aided schools". They had declined in importance during the mid-nineteenth century but financial assistance from the Arts and Science and Technical Education grants improved their position. However, at the turn of the century, as has been explained, their financial status was uncertain as they were no longer able to continue on the basis of fees and endowments, but had not yet advanced to the whole-hearted acceptance of State aid and control. Furthermore, their scholarship provisions were inadequate, and they had developed no systematic relation with the elementary schools. "... the old foundation schools still hang in the air", wrote Booth in 1890, "with little organic connection with the vast system of State-aided primary education which has grown up underneath it."

ENDOWED SCHOOLS, 1909: BOYS

School	Founded	Borough	Number of Pupils	Annual Fees
				£ s. d.
Archbishop Tenison's	1685	Westminster	167	7 7
Westminster City	1594	Westminster	565	4 7 to 6 15
Dame Alice Owen's	1613	Finsbury	415	10 0
Haberdashers' Aske's	1690	Hampstead	424	11 11 to 12 12
Parmiter's	1681	Bethnal Green	376	5 8
Cooper's	1538	Stepney	468	4 4 to 6 6
St. Olave's	1561	Bermondsey	435	7 10 to 10 0
Battersea Grammar	1700	Battersea	250	7 10 to 10 0
Emanuel	1594	Battersea	427	10 2 6
Alleyn's	1619	Camberwell	613	11 10
Colfe's	1656	Lewisham	290	9 9 to 15 15
Roan	1643	Greenwich	373	3 to 6
St. Mark's College	1841	Chelsea	246	6 6 to 7 16
William Ellis	1889	St. Pancras	292	6 6
Central Foundation	1866	Finsbury	598	6 6
Grocers' (Hackney Downs)	1873	Hackney	460	9 9 to 12 0
Whitechapel Foundation	1854	Stepney	200	4 1
Sir Walter St. John's	1700	Battersea	210	4 11 to 5 12
Wilson's	1615	Camberwell	333	10 0 to 11 10
St. Dunstan's	1446	Lewisham	463	9 0
Haberdashers' Aske's (Hatcham)	1690	Deptford	442	9 9
Latymer Upper	1624	Hammersmith	524	7 10
Raine's Foundation	1719	Stepney	141	2 8
Strand	1893	Westminster	469	7 10 to 18 0

ENDOWED SCHOOLS, 1909: GIRLS

School	Founded	Borough	Number of Pupils	Annual Fees
				£ s.
James Allen's	1741	Camberwell	334	8 8
Camden	1871	St. Pancras	337	7 to
				9 9
Dame Alice Owen's	1886	Finsbury	300	10 0
Roan's	1878	Greenwich	360	3 6 to
				6 6
Haberdashers' Aske's (Hatcham)	1876	Deptford	300	9 9
Grey Coat	1698	Westminster	386	5 5 to
				6 15
Burlington	1699	"	215	4 10 to
				6
St. Martin's	1699	"	155	4 10 to
				5
Coborn	1701	Poplar	300	4 4 to
				6 6
Highbury Hill	1844	Islington	253	6 6 to
				15 15
Central Foundation	1726	Stepney	403	4 10 to
				6 6
Raine's Foundation	1719	Stepney	117	2 8
St. Saviour's	1561	Southwark	337	6 0

By 1909 the London County Council had opened nineteen new schools, four for boys, fourteen for girls, and one mixed, which corresponded in many ways to the old endowed schools, but which had no other source of income, apart from fees, except from the Council and Board of Education. These were the maintained grammar schools, which were eventually to become second in importance to the endowed schools.

Associated with them were the secondary departments of the polytechnics, which had grown up in the 1890's and provided education for about 1,500 pupils in 1909:

POLYTECHNICS: SECONDARY SCHOOL DEPTS. (1909)

		Borough	Number of Pupils	Annual Fees
				£ s. d.
Northern	(M)	Islington	254	6 19 6
Wandsworth Technical Institute	(B)	Wandsworth	148	4 10
Woolwich	(M)	Woolwich	411	4 10
South West	(B)	Chelsea	176	6 0
Regent Street	(B)	St. Marylebone	430	5 5 to
				12 12
Battersea	(B)	Battersea	161	?

Another group was the private schools, which are believed to have been very numerous and probably provided education for many thousands of London children at the beginning of the century.[1] These schools had arisen to meet the needs primarily of the middle and lower middle classes, and were run mainly with the object of making a profit for their owners. Some were preparatory institutions for the bigger endowed schools, many resembled "dame" schools, and a few were survivors of private elementary schools of the pre-School-Board era. Most were in financial difficulties towards the end of the nineteenth century owing to rising costs, competition from State-aided schools, and the movement of middle-class population into the suburbs. They were not controlled or inspected in any way by the central or local authorities, and it is generally believed that the education they provided was usually inadequate. The first comprehensive survey of accommodation at these schools was made by the London County Council in 1909, and even then it was estimated that only about one-quarter of the schools replied to the Council's inquiries. It was reckoned that approximately 27,000 children were attending private schools in that year, of whom a majority were under secondary-school age.

A further group that fitted into none of these categories was the Roman Catholic secondary schools, which were maintained by fees, church subscriptions and endowments, and in certain cases by aid from the London County Council and Board of Education. There were ten such schools with attendance, mainly of girls, of about 1,400 pupils:

ROMAN CATHOLIC SCHOOLS: BOYS AND GIRLS

School		Borough	Number of Pupils	Annual Fees
				£ s.
Hammersmith	(G)	Hammersmith	103	6 6
St. Aloysius	(G)	St. Pancras	153	9 9
Notre Dame, Eden Grove	(G)	Islington	104	6 6 to 8 8
Howrah House	(G)	Poplar	152	5 5
Notre Dame, Southwark	(G)	Southwark	235	6 6 to 9 9
Notre Dame, Battersea	(G)	Battersea	133	3 3 to 6 6
Ave Maria	(G)	Wandsworth	118	6 6
St. Angela's	(G)	Wandsworth	91	6 6 to 9 9
Convent School, Highgate	(G)	St. Pancras	101	9 9 to 15 15
Clapham College	(B)	Wandsworth	163	6 0 to 9 0

[1] Not much information is available about these schools.

20

Administrative Chaos

When the London County Council took over responsibility for secondary education in 1904, it found not only an inadequate number of grammar-school places and a marked bias in favour of the middle classes, but also a state of administrative muddle and confusion.

The grammar-school system was in a stage of transition from private or semi-private enterprise to State control; and as the old system was breaking down before the new system had taken definite shape the result was a series of stopgap measures and typically English compromises, which worked effectively for a period, but did not make, in the early stages at least, for administrative tidiness or financial clarity.

The general administrative as well as philosophical confusion that prevailed can best be illustrated by the comments of two eminent contemporary observers. "Chaos" was the term used by both Robert Morant and Sidney Webb to describe the situation as it existed at the beginning of the century.

> Looked at as a mere matter of civic administration, London's educational service, is, at this moment, plainly inferior to its police or its fire brigade, or even its water supply. The educational provision is scrappy and disjointed; its fragments are ill-adjusted and unco-ordinated; it is uninspired by any vivifying principles; there are great gaps in some directions, and redundancies or duplications in others,

wrote Sidney Webb.[1]

> The organization and development of the education given in secondary schools is the most important educational question of the present day,

commented Robert Morant, who continued.[2]

> It is the pivot of the whole situation, as it affects the efficiency, intelligence, well-being of the nation. The scope and character of primary education are now pretty well settled. Much remains to be done in improving it; but the problems, so far as they are strictly

---

[1] Preface to *London Education*, by Sidney Webb, 1903.
[2] Report of Board of Education, p. 45, 1906.

educational, are uncontentious and admit of approximate solution. Further advance will be on well ascertained lines. The experience of thirty-five years' working has borne fruit. . . . But as soon as we pass beyond the sphere of Elementary Education proper . . . beyond what is provided and compelled by law for the whole child population of the nation, we plunge into chaos. Higher education has grown up in this country almost of itself, without any continuous or uniform guidance from the State. It takes innumerable forms. . . . The provision and aid of this super-primary education is now a function of all Local Education Authorities. But the essentials of the problem are not yet authoritatively settled or even clearly stated. Great confusion of thought still exists throughout the country . . . it is inevitable that there should be many false starts, much waste of labour, and misapplication of machinery.

The chief administrative problem was that of finance. Generally speaking, the division into famous old endowed, lesser endowed, proprietary, and private schools was as much a social and financial division as an educational one, but there was great variety in the methods used to finance the schools, as well as considerable overlapping between them. Some schools, such as St. Paul's, were richly endowed and also charged high fees, with the result that they were very wealthy; others, such as Dame Alice Owen's Schools, were poorly endowed and charged lower fees, and consequently were chronically short of money; a few, such as Mercers' were largely supported by rich City Livery Companies, and did not have to look to the State for financial aid; while others, such as the proprietary schools, were almost entirely self-supporting out of fees.

Prior to the 1902 Education Act, the two main sources from which the "aided" secondary schools drew financial assistance were the Arts and Science grants paid by the Board of Education, and the Technical Instruction Board grants of the London County Council. The former had been paid since 1853 when the Art Department of the Board of Trade was set up, and the latter since the Local Government Act of 1888 and the Local Taxation, Custom, and Excise Act of 1890 (the famous "whisky money"), which enabled the local authorities, by stretching a legal point, to spend money on secondary education. Then came the celebrated Cockerton judgment, which declared it to be illegal for the local authorities to spend money on certain types of secondary school. It was this incident, together with the other circumstances already mentioned, that forced the Government to introduce the Education Act of 1902. Henceforward, the amount of money spent on secondary education by the London County Council rapidly increased, and by 1907–8, for example, over two-fifths of the income of aided schools was coming from Council or Board of Education sources.[1]

Fees varied greatly from school to school, and seem to have been arranged according to no other principle than that of charging "what the traffic would bear". Highest fees in London at that time were those of Westminster School, which charged £31 10s. per year for day pupils, while the lowest were those of Raine's Foundation School, which charged £2 8s. annually. The average fees for the lesser endowed schools were about £8 to £10 per year. Generally, fees brought in about one-quarter to one-third of total income for the aided schools. It was difficult to raise fees owing to the weight of tradition, and also because the fee-paying community was tending to dwindle steadily, both absolutely and proportionately.[2]

Similarly, endowments had tended to reach an upper limit in their value because they were invested either in Government securities, which paid a fixed rate of interest, or else in land and property, which had appreciated considerably in value during the nineteenth century, but the rentals of which in some cases reached a peak during the first decade of the twentieth century. These endowments were an extremely important source of income for some schools, and in certain cases determined their whole educational status and social traditions, but for other schools they were only worth a few thousand pounds per year.[3]

The dilemma facing the secondary schools was, therefore, very acute. On the one hand, their traditional sources of income had reached a maximum level, and could not easily be increased. On the other hand, the costs of administering the schools steadily mounted as teachers' salaries were raised, new buildings erected, and as the Board

[1] According to the L.C.C. Education Report of 1907–8, 28·42 per cent. (£73,447) of the income of 42 aided schools came from L.C.C. grants, and 12·98 per cent. (£33,540) from the Board of Education. Fees comprised 29·97 per cent. (£77,439) of the total.

[2] "... there is abundant evidence that in poorer districts, such as nearly the whole of the poorer eastern postal district, an inclusive fee of £5 is the upper limit of the fee which can be charged in order to fill the schools", commented Booth, *Life and Labour of the People in London*, p. 268 (Macmillan, 1904).

[3] Considerable reorganization of charitable endowments had occurred during the nineteenth century to bring them into accord with modern requirements, but they still remain very unevenly distributed. The endowment of Christ's Hospital, for example, was said to be worth about £80,000 per year in 1912, whereas the endowment of Owen's Schools was worth £2,900, and of William Ellis School, £1,053 yearly in 1907–8. (See Annual Report of L.C.C. Education Officer for that year.)

of Education required improved standards of equipment and accommodation. It was this dilemma, combined with the necessity to provide for the very largely increased number of scholarship entrants, that forced acceptance of increased State aid and control. Henceforward, the Board of Education and the London County Council paid the piper (and to a growing extent called the tune) in the grammar schools. The death of Queen Victoria marked the end of an educational as well as a constitutional epoch.

Chapter 2

THE GROWTH OF
LONDON GRAMMAR SCHOOLS
1910–54

The educational aim of capitalist democracy has always been the training of an élite. Admission to this élite was restricted to the children of parents who could afford school fees, together with a small proportion of the ablest children born into working-class homes.—St. John Reade.[1]

. . . is not the only hope for the continued existence of a democratic State to be found in an increasing need for voluntarily submitting the impulses of the many ignorant to the guidance and control of a few wise, and thus to the willing establishment and maintenance by the democracy, of special expert governors and guides and leaders deliberately appointed by itself for the purpose?—Robert Morant.[2]

THE prolonged and bitter controversy aroused by the 1902 Education Act was mainly centred on the question of providing State aid for Church elementary schools. In contrast, the proposals to reorganize secondary education met with very little criticism; and it is this fact, probably more than any other, that indicates how urgent was the need to reform the grammar schools.[3] People who differed violently in their approach to other educational issues were unanimous in the view that a comprehensive reorganization of secondary schools was required. A growing volume of public opinion recognized, for

[1] St. John Reade in the *Bulletin* of the English New Education Fellowship, November, 1946.

[2] *Sir Robert Morant*, by B. M. Allen, pp. 25–26 (Macmillan, 1934).

[3] ". . . there was another great thing the (1902) Act achieved. It secured that, for the first time in this country, provision should be made for an adequate supply of secondary schools to which parents who desired their children to receive a higher type of education could send them at moderate cost and to which children who obtained scholarships from the elementary schools could proceed for a more advanced course of instruction.

"This important and indeed fundamental feature of the Act was obscured by the bitter wranglings which took place over the religious question." (*Sir Robert Morant* by Bernard M. Allen, p. 200 (Macmillan, 1934).)

25

example, that the existing grammar schools were too few and too small, that administration and finances were in a state of confusion, and that unfair class privileges were the rule.

But while the ills of the old system were widely realized, there was less agreement as to proposed cures and remedies. For instance, it was plain to everyone that the number of secondary-school places was insufficient to meet the needs of the population, but it was not at all clear how many new places should be provided. It was accepted that the administration of the schools needed to be improved, but the authorities disagreed as to how the financial burden should be redistributed. The majority of progressive people wanted an expansion of the scholarship system and the opening up of opportunities to the children of the poor, but there was controversy about the merits of the "County scholars", and few educationists were prepared to be dogmatic about the ratio of fee-paying to scholarship entrants. Certainly in these early days only a small minority envisaged the complete abolition of all fees in aided and maintained schools such as occurred under the terms of the 1944 Act.

It has taken fifty years' experience of State intervention in the field of secondary education to evolve a more clear-cut grammar-school policy. But even today, after all the experience that has been gained and the prolonged controversies that have taken place, it would be very rash to claim that all the early defects have been overcome or that agreement has been reached upon every aim and policy. On the contrary, modern social and technical developments and the controversy over the comprehensive school have focused attention on the need for far-reaching reforms of the present tripartite system.

Grammar-School Places and the Trend of Population

Fifty years ago there was no clear agreement as to what percentage of children should go to grammar schools. Traditionally, it depended upon the number of available fee-payers, and to a lesser extent upon the number of local scholarships.

The number of grammar-school places developed haphazardly in London, dependent, on the one hand, upon middle-class willingness to pay fees, and, on the other hand, upon the charitable but rather arbitrary decisions of philanthropists such as Edward Alleyn, the Shakespearean actor, who founded both Alleyn's and Dulwich Schools in the seventeenth century; Dame Alice Owen, widow of a Tudor merchant, who founded two schools near the Angel, Islington; or George Green, a retired sea captain, who founded a school for boys in East India Dock Road in the early nineteenth century. City Livery Companies and various religious organizations were also concerned with providing secondary schools.

The question of how many grammar-school places should be provided in various districts was not a serious theoretical problem until the Government and local authorities assumed responsibility for secondary education—at least, some schools were provided, whatever the reason. But as soon as the State intervened, a decision had to be made as to how many new secondary-school places should be provided and what proportion of children should stay at school after the age of twelve or thirteen years. The taking of this decision was an extremely complex matter as it meant trying to reach a compromise between the traditional viewpoint and the new political forces then stirring.

During the last forty-five years there have been two World Wars and a series of economic depressions, which have naturally affected the decisions taken on this matter. It has been against this background of recurring political and economic crises that the conflicting viewpoints about the necessity to expand educational facilities—what the Spens Report described as the "liberal or conservative" attitude to education—have been debated. This clash of opinions has continued to be fought out in Parliament and at County Hall with varying degrees of success, depending upon the ebb and flow of political battle. There have been various skirmishes on religious issues, and many diversions on purely educational themes cutting across political lines, but the main conflict has always been between those who believed, like Sidney Webb and Graham Wallas, that there was a great deal of talent going to waste among the poorer children, and therefore wanted a better scholarship system and greater opportunities of secondary education for every child, and those who held firmly to the conservative view that matters were all right as they were, that changes, if they were to come at all, should be slow and cautious, and that the rate-payers must be protected at all times against municipal extravagance.

These political aspects of the problem are discussed more fully elsewhere, but meanwhile it is revealing to see how the London County Council's attitude towards the provision of grammar-school places developed over four or five decades.

At the beginning of the century there was no precise official guidance as to the number of places that should be provided. In 1868, the School Inquiry Commission had come to the conclusion that accommodation ought to be provided in the first instance for ten *boys* per 1,000 population, and ultimately sixteen per 1,000, of whom one half would be at "third-grade" (corresponding to higher-grade elementary schools). The 1895 Royal Commission on Secondary Education refused to commit itself on a figure, stating:

The demand for secondary education in any district will vary not only with the character and wealth of the population, but with the grade and quality of the education offered, and the price at which it is provided.[1]

This rather vague statement of official policy was not of much help to the local authorities in 1904. The London County Council, particularly, was left in the air because it did not at that time even know how many secondary-school places existed in the area under its control. The Council's first task, therefore, was to make a survey of accommodation, and this it did in 1909. The Report published on this subject estimated that there were 30,543 pupils in attendance at 108 secondary schools, or 6·5 per 1,000 of the population. There were another 9,000 children attending private secondary schools, but over half of these were under twelve years of age. Furthermore, out of this total of 30,543 nearly 4,000 came from outside the County boundary, and about 12 to 15 per cent. were under twelve years of age, so it would appear that the figure of 6·5 per 1,000 probably over-estimated the true position.

This Report was also of considerable significance because for the first time the Council committed itself to a target of ten secondary-school places per 1,000 population.

However, it went on to say:

Such provision, however, cannot be regarded as being sufficient as a permanent provision for London.

It will be sufficient to meet the more pressing requirements, but it cannot be regarded as being a final settlement of the question. The general expansion of knowledge and the demand for improved conditions of life will, there is little doubt, bring about a continued upward movement in education, and it must always be the duty of

[1] Report of the Royal Commission on Secondary Education, pp. 156–7, Vol I, 1895.

the education authority of London to keep pace with the growing intellectual and social needs of the people.

It is not proposed, however, in the present Report to put forward a scheme of secondary accommodation that can be regarded as holding good for more than a limited number of years.

In dealing with any educational problem in London it is important not to introduce changes of too extensive a nature, since the distribution of the population within the County is subject to constant changes, and the character of a district, whether as regards the number or character of the inhabitants, may change very considerably within the course of a few years.[1]

Expansion in Number of Grammar-School Places

Though in 1904 the Council had not made up its mind as to what its ultimate target should be, nevertheless it was plain to everyone connected with the work, both Councillors and full-time officials, that more grammar-school places were urgently needed, particularly for girls, and in certain districts of London where accommodation was quite inadequate. In 1905, therefore, an ambitious scheme of expansion was launched, and during the next four years the Council took control of or opened nineteen new grammar schools, fourteen for girls, four for boys, and one mixed. Their geographical location can be judged from the list of their names:[2]

Dalston (G), Bermondsey (G), Clapham (G), Eltham (G), Fulham (G), Putney (G), Sydenham (G), Forest Hill (G), Peckham (G), Stockwell (G), South Hackney (G), Kentish Town (G), St. Pancras (G), Chelsea (G), Brockley (B), Holloway (B), St. Marylebone Grammar (B), Hackney Downs (B), and George Green's (Mixed).

By the opening or extension of these schools, 5,636 additional places were created, and between 1909 and 1919[2] another 2,253 places were

---

[1] Report of the L.C.C. Education Officer upon Secondary School Accommodation in London, p. 11, 1909.

[2] Four of these schools were not, strictly speaking, new foundations; they were schools established in the nineteenth century that had fallen into financial difficulties and been taken over by the L.C.C. Hackney Downs had been known as the Grocers' School, St. Marylebone Grammar as the Philological School, and Brockley as West Kent Grammar. George Green's School had been founded in Stepney by a sea captain early in the nineteenth century. They were all described as "County Secondary Schools" with the exception of Hackney Downs, St. Marylebone, and George Green's.

added. Kentish Town and St. Pancras Girls' Schools were amalgamated and moved to new buildings at Parliament Hill in 1913; Highbury Hill School for Girls was taken over from the Home and Colonial School Society in 1912; Carlyle School for Girls, which had originally been part of the Chelsea Polytechnic, was opened in 1908, and transferred to new buildings in 1914;[1] Plumstead School for Girls took over the girls' department of Woolwich Polytechnic Secondary School in 1913; Stockwell School for Girls was absorbed by the Streatham County School for Girls, which opened in 1913; and in the same year the Strand School for Boys was taken over by the Council, and moved to Brixton.

During the First World War the Paddington and Maida Vale High School was sold to the Council by the Girls' Public Day School Trust. South Hackney School for Girls was renamed Clapton County Secondary School and moved to new buildings in 1916, and Forest Hill School was amalgamated with Sydenham County School for Girls in 1917.

Accommodation in the aided schools was also substantially increased during this period, as can be seen from the following figures:[2]

| | Maintained | | Aided | | |
Year	Boys	Girls	Boys	Girls	Total
1905	—	—	9,874	4,841	14,715
1909	1,042	3,434	9,244	5,468	19,188
1914	1,863	4,866	8,104	3,428	18,261
1919	2,691	5,773	11,078	7,376	26,918

Post-war Plans

Towards the end of the First World War the general deterioration in material conditions of life affected education to an ever increasing extent. School buildings grew shabbier and more overcrowded, equipment and furniture wore out, and there was a severe shortage of paper and text-books. Many young men teachers joined the armed forces, and classes in all types of schools tended to become bigger.

However, as also happened in 1943–4 (when the campaign for reform of secondary schools culminated in a new Education Act), the War had

---

[1] It was closed again for the duration of the War.
[2] Figures for 1914 and 1919 are taken from the Report of the L.C.C. Higher Education Sub-committee, 31-1-1924.

the effect of turning people's minds towards the deeper and more creative aspects of life, among them the care and training of children. The more terrible the suffering and degradation of war, the more determined were people that something nobler should emerge from it. In education, as in other forms of social activity, there was a rejection of many ancient shibboleths, and vigorous rethinking of traditional ideas. Many new plans were made for secondary schools as victory appeared on the horizon and the Armistice was signed.

Political and educational forces striving for a more democratic school system, such as the Labour Party, Trades Union Congress, the radical wing of the Liberal Party, National Union of Teachers, and Workers' Educational Association, pressed strongly for more secondary-school places, increased scholarships, new buildings and equipment, reduction in the size of classes, and higher pay for teachers. Even the majority of Conservatives, who preferred the *status quo* in education, realized that the grammar schools must be expanded in order to train more youths and girls for jobs in commerce and in the rapidly expanding professions. Indeed, it was an important point of Conservative educational policy to encourage the most intelligent working-class children to go to the grammar schools, and so to help them climb into the middle or lower middle classes.

In London, the main criticisms of secondary education were that:

a. the private schools were often inefficient;
b. the public secondary schools were overfull; and
c. it was desirable to raise the target of 10 places per 1,000 population.

The London County Council was moved by these social currents, as were other local authorities, and in 1919 published another report on secondary-school accommodation. This pointed out that many private schools more closely resembled primary than secondary schools, and, therefore, should properly not be included in the target of 10 per 1,000 population. It was recommended that the figure of 10 per 1,000 should apply only to publicly controlled secondary schools. The Council's report concluded:

Detailed examination of the returns from the private schools makes it clear that their contribution to effective secondary education cannot be regarded as anything like so considerable as would be indicated by the old record of numbers in attendance. Great events have happened since 1909. The general expansion of knowledge and the demand for improved conditions of life foreshadowed in the 1909 report have recently enormously accelerated, and in any case, a period of 10 years might even in normal times be regarded as sufficiently long to admit of an expansion of the requirements in regard to secondary education. The time has, therefore, now come when the Council should aim at accommodation of at least 10 per 1,000 in publicly recognized schools. The growing demand for education suggests that the standard of 10 per 1,000 is too low. It is advisable, however, to proceed cautiously.[1]

On March 20, 1920, the Council decided officially to accept the recommendation of 10 places per 1,000 population, and to increase accommodation for boys from 18,000 to 21,000, and for girls from 19,000 to 20,000.[2] Within a few months, however, the onset of economic depression put a temporary stop to the plans for expansion,[3] and instead of the increase that had been visualized there was a small decline in attendance at both maintained and aided schools. Between 1921 and 1923, attendance in boys' schools fell by 2 per cent. in the case of both maintained and aided schools. For girls' schools, the fall was 13 per cent. and 3 per cent. respectively. The actual decline was somewhat worse than these figures would suggest because the over-all decrease in entrants was masked by the longer average school life and later age of leaving. (Incidentally, this was a phenomenon that also marked the economic crisis of 1931–33.)

The London County Council Education Officer attributed this fall in numbers to various factors, such as the depression of trade (which, paradoxically, encouraged pupils to stay longer once they were *in* the grammar school), the increase of fees (which averaged about eight guineas before and during the War but were increased to an average of about fourteen guineas in 1921), the reduction in the number of out-county pupils (largely because of the higher out-county fee), and the reduction in the number of scholarships owing to the operation of the Board of Education six-shilling limit.

[1] Report on Secondary School Accommodation in London, L.C.C. Higher Education Sub-Committee, p. 2, 1919.

[2] The 1919 Report estimated that there were about 36,000 attending public secondary schools of various kinds (including "public" schools) in London, or 8·1 per 1,000 population. (1911 figure.)

[3] All over the country, post-war schemes for educational reconstruction were scrapped during this period.

By the mid twenties the economic crisis was partly alleviated, and there was a further expansion of maintained schools.[1] Bec School and Wandsworth School were opened in Wandsworth in 1926, Shooter's Hill in Woolwich in 1928, Henry Thornton in Wandsworth replaced Battersea Grammar School in 1927 (all were for boys), and King's Warren School for Girls in Woolwich replaced Plumstead in 1928. The aided schools remained fairly stable in numbers (51 in 1921, 50 in 1924, 51 in 1926, 52 in 1928); but the increased financial aid granted then by the Council enabled them slightly to expand their accommodation. The result of these changes was a small addition to the total number of pupils in attendance at both types of grammar school as can be seen from the following figures:

LONDON GRAMMAR-SCHOOL ATTENDANCE[2]

Year	Maintained		Aided		Total
	Boys	Girls	Boys	Girls	
1920	(No figures available)				
1921	2,964	6,560	13,078	7,733	30,335
1922	3,450	6,419	11,456	6,418	27,743
1923	(No figures available)				
1924	3,505	5,837	11,408[2]	8,125	28,875
1925	3,550	6,037	11,408	8,125	29,120
1926	3,733	6,135	12,392	8,230	30,490
1927	4,337	6,183	12,392	8,230	31,142
1928	4,619	6,150	12,392	8,230	31,391
1929	4,595	6,111	11,261	9,323	31,290
1930	4,807	6,180	11,409	9,394	31,790

By the end of the 1920s the main period of expansion had been completed. No new maintained schools have been opened since 1928,[3] and the number of aided schools reached a maximum of fifty-two in the same year The year 1930 may, therefore, conveniently be taken as a milestone on the road of grammar-school development in London, for, not only was the main structure of Council maintained and aided schools completed during that period, but it was also about then that the number of scholarship entrants began for the first time to exceed fee-payers.

[1] Highbury County School for Boys replaced Northampton Polytechnic Day School in 1921–22.

[2] Figures for maintained and aided schools were not always counted at the same time. Frequently, aided schools were only enumerated every second year.

[3] Forest Hill School for Boys was opened in 1930 and closed the following year because of the economic crisis.

In 1930, according to London statistics, the population of the County of London was approximately 4,400,000, and the attendance at 80 maintained and aided grammar schools was approximately 32,000 with another 11,000 attending other secondary schools recognized by the Board of Education.[1]

In other words, attendance had reached 7·3 per 1,000 population for publicly controlled schools, or 9·8 per 1,000 if we include those schools over which the L.C.C. had no control. These figures may be compared with 10·3 for administrative counties and 9·5 for county boroughs of England and Wales.[2]

They fell considerably farther short of the target of 10 per 1,000 if both (a) the number of children under ten years of age attending these schools, and (b) the out-county pupils are deducted.[3]

During the next nineteen years the attendance at grammar schools rose slowly, as may be seen in the following table:

Year	Maintained Boys	Maintained Girls	Aided Boys	Aided Girls	Total
1931	(No figures available)				
1932	5,262	6,491	11,972	9,509	33,234
1933	5,266	6,499	11,920	9,302	32,987
1934	5,359	6,569	11,634	9,589	33,151
1935	5,452	6,675	11,903	9,714	33,744
1936	5,394	6,819	11,943	9,864	34,020
1937	5,359	6,777	11,927	10,074	34,137
1938	12,136		22,002		34,138
1939	11,950		22,047		33,997
1949 (Jan.)	13,117		22,223		35,340

Nevertheless, though attendance increased by only 10 per cent. between 1930 and 1949, the target of ten places per thousand population was reached before the Second World War and surpassed during it. In 1951, there were approximately 3,350,000 persons living in the County of London, which would give a ratio of about eleven grammar-

[1] Including public, direct-grant, private, and religious schools.
[2] These figures are for "secondary schools on grant list", 1928–29.
[3] In 1930 there were 2,224 pupils (7 per cent.) under ten years of age attending aided and maintained schools, probably more at the private schools. There were also between 3,000–4,000 out-county pupils attending the L.C.C. schools. In 1934–35 there were 3,824 and in 1938, 2,650 such pupils.

school places per thousand people. London had for long lagged behind the rest of the country in its provision of grammar-school places, but by that year its figures were just above the average for the country as a whole. In 1951, according to official Ministry of Education figures, 20·3 per cent. of the thirteen-year-old boys and 21·5 per cent. of girls of the same age in London were attending grammar schools, compared with 19·7 per cent. of the boys and 20·7 per cent. of the girls in England and Wales.

Paradoxically, despite the Council's large-scale building programme and its determination to reach the goal set by the pioneers of secondary-school reform so many years before, it was circumstances outside the Council's control that eventually led to the successful conclusion of their plans, namely, the substantial fall in child population that occurred between 1931–51.

Fall in London's Population

The population of the metropolitan area, which had risen steadily during the nineteenth century, reached its peak soon after 1901, and then began to decline, slowly at first but later with increasing rapidity. The twenty years from 1931 to 1951 were a period of particularly substantial decline as may be seen in the following table:

Year	Population of County of London
1901	4,536,500
1911	4,521,600
1921	4,484,500
1931	4,397,000
1951	3,348,300

The child population fell to an even greater extent, the age-group 11–15, which is approximately the secondary-school age-group, declining by between one-third and one-half within a period of twenty years. The eleven-year-olds, who are the most important from the point of view of grammar-school entrance, numbered only 35,000 in 1951 as compared with 79,000 in 1931—a decline of over half in two decades, as the table on the next page shows:

35

POPULATION OF LONDON (AGED 11–15), 1901–51

Year	11[1]	12	13	14	15	Total
1901	84,000	84,000	83,093	84,399	84,486	419,978
1911	80,740	80,874	80,298	76,990	79,269	398,171
1921	81,775	81,702	83,508	81,446	81,477	409,908
1931	79,141	50,690	51,335	64,113	70,013	315,292
1951	35,413	35,651	35,443	34,818	34,652	175,977

The causes of this remarkable decline, which has not been equalled in extent though it has been paralleled in direction in any other large urban area in Britain, were twofold. First, the birth-rate fell fairly steadily, with the exception of the years 1919–20, for the first four decades of the century, and never recovered the high levels reached in the 1900s and earlier. Secondly, large numbers of people have tended to migrate from the centre to the suburbs of London. There is no space here to go into all the reasons for the decline in the birth-rate, but briefly they were much the same in London as in other parts of the country—the spread of birth-control, desire for a higher standard of living, wish of parents to give their children better opportunities in life, or the fear of unemployment and war.

The sudden reversals of the population trend experienced in 1919–20 and 1946–7 were apparently only temporary phenomena, and can probably best be explained by the return of soldiers home after demobilization and the hope of families for a happier future following the two World Wars.

The migration of population to the suburbs has been a feature of most large urban communities in Britain during this century, and London has been particularly affected because of the enormous size of its built-up area. There are about eight million people living within a short radius of Charing Cross, and the metropolis has tended to spread in ever expanding concentric circles. A few figures will illustrate the great size of this outward movement of people. Between 1921 and 1931 the County of London lost 2 per cent. and between 1931 and 1951 a further 23·8 per cent. of its population. During the same decades the "Outer Ring" gained 27·1 per cent. and 30·9 per cent. respectively; that is to say, the County of London lost about one million and the "Outer Ring" gained about two million people.

Within the County itself there have been many *local* fluctuations in population, creating all kinds of difficulties and problems for the

[1] These are approximate figures.

36

educational service. In some boroughs the population has been falling steadily for over one hundred years, in others it reached a peak half a century ago and has fallen since, while in a few areas it has remained stationary or even increased slightly. For example, the City, Stepney, and Shoreditch have lost more than 50 per cent., and Islington, Poplar, St. Pancras, Southwark, Battersea, Bermondsey, Bethnal Green, Camberwell, Deptford, Finsbury, and Holborn between 25 and 50 per cent. of their population during the last twenty years, whereas Hampstead, Lewisham, and Woolwich have gained slightly in numbers during the same period.[1]

Out-county Pupils

In all these calculations allowance must also be made for those pupils who, living under one local authority, go to school under another. These "out-county" pupils, as they are called, have always been numerous in London, and in recent years have amounted to about one-tenth of the total grammar-school attendance. In 1909 there were 2,678 such pupils, and by 1919 the numbers had risen to 3,929 boys and 1,874 girls. About half were attending independent, and half Council-aided or maintained schools. It is not known how many London boys and girls were then going in the reverse direction to schools outside the County boundary, but it is believed that the numbers were small, except for a few children of wealthy parents attending boarding-schools in the country.

After the First World War the London County Council became concerned at the heavy burden on rates occasioned by this daily influx of children into London, so in 1921 it was decided that the total cost of providing schooling for these pupils (and not merely the fees, which

[1] To illustrate some of the problems created by changes in population—either over short periods of time or else in different neighbourhoods— we may quote the following examples:

(a) The number of admissions to London grammar schools in September, 1945, was 6,407, and in September, 1950, was 6,575. Yet in the latter year the percentage of 11-year-old children admitted was only 20·0 per cent. as compared with 25·6 per cent. in 1945. The higher degree of selectivity was due to changes in child population rather than changes in the number of grammar-school places.

(b) In the case of two particular boroughs in north London, Islington and St. Pancras, we find that in 1919 there were 2,700 grammar-school places for 56,000 children aged 10-15 years inclusive, or one place for every twenty children. In 1950 there were 3,800 places for 24,500 children, or one place for every six. In other words, because of the combined effect of changes in population and number of school places the proportion of grammar-school places available for the secondary age-group has more than trebled during the last thirty years.

only covered about one-third of the total cost) should be paid by the local authority of the county from which the pupils came. Agreements were made in this respect with Essex, Middlesex, and Kent County Councils, but not with Hertfordshire and Surrey. Simultaneously with the introduction of those new regulations, all the Councils concerned were rapidly expanding the number of places in their own grammar schools. The general effect of the changes was to reduce the number of out-county pupils in the aided and maintained schools in London as a whole, though the result varied from school to school depending largely upon the distance of the school from the County boundary. The schools most affected by the change were those in the East End boroughs and the City and Westminster, which had previously drawn a considerable number of their entrants from non-local sources. Those least affected were schools situated within easy reach of the surrounding suburbs, such as Latymer Upper in Hammersmith and Haberdashers' in Hampstead.

There was general agreement among inspectors and teachers that the reduction in the number of out-county pupils was bad for the schools concerned.[1] Parents were also irritated by what they regarded as the artificiality of county boundaries. On grounds of both convenience and common sense it was felt that children should usually attend the nearest secondary school, irrespective of the local authority under which they lived. In recent years, therefore, a more liberal policy has been adopted, and in 1950–1 there were 3,770 non-London County Council children attending London grammar schools, and about 1,500 London children attending grammar schools in the Home Counties.[2]

Size of Educational Elite

The emphasis in this chapter on population trends and similar demographic aspects of education may surprise some persons accustomed to think in conventional terms of the "grammar-school type". Theoretically, according to the Norwood Committee, the Ministry of Education, and others who officially support the tripartite system of

---

[1] It was reported, for example, by an inspector of a grammar school situated in the East End in 1926: "The school has suffered seriously from the falling-off in out-county pupils and the deterioration of the neighbourhood . . . the out-county scholars . . . at one time amounted to over a hundred. They are now reduced to seven. As these scholars were often the best pupils their loss is a serious matter, especially as the pupils coming from the locality itself are also of a lower standard than their predecessors owing to the neighbourhood having deteriorated."

[2] London children attending boarding-schools in the country were not, of course, included in this total.

secondary education, there is a well-defined and clearly distinguishable type of intelligent boy or girl who comprise the country's educational *élite*. By means of carefully prepared and scientifically planned tests at the age of eleven it is possible to select this *élite* with a high degree of accuracy, largely irrespective of environmental circumstances. Indeed, the whole argument in favour of the tripartite system depends upon the theory that only a small minority of children are suitable for the advanced academic curricula of the grammar schools, and that these comprise a fairly stable and fixed proportion (officially estimated at about one in five or six) of the total child population.

In practice, however, it is found that, far from there being uniformity throughout the country, as might logically be expected if the Norwood theory is accepted, the percentage of children chosen for grammar schools varies widely from county to county and from town to town. Some of the more extreme examples of these variations are given in the table below:

PERCENTAGE OF 13-YEAR-OLD CHILDREN ATTENDING MAINTAINED AND ASSISTED GRAMMAR SCHOOLS IN VARIOUS PARTS OF ENGLAND AND WALES (1951)[1]

Area	Boys	Girls
Merionethshire	62·3	65·0
Cardiganshire	49·2	61·5
Westmorland	40·7	45·5
Gloucestershire	28·0	30·5
Dorset	33·6	31·5
Northumberland	13·7	13·5
Nottinghamshire	14·0	13·0
Durham	12·5	13·1
Lincoln	36·3	30·0
Canterbury	29·6	30·4
Sunderland	8·7	10·6
Gateshead	8·4	7·2
London	20·3	21·5
England	18·9	19·8
Wales	30·3	34·2

[1] Allowances must be made for children who live under one authority but go to school under another, and also for children attending independent schools of the grammar-school type. But even with these qualifications the differences are startling. For further discussion of this matter see "Anomalies in Grammar School Placing", by F. C. Campbell, *The Schoolmaster*, Dec. 12, 1952.

What are we to conclude from these wide differences in the proportionate number of children attending grammar schools? Are the children of Wales nearly twice as intelligent as the children of England? Does the mountain air of Merionethshire breed a race of superior intellects? Are the people of mining Durham and Northumberland slower witted than the farming folk of Gloucestershire and Westmorland? Is the academic pace much quicker in the cathedral towns of Lincoln and Canterbury than it is in the industrial towns of Gateshead and Sunderland?

On the contrary, it would appear that the number of grammar-school places depends less upon the intelligence of local pupils than upon historical circumstances or administrative convenience; and furthermore, that little allowance appears to be made, at least over comparatively short periods of time, for substantial changes in child population. It is hard statistical facts like these, perhaps, more than arguments based on philosophy or psychology, that reveal how false are the claims made about the allegedly scientific selection of the "grammar-school type".

London's figures for grammar-school attendance, as was previously explained, have now risen above the average for England and Wales, mainly as a result of the dramatic fall in child population during the last twenty years.

But instead of there being any prospect of stability within sight, the London County Council will again be confronted with new population problems as the post-war "bulge" in the birth-rate begins to be felt in the secondary schools about 1957–8. For example, in 1951 there were nearly twice as many children in the 3–4 age-group (120,384) as compared with the 11–12 age-group (71,064). To make matters more complicated there were only 98,535 children in the 0–1 age-group. All these changes will create serious administrative problems in the schools, but at least they have the merit of focusing attention on the way in which wider sociological factors influence secondary-school selection.

In the long run it is hoped that non-selective comprehensive high schools will provide a partial solution to the problem of a secondary-school entry that fluctuates in both quantity and quality. In the meantime it is obvious that no one concerned with grammar schools—administrators, teachers, or psychologists alike—can afford to ignore the many important ways in which changing demographic conditions affect their schools. It is not merely a question of providing more or fewer secondary-school places in accordance with fluctuations in the birth-rate or the movement of children in or out of London, but of taking into account much wider educational considerations, particularly in relation to the grammar schools. Many of the outstanding issues with which the latter schools are faced (including abilities of pupils, types of curricula selected, standards achieved in examinations, size of sixth forms, and eventual careers of leavers) are closely bound up with the degree of selectivity practised in the choice of pupils; and this selectivity may vary as much from place to place, and from time to time, in the future as in the past.

Chapter 3

THE CHANGING SOCIAL STRUCTURE
OF THE GRAMMAR SCHOOLS

*. . . the social aspects and consequences of an educational system
are not less important than the pedagogic. . . . What we wish to do
in the field of education should not, and cannot, be kept apart from
our broader social objectives—from our ideas of the kind of
society we wish to see develop.*—Professor D. V. Glass.[1]

*. . . there is truth in the paradoxical statement of a modern
writer that progress in English education has owed less to the zeal
of its advocates than to changes in the structure of social life
which have often no apparent connection with educational movements. . . .*—A. E. Dobbs.[2]

THE question of how many London children should attend grammar
schools was not, as we have seen, the only problem in secondary
education confronting the London County Council at the
beginning of the century. There was also the problem—which,
incidentally, has proved more difficult to solve—of what type of children should attend, and how they should be chosen. As the grammar
schools were selective rather than comprehensive, a decision on methods
of selection had to be reached. Quality must be measured as well as
quantity. Once the traditional method of entry was altered all kinds of
difficult questions, involving the most complicated social and educational issues, were raised. Should the new basis of entry be willingness
to pay fees or ability to win a scholarship? How many scholarships
should be awarded? Should the middle-class bias of the grammar
school be retained or should the doors be opened wider to children
of the working class? For whom were the scholarships intended—the
very poor who could afford no fees or the better-off artisans and lower-
middle-class children who might fit more easily into traditional gram-

---

[1] *Social Mobility in Britain*, edited by D. V. Glass, p. 27 (Routledge and Kegan
Paul, 1954).
[2] A. E. Dobbs, *Education and Social Movements* (Longmans, Green and Co., 1919).

42

mar-school ways? Should allowances be made for environmental differences between schools' catchment-areas, and should the number of school places vary with local social conditions? Should curricula be adapted to take into account possible changes in the family background of pupils? These were questions that vexed the pioneers of State secondary education at the beginning of the century, and continue to provoke controversy today.

The main difficulty confronting the Council in this respect, was not the immediate practical problem of devising a suitable selection examination (though that difficulty has never effectively been overcome), but the broader social problem of introducing larger numbers of working-class children into the grammar schools. This was not, of course, a new problem as the need for "democratizing" secondary education had long been recognized, but it became more urgent as a result of the 1902 and 1907 Education Acts. These Acts were attempts to remedy some of the more glaring deficiencies of secondary education on a national scale. Locally, the London County Council's plan to push ahead with the expansion of grammar-school places and to provide an improved scholarship system was evidence of its determination to extend the benefits of grammar-school education to larger numbers of London children, irrespective of their social origin.

Nevertheless, despite the more democratic approach to secondary education advocated by reformers such as Sidney Webb, it is revealing to see how the old middle-class prejudices lingered on among many councillors and education officials at County Hall. In the early days of the new Council scheme a district's suitability for secondary education was assessed in terms not only of child population, but also of social status. When it was proposed to build a new grammar school or extend an old one in a particular neighbourhood, that neighbourhood was carefully surveyed from the social viewpoint, and all the economic factors involved, especially the number of potential fee-payers, were carefully studied. The first comprehensive report on secondary-school accommodation in London, which was presented to the Council in 1909, contained a detailed analysis of each borough in terms of the proportion of inhabitants engaged in professional, commercial, and manual occupations. Rateable value was also assessed. Boroughs were listed as suitable or unsuitable for the expansion of secondary schools according to their relative wealth or poverty. Thus, for example, well-to-do residential boroughs such as Hampstead and Lewisham were areas in which, in the Council's opinion, a person "would naturally expect a demand for secondary education", whereas poverty-stricken Shoreditch, Bethnal Green, and Poplar were dismissed as areas where the demand for grammar schools was "likely to be small". The need to relate grammar school facilities to local environmental conditions was stated with surprising frankness in the 1909 Report:

> The demand for secondary education will vary not only with the character and wealth of the population but with the grade and quality of the education offered, and the price at which it is afforded . . . the various local authorities differ greatly in the character of their population and therefore differ in their educational requirements. One form of higher education may be better suited to one district, another form to another. . . . It is, therefore, not possible or desirable to adopt a definite standard for the provision of secondary education for the country generally. Each town, and in the case of London, each district, must be considered as to its special needs and requirements.[1]

Ten years later, when the Council made a similar survey, more enlightened views were held about the undesirability of confining grammar schools to a particular social class. By the time the First World War was over it was widely felt that to debar children from the benefits of secondary education solely because of their poor background was unfair to the children concerned as well as a loss to the community as a whole. To accept the social *status quo* in this way was to reject the educational hopes aroused at that time. However, even as late as 1919, it was apparently still officially agreed that the poorer areas of London needed fewer grammar-school places than the richer ones. In its Report for that year, the Council stated:

> It will be observed that the proportion of population in attendance at public secondary schools has a fairly close relation with the general social and economic conditions of the boroughs.[2]

There was, of course, a good factual basis for the Council's attitude on this point.

For example, Lewisham (16·9 per 1,000), Wandsworth (13·8), and

---

[1] Report of the L.C.C. Education Officer upon Secondary School Accommodation in London, p. 9, 1909.
[2] "Secondary School Accommodation in London," p. 2, Report to London County Council Higher Education Sub-Committee, Dec. 11, 1919.

Hampstead (13·4) had the highest average attendance at secondary schools for three selected years. They were also among the boroughs where there was least poverty, least overcrowding, the lowest rates for infantile mortality, and the highest proportion of persons engaged in commercial and professional occupations. Shoreditch (1·5 per 1,000), Bethnal Green (2·3), and Southwark (2·5) were at the bottom of the table for attendance, and were also among the poorest, most over-crowded, and unhealthy boroughs, with the smallest proportion of middle-class population. In statistical terms, the correlation coefficient between those attending secondary schools in various boroughs and the percentage of people living in poverty was —0·59. The correlation of this factor with overcrowding was —0·92, with infantile mortality —0·73, and with the percentage of people engaging in professional or commercial occupations +0·67, as may be seen in the table on page 46.

An analysis from other sources of the demographic and social structure of the schools themselves confirms that at the end of the First World War the London grammar schools were still predominantly middle-class institutions. Poverty and lack of school places were still preventing large numbers of children from getting the secondary education they deserved. In 1919, for example, only one London child in thirteen out of the age-group 10–15 years was attending a secondary school, and the figure is reduced to one in eighteen if we consider only the aided and maintained schools. Less than one place in three was free in these schools, and there is some evidence to suggest that such scholarship winners as there were came from lower-middle-class or artisan rather than very poor homes.[1] Moreover, in three north London grammar schools for which we have detailed information in the early 1920s, less than one in ten of the pupils came from homes where parents were in unskilled or semi-skilled occupations. In other words, despite the reforms of the previous fifteen years, the grammar schools were still heavily weighted towards the better-off sections of the population.

Influx of Working-Class Pupils

During the next twenty-five years, however, this picture was significantly changed. The aided and maintained grammar schools altered considerably in their social structure, and the middle-class predominance,

---

[1] See chapter on Scholarships.

CORRELATION OF SECONDARY-SCHOOL ATTENDANCE
WITH SOCIAL FACTORS IN LONDON

Borough or City	Attendance at secondary schools per 1,000 population				% of population			Infant mortality per 1,000 population
	1909	*1919*	*1926*	*Average*	*living in poverty*[1]	*over-crowded*	*in professions or commerce (1919)*	
Lewisham	11·9	18·8	19·9	16·9	4·8	4·7	8·0	59·3
Wandsworth	9·5	15·7	16·3	13·8	4·4	6·8	6·8	64·3
Hampstead	11·9	14·5	13·9	13·4	1·4	6·5	8·0	56·6
Stoke Newington	8·7	12·6	14·2	11·8	5·4	8·1	8·1	67·1
City	10·4	9·7	11·8	10·6	8·9	6·6	5·5	79·4
Woolwich	6·8	10·1	9·7	8·9	8·8	7·8	2·5	62·0
Camberwell	7·7	9·4	9·7	8·9	8·2	12·8	5·4	74·3
Greenwich	6·0	7·9	9·9	7·9	11·8	13·8	3·0	68·0
Hackney	7·8	7·0	8·8	7·9	7·4	11·5	5·5	73·4
Battersea	6·3	7·7	9·4	7·8	8·1	12·4	4·5	75·2
Deptford	6·4	7·2	8·5	7·4	14·6	12·8	4·4	80·3
Kensington	5·7	5·2	9·0	6·6	7·9	16·7	4·8	91·6
Fulham	5·2	6·0	7·7	6·3	7·2	13·1	4·7	75·7
Hammersmith	6·2	6·0	6·8	6·3	7·2	13·8	5·3	75·2
Chelsea	4·9	5·6	8·0	6·2	4·5	13·7	3·9	66·6
Westminster	5·1	5·4	6·8	5·8	4·2	10·1	5·1	69·7
Lambeth	4·9	5·3	6·0	5·4	8·5	12·7	6·0	74·1
Holborn	4·1	4·7	6·6	5·1	4·6	19·8	7·2	72·7
Islington	4·7	4·3	5·8	4·9	9·6	19·4	4·9	76·6
Paddington	4·2	5·1	5·2	4·8	6·2	15·4	5·1	79·7
St. Pancras	3·9	3·7	5·8	4·5	11·8	22·4	4·6	74·6
St. Marylebone	2·8	5·2	5·4	4·5	4·6	17·9	4·8	69·3
Stepney	3·2	4·5	5·0	4·2	15·5	29·0	2·0	85·5
Poplar	3·3	3·3	5·0	3·9	24·1	21·2	2·0	81·3
Bermondsey	3·7	2·7	3·5	3·3	17·5	23·2	2·5	92·6
Finsbury	2·8	2·7	3·1	2·9	13·2	34·0	2·4	83·3
Southwark	2·6	2·3	2·7	2·5	13·5	23·5	2·9	85·4
Bethnal Green	1·5	2·2	3·3	2·3	17·8	27·8	1·5	95·5
Shoreditch	1·3	1·3	1·9	1·5	18·0	32·0	1·3	101·8
Coefficient of Correlation					−0·59	−0·92	+0·67	−0·73

[1] Statistics relating to social conditions for various years in the 1920s are quoted in *The Backward Child*, by Sir Cyril Burt, pp. 100–1 (Univ. of London Press, 1950).

which was such a characteristic feature of these schools in earlier days, was seriously challenged. Not only did the number of fee-payers gradually decrease, to be eventually wiped out altogether under the terms of the 1944 Education Act, but the proportion of working-class children rose steadily until today in many grammar schools they comprise a majority, or at least a substantial percentage, of the pupils. A detailed account of the social transformation that occurred in four fairly typical north London grammar schools is given in the tables that follow. These are based on an analysis of the occupations of parents, going back in some cases as far as the years 1900–9. Approximately 13,000 items were classified, so it cannot be argued that the sample was a small one.[1]

Broadly speaking, the social classes have been divided as follows:

1 and 2.

Higher administrative, commercial, and professional grades such as company directors, higher Civil Servants, doctors, architects. Executive, technical, and lower professional grades such as managers, teachers, bank clerks, parsons, small employers.

3 and 4.

Shopkeepers, persons in supervisory capacity and skilled clerical jobs, inspectors, jobbing builders.

5.

Skilled workers, artisans and craftsmen, routine clerical workers.

6 and 7.

Semi-skilled, unskilled, and casual workers, labourers, watchmen.

The most striking fact that emerges from these tables is the steady decline in the proportion of pupils coming from middle- or lower-middle-class homes, and the corresponding increase in pupils from working-class homes. In the case of the two schools, A and D, for which we have the longest records, the percentage of parents in categories 1 and 2 (broadly speaking, the middle class) fell from 16 to 6, and from 15 to 1 respectively between 1900–9 and 1945–9, whereas the percentage of parents in categories 6 and 7 (broadly speaking, the semi-skilled and unskilled workers) rose from 4 to 15, and from 2 to 21 respectively, during the same period. In both these schools the lower middle class, which was formerly the largest single group represented, has long since lost its leading position to the skilled-worker category. Similar trends

[1] The defining of a social class is a complex matter, and decisions on borderline cases must often necessarily be somewhat arbitrary. For purposes of convenience, therefore, a modified version of a classification recently approved by the sociological department of the London School of Economics and Political Science has been used, see "Social Grading of Occupations", by J. Hall and C. Jones, *British Journal of Sociology*, Vol. I, No. 1, March, 1950. In view of the fact that precise and detailed information about parents' occupations was sometimes lacking in the original school records (from which data were taken) a fourfold classification has been used.

E

PARENTS OF PUPILS IN FOUR LONDON GRAMMAR SCHOOLS
CHANGES IN SOCIAL CLASS, 1900-49

SCHOOL A

Class	1900-09		1910-19		1920-4		1925-9		1930-4		1935-9		1940-1		1946-9	
	No.	%	No.	%	No.	%	No.	%	No.	%	No.	%	No.	%	No.	%
1-2	289	15·99	227	17·29	149	19·13	81	13·87	75	13·35	47	8·56	14	5·24	23	6·18
3-4	783	43·02	562	42·80	315	40·44	210	35·96	226	40·21	199	36·25	82	30·71	116	31·18
5	573	31·48	376	28·64	226	29·01	183	31·33	179	31·85	191	34·79	111	41·57	169	45·44
6-7	68	3·74	65	4·95	40	5·13	71	12·16	67	11·92	85	15·48	32	11·99	57	15·32
Unclassified	105	5·77	83	6·32	49	6·29	39	6·68	15	2·67	27	4·92	28	10·49	7	1·88
Totals	1,818	100·0	1,313	100·0	779	100·0	584	100·0	562	100·0	549	100·0	267	100·0	372	100·0

SCHOOL B

Class	1922-4		1925-9		1930-4		1935-9		1941-3		1945-9	
	No.	%	No.	%	No.	%	No.	%	No.	%	No.	%
1-2	35	14·9	50	11·8	31	6·2	17	7·8	4	2·1	12	2·3
3-4	87	37·0	173	40·5	188	37·75	74	33·9	31	16·3	79	14·8
5	92	39·15	160	37·6	226	45·4	99	45·4	84	44·2	277	52·2
6-7	17	7·25	38	8·9	47	9·4	25	11·5	25	13·2	112	21·1
Unclassified	4	1·7	5	1·2	6	1·25	3	1·4	46	24·2	51	9·6
Totals	235	100·0	426	100·0	498	100·0	218	100·0	190	100·0	531	100·0

PARENTS OF PUPILS IN FOUR LONDON GRAMMAR SCHOOLS
CHANGES IN SOCIAL CLASS, 1900-49

SCHOOL C

Class	1934 No.	%	1935–9 No.	%	1940–4 No.	%	1945–9 No.	%
1–2	2	2·25	14	3·7	27	4·25	25	3·8
3–4	31	34·85	106	28·3	147	23·1	172	26·05
5	33	37·1	160	42·7	270	42·35	285	43·2
6–7	10	11·2	57	15·2	90	14·1	82	12·45
Unclassified	13	14·6	38	10·1	104	16·2	96	14·5
Totals	89	100·0	375	100·0	638	100·0	660	100·0

SCHOOL D

Class	1905–9 No.	%	1910–14 No.	%	1915–19 No.	%	1920–4 No.	%	1925–9 No.	%	1930–4 No.	%	1935–9 No.	%	1940–4 No.	%	1945–9 No.	%
1–2	13	14·9	19	10·1	39	8·3	37	7·7	25	5·5	14	3·3	26	6·3	11	3·25	6	1·0
3–4	28	32·2	77	40·95	195	41·6	193	40·3	150	33·3	140	32·8	97	23·55	70	20·7	112	19·1
5	20	23·0	67	35·65	157	33·5	167	34·9	190	42·1	193	45·2	184	44·65	159	47·05	315	53·8
6–7	2	2·3	17	9·05	34	7·2	55	11·5	42	9·3	52	12·2	69	16·75	66	19·5	124	21·2
Unclassified	24	27·6	8	4·25	44	9·4	27	5·6	44	9·8	28	6·5	36	8·75	32	9·5	29	4·9
Totals	87	100·0	188	100·0	469	100·0	479	100·0	451	100·0	427	100·0	412	100·0	338	100·0	586	100·0

49

were experienced by Schools B and (though to a somewhat less extent) C during recent years.[1]

When the four schools are taken together for the years immediately following the Second World War, it is clear that a. the professional and administrative class contributed on the average less than one in twenty of the school's entrants, b. the skilled working-class share has risen from under one-third to about one-half, and c. one in five or six of all entrants came from the poorer homes. In other words, bus drivers, factory hands, engineers, postmen, railway porters, carpenters, electricians, printers, and similar manual workers predominate among the parents of pupils attending the majority of London grammar schools rather than shopkeepers, teachers, businessmen, clerks, doctors, and other professional persons as was the case a generation ago.

Contrast with Suburban Grammar Schools

It is important to realize that grammar schools situated in the suburbs of Greater London, where the population is more noticeably middle class in social composition, have not been affected by this "proletarianizing" trend to the same extent as the grammar schools in the metropolitan boroughs. A recent investigation by research workers from the London School of Economics and Political Science of the social class of a representative sample of pupils in four grammar schools (in East Ham, Battersea, Surrey, and Middlesex) showed that the class structure of two London County Council schools corresponded broadly with those already described in Islington and St. Pancras, but that the suburban schools were much more middle class in their background.[2] In the case of one such suburban school situated in a prosperous area in Surrey the pupils classified as upper middle class comprised 33 per cent., and lower middle class 22 per cent., of the total. In another case,

[1] School D is a maintained school drawing the greater bulk of its entrants from Islington and St. Pancras. School B is also a maintained school, and draws most of its pupils from Islington. School A is an old Jacobean foundation drawing partly on Islington, and also to some extent on Middlesex, where its playing fields are situated. All three are situated in predominantly working-class areas. School C is situated in comparatively new buildings on the edge of Parliament Hill. It draws its pupils from Hampstead and Hendon as well as St. Pancras. Schools A and C are both aided schools.

[2] See "Selection for Secondary Education and Achievement in Four Grammar Schools", by A. H. Halsey and L. Gardner, *British Journal of Sociology*, Vol. IV, No. 1, March, 1953; "Social Status and Secondary Education", by H. T. Himmelweit, *Social Mobility in Britain*, p. 144 (Routledge and Kegan Paul, 1954).

where the school drew upon a well-to-do residential area of Middlesex for its catchment-area, the upper middle-class pupils comprised 34 per cent., and the lower middle-class 24 per cent. of the total.

In the table given below, the four categories correspond broadly, though not exactly, with the categories already described for the schools in Islington and St. Pancras:

PERCENTAGE DISTRIBUTION OF THE SOCIAL STATUS COMPOSITION OF THE THIRD FORMS OF FOUR GRAMMAR SCHOOLS IN THE GREATER LONDON AREA

Schools	Upper Middle	Lower Middle	Upper Working	Lower Working
E	7·2	25·5	46·9	20·4
F	18·0	33·7	34·8	13·5
G	33·3	21·8	29·9	14·9
H	34·5	24·1	34·5	6·9

Direct-grant schools, which accept a certain proportion of fee-payers as well as very carefully chosen scholarship entrants, continue to be highly selective, both socially and academically.[1] In an analysis made by the present writer of the social class of pupils entering such a school formerly situated in London but now in the Home Counties, it was found that the school's middle-class character had become even more accentuated as the years went by, as may be seen in the following table:

SOCIAL STRUCTURE OF DIRECT-GRANT GRAMMAR SCHOOL

Year	1–2	(% in each social class) 3–4	5	6–7	Unclassified
1905	33	44	14	2	7
1925	36	39	18	2	5
1935	52	31	14	3	0
1944	58	32	9	0	1
1950	53	42	3	2	0

[1] Under the terms of the 1944 Education Act certain old-established and well-known secondary schools were given direct-grant status. This meant that they got financial aid directly from the Ministry of Education and not from the local authority. They could continue taking fee-payers but also had to take a certain proportion of scholarship entrants; the latter usually being the best of the successful candidates in the Common Entrance test.

It is clear, therefore, that the relative proportions of the different social classes in various schools will depend not only upon general social conditions in the catchment-area, but also upon the degree of selectivity permitted in the choice of pupils.[1] A further important point that emerges from these conclusions, and one that is stressed by contributors to recent studies of social mobility in Britain is that the social class structure of the grammar schools even ten years after the 1944 Education Act does not correspond exactly with the social class structure of the catchment-area from which the schools draw their pupils.[2] Such figures as are available show that, despite the abolition of fees, the middle class are relatively over-represented and the working class under-represented in the grammar schools. The reasons for this, and its bearing upon the question of providing secondary education for all children, regardless of their social background, are discussed elsewhere in this book.

Causes of Changing Social Structure of Grammar Schools

There are three main causes why the proportion of middle-class pupils has declined so substantially in many London grammar schools during the last thirty years. First, there has been the great expansion of school places in relation to child population that was described at length in the last chapter. Secondly, there has been the development of the scholarship system, enabling larger numbers of poorer children to take the places formerly occupied by fee-payers. This point is discussed in detail in the next chapter.

The third cause of the social transformation of the grammar schools is the internal change in the class structure of the population itself. Not only has the number of children varied greatly during the last half-century but there have been significant changes in the relationship

[1] Under present conditions, as has been pointed out, the degree of selectivity varies widely from county to county, from school type (direct-grant, aided, maintained) to school type, and, even within the same type, from school to school. Other things being equal, it is probably true in most cases that a headmaster or headmistress interviewing pupils for entry to a grammar school (and it must be appreciated that they still retain certain powers of choice in this respect) will tend to choose those boys or girls who are considered to have the best family and cultural background. It is not surprising, taking into account the traditions and general ethos of the grammar school, that "best" may sometimes in these circumstances be equated with "professional" or "middle class".

[2] For further discussion of this point see Chapters V and VI in *Social Mobility in Britain*, edited by D. V. Glass (Routledge and Kegan Paul, 1954).

of social classes, and the relative importance of various occupations.[1]

During the first quarter of this century the number of persons employed in commerce, finance, administration, or the professions in Greater London increased substantially, both absolutely and proportionately. In more recent years, however, the number of "white-collar" workers actually living in the central area has tended to decline, even though they continue to form a relatively high percentage of the suburban population. In 1951 there were, in fact, fewer clerical workers living in the County of London as compared with 1931, although this occupational group has increased considerably in the country as a whole. Furthermore, the percentage of population in social classes 1 and 2 (broadly speaking, the middle and lower middle classes) is nowadays less in London than in England and Wales, and much less than in the surrounding counties of Hertfordshire, Middlesex, Surrey, and Kent, as the following table based on the One Per Cent. Sample of the 1951 Census shows.

	Social Classes 1 and 2 as percentage of total number of households, 1951
London	17
Middlesex	24
Surrey	28
Kent	22
Herts	24
England and Wales	18

The reasons for this exodus of hundreds of thousands of shopkeepers, clerks, doctors, teachers, technicians, Civil Servants, bank officials, and other professional workers from the old City centre to newer suburbs are well known. Improved methods of transport have made it possible to travel longer distances to work. The spread of dormitory estates, largely financed by building societies, encouraged the family man with reasonably high income but little capital to buy his house by mortgage payments. Wives wanted easily run houses for themselves and gardens for their children. Residential accommodation in the central boroughs became increasingly expensive for the middle classes as rents rose. The

[1] For a more detailed study of changing social class relationships in two London boroughs see "The Changing Environment of the London Grammar School 1900–50", by F. C. Campbell, Ph.D. thesis, Univ. of London, 1953.

new Council flats were reserved for working-class families. The large, old-fashioned Victorian houses mainly built between 1850 and 1900 near the County boundary were increasingly split into rooms and apartments for poorer sections of the community. Once a neighbourhood in these circumstances began—in the estate agent's phrase—to "go down" it was not long before the whole social character of a district changed.

However, although the local schools were inevitably affected by their altered environment, the changes were not all loss from the grammar schools' point of view. On the contrary, among broad sections of the population hitherto barely touched by secondary education, there was a new intellectual stirring and eagerness for the cultural and vocational benefits conferred by the grammar school.

Simultaneously, as the influence of the middle and lower middle classes declined economically (and also politically, if we consider the Labour Party's large majority on the London County Council) that of the working class increased. It has already been pointed out how slight was the contact of the children of manual workers—except for a few brilliant scholarship winners—with secondary schools at the beginning of the century; but gradually over the years more and more working-class boys and girls entered the grammar schools as living standards rose and educational opportunities were opened up. Real wages for both skilled and unskilled have increased steadily, hours of work have shortened, and unemployment, in recent years at any rate, is less than formerly. Slum clearance and the building of new Council houses have reduced overcrowding—a process helped by the fall in the size of the average family. Holidays with pay have become more widespread, and there are greater facilities for leisure and recreation than ever before. The social services have alleviated the worst aspects of sickness, old age, accidents, widowhood, and orphanhood, especially for the very poor. The skilled manual worker nowadays often has a higher money income and sometimes greater social prestige than the clerk or minor Civil Servant. Life for the mass of the adult industrial population, in other words, despite the set-backs of cyclical unemployment and two world wars, has tended to become more comfortable, more spacious, and more "civilized" in every way than it was two or three generations ago. Similarly, with the great majority of children there have been substantial advances in physique, nutrition, and also (despite what some of our educational Cassandras say!) in manners and behaviour. Certainly, modern children on the average are healthier and stronger, and most probably mentally more lively and alert than were their parents and grandparents.[1]

Decline of Fee-payers

The consequences that flowed from these long-term social and economic developments affected secondary schools in London in many other organizational ways, apart from the changed intake of pupils. As their middle-class basis was undermined so both grammar and independent schools were faced with new problems of finance and administration. A number were compelled to abandon their independent status and accept Council control. Several private schools were forced by the loss of their traditional fee-paying clientele to move lock, stock, and barrel into the suburbs. Practically every school situated in the centre of London was confronted with serious building difficulties because of the spread of industry and commerce, and the absorption of open space for non-educational purposes. The physical deterioration of certain neighbourhoods because of noise, smoke, and traffic congestion was another problem. Only the wealthiest and most firmly established schools proved strong enough to resist these pressures and even they were forced in different ways to adapt themselves to the new circumstances.

The most direct and obvious financial result of the "flight of the middle classes" was the decline in the number of school fee-payers in central London. It is not possible, owing to the lack of published data and wide variations in methods of obtaining and spending income, to provide a full account of the changing finances of the grammar schools, but sufficient data is available to give an outline picture of what happened to the fee-paying contribution during the forty years between the Council's intervention in 1904 and the abolition of fees in 1944.

At the beginning of the century more than nine out of ten pupils in London secondary schools were fee-payers. This proportion was rapidly reduced to just under two out of three as a result of the expansion of the Council's scholarship scheme between 1904-10. It rose again to nearly three out of four during the next fifteen years, and then fell

---

[1] In London the infant mortality rate, which is an excellent index of maternal and child poverty, fell from 139 per 1,000 in 1901–3 to 31 per 1,000 in 1948. The average height of 13½-year-old boys has risen from 56·3 inches (57·8 inches for girls) in 1905–12 to 60·0 inches for boys (and 60·5 inches for girls) in 1949. Weights of both boys and girls have also risen proportionately.

steadily until at the outbreak of the Second World War less than half of the pupils entering the grammar schools were fee-payers.

Generally speaking, the proportion of fee-payers was higher in the aided than in the maintained schools, but this to some extent depended upon the nature of each school's catchment-area. A school situated in a poor working-class area, for example, tended to have more scholarship entrants, irrespective of its status, whereas a school drawing its entrants mainly from a more prosperous residential area tended to keep up its proportion of fee-payers.[1]

The detailed figures for four schools situated in a district of north London where social conditions were changing fairly rapidly between the two World Wars are given below:

DECLINE OF FEE-PAYERS IN FOUR LONDON GRAMMAR SCHOOLS

Boys	Pupils entering schools				
	1908–9		1928–9		1948–9
Owen's	No. %		No. %		No. %
Scholarships	69 27·7		102 46·15		164 100
Fee-payers	180 72·3		119 53·85		— —

	1908–9	1918–19	1928–9	1938–9	1948–9
Holloway	No. %	No. %	No. %	No. %	No. %
Scholarships	— —	89 44·5	102 60·4	100 80·6	194 100
Fee-payers	43 100	111 55·5	67 39·6	24 19·4	— —

Girls	Pupils attending schools				
	1913	1923	1934	1938	1950
Highbury Hill	No. %	No. %	No. %	No. %	No. %
Scholarships	102 31	83 28	200 59	253 70	470 100
Fee-payers	232 69	214 72	138 41	110 30	— —
Parliament Hill	No. %	No. %	No. %	No. %	No. %
Scholarships	186 55	143 38	296 56	358 71	530 100
Fee-payers	152 45	237 62	236 44	143 29	— —

Fees, of course, never covered all the costs of maintaining the grammar schools, but before the First World War they comprised about one-third of the schools' total income.[2] Gradually, however, as the costs

---

[1] Many of the old aided schools were situated in the centre and East End of London.

[2] In 1908–9 the total income of forty grammar schools aided by the London County Council was £223,598, of which fees brought in 29·82 per cent., endowments 19·69 per cent., Council grants 28·09 per cent., and Board of Education grants 22·40 per cent. (See Summary of Accounts of Secondary Schools, etc., aided by the London County Council, 1908–9.) It should be noted that there were then, and continued to be, wide variations in sources of income between different schools.

of running the schools increased, and more and more scholarship pupils were introduced, their share in the total income declined. Between 1909 and 1939 the total expenditure on the London grammar schools rose from about £280,000 to about £1,300,000 annually, which, allowing for changes in the price-level, represents approximately a doubling of expenditure. During the same period the cost per pupil rose from about £15 to about £40.[1]

After the First World War, fees were raised to meet this increased expenditure from an average of about £9–£12 for boys (£6–£8 for girls) to about £13–£15 for both sexes in the mid 1920s.[2] Nevertheless, their share in total income dropped substantially, particularly after 1920, as the following table shows:

INCOME FROM FEES AS PROPORTION OF TOTAL EXPENDITURE IN GRAMMAR SCHOOLS MAINTAINED BY THE COUNCIL

Year	Expenditure	Income from fees	Fees as percentage of total expenditure
1912–13	£88,050	£17,221	19
1919–20	£208,534	£39,318	19
1924–5	£366,542	£64,583	17·5
1928–9	£449,242	£70,861	16
1936–7	£524,323	£61,528	12

So far as the aided schools are concerned, it has already been pointed out that in 1908–9 approximately one-third of their total income came from fees. By 1938–9 the total expenditure on these schools had risen to approximately £806,000 annually, of which fees brought in £164,000 or about one-fifth.

The aided schools, unlike the wholly maintained, which had to rely for their income upon what they could persuade parents to pay or the Council and Board of Education to grant, had another source of income in endowments. In some cases these were very valuable, bringing in an annual income of several thousand pounds, but in others they were

[1] In 1937–8 the cost was £44 9s. 11d. per pupil in maintained and £35 18s. 2d. in aided schools.
[2] Differences in fees continued to exist after the First World War, but they were not quite so wide as previously. In 1926 the highest annual fees for aided schools were £21 for Emanuel, £21 for Strand, £18 for Alleyn's, and £18 for Holloway (maintained). The lowest fees were £9 9s. for Raine's and £9 for George Green's, with the exceptionally low figure of £4 10s. for Bermondsey County Secondary School for Girls. Fees in the London public schools ranged up to £50, and in the proprietary schools up to £63 a year for day pupils.

worth only a few hundreds yearly. The endowments, whatever their size, also became relatively less important as the years went by. Ultimately, their main advantage was not so much their financial value as the special status they gave the schools possessing them.

Since the Second World War the London County Council has published no figures relating separately to grammar-school finances. Such information as has been made available relates to secondary schools as a whole. This policy of lumping together the budgets of technical, modern, secondary, and grammar schools may be convenient to the Council's administrators (and may also, one suspects, be part of the policy of conceding "parity of esteem"), but it has distinct disadvantages to the outside observer. It would be valuable, for example, to know precisely how much per head the Council is spending on its grammar-school pupils today as compared with pre-war, and how the figures compare with other types of secondary school.

But in other respects this reticence on the part of the Council is not so important. The abolition of fees was merely the logical conclusion of a trend that had been going on for a long time; and even if there had been no 1944 Education Act the Council would probably have found it difficult to increase or even maintain the fee-paying income of the grammar schools. It is known that since 1945 all the income of the maintained schools comes from the State or local authority, and it can be deduced from other evidence that the aided schools now obtain at least 95 per cent. (and probably more) of their income from the same sources.

The fact that fees were abolished, and grammar schools are now almost completely State-supported, is of much more social and educational than strictly financial significance.

Plight of Independent Schools

The independent or semi-independent schools, having fewer sources of State aid to fall back on, naturally also proved sensitive to the migration of potential or actual fee-payers from central London. Broadly speaking, there are three categories of these schools (though there is some overlapping of type and function, and even considerable variety within each category), and they reacted in different ways according to their own social and economic circumstances or peculiarities of sites and buildings.

The famous old public schools[1] such as St. Paul's, Westminster, Mercers', Merchant Taylors', Dulwich, Charterhouse, and City of London possessed wealthy endowments and drew upon a prosperous and fairly widely scattered community for the majority of their entrants. As the cost of providing first-class facilities for their pupils steadily rose so they drew increasingly upon their endowment income and also increased fees—a policy that, of course, could only be adopted in their own exceptionally favourable circumstances.

Although only a small minority of the population could afford the high fees charged by these schools, the demand for them, in the economist's phrase, proved highly inelastic, i.e. the buyers' willingness to pay was not much reduced by the higher prices charged. Despite the fact that fees doubled during the First World War and again during the Second World War (see table) there is still a long waiting list of parents anxious to get their children admitted.

ANNUAL FEES IN LONDON BOYS' PUBLIC SCHOOLS

	1909	1942	1953
	£ s.	£ s.	£ s.
City of London[2]	15 15	25 4 to 31 10	78 15
Dulwich	24	45	78
St. Paul's	24 9	45	90 (day)
Mercers'	10 10	30	64 10
Westminster	31 10	74 10	170
Merchant Taylors'	12 12 to 14 14	—	102 (day)

The strong social and financial basis of these schools enabled them to refuse a large amount of State aid, and they have accordingly also rejected much State control. On the other hand, in the nature of things they were unable to resist the relentless encroachment of commerce and industry, and even in some cases the spread of slums or public buildings,

[1] A discussion of the history of these schools in recent years lies outside the scope of this book. For an account of the London County Council's attitude towards them the reader should see the Report of the London County Council Education Officer on the Board of Education Committee on Public Schools, Nov. 16, 1942.

[2] Dulwich, City of London, and Mercers' accept a small number of the best scholarship pupils selected at the Council's Common Entrance Examination (possibly as many as one-fifth of all entrants), but the income thus received is not a large part of the total.

upon their school sites and playing spaces.[1] As a result of this pressure they were faced in several cases (some of them in the nineteenth, others in the twentieth century) with the necessity to move to new sites, either to more spacious and open districts of London away from the City and West End, or else, if they were mainly boarding-schools, to completely different surroundings in the country. Thus, Charterhouse moved from Smithfield to Godalming in 1872; St. Paul's from the City to Hammersmith in 1884; St. Dunstan's from the City to Catford in 1888; Christ's Hospital (Girls) from the City to Hertford in 1898, and Christ's Hospital (Boys) from the City to Horsham in 1902; University College from Bloomsbury to Hampstead in 1907; Haberdashers' Aske's from Hoxton to Hampstead in 1907; Merchant Taylors' from Smithfield to Northwood in 1933; and North London Collegiate from St. Pancras to Edgware in 1940.

The uprooting of such a large number of ancient foundations and the breaking of centuries-old traditions must clearly have been done only for very good and pressing reasons. A vivid account of one of those reasons —the encroachment of buildings upon the school site—is given in this quotation[2] from the history of Charterhouse School:

When Sutton selected Howard House as the best site for his Hospital, this house was then on the very outskirts of the city. It was surrounded on all sides by open spaces. On the north, the village of Islington lay about a mile distant from the walls of Charterhouse, and the walk between them was through green fields; further to the north was the neighbouring village of Hackney. On the west the houses of Snow Hill and Newgate Street were not yet built; no buildings were to be seen in the Strand. On the south the left bank of the river was only sparsely occupied by the mansions of peers

[1] Lack of space for expansion, the spread of commerce, and reduction in local residential population were also reasons for the removal of five aided grammar schools from central London to sites nearer the County boundary. In 1913 the Strand School for Boys moved from King's College in the Strand to Brixton. In 1928 St. Martin's School for Girls moved from Charing Cross Road to Tulse Hill, Archbishop Tenison's School for Boys moved from Leicester Square to the Oval, and Holborn Estate (St. Clement Dane's) School for Boys from Aldwych to Hammersmith. "The transference here recorded in one year of three ancient schools from the centre of London to suburban districts reflects the rapid absorption of the centre for business purposes. It illustrates the constant change which takes place in the educational provision for London", comments the London County Council. (Annual Report of the London County Council Education Officer, p. 33, 1928). The last school to be thus moved was the Burlington School for Girls, which went from a site near Piccadilly to Hammersmith in 1936. From time to time other aided schools have requested permission to move but this has been refused.

[2] *Charterhouse—Past and Present*, by William Haig Brown, pp. 169–71, 1879.

and wealthy merchants. And even for 200 years after the Founder's death Charterhouse School was on the borders of a rural locality. But the condition of things was altogether changed when the site, once so admirably adapted for its purpose, was closely surrounded by a densely crowded population, when every trace of rural freshness was abolished and the boys were of necessity closely confined within five acres surrounded by high brick walls and overlooked from the upper storeys by Goswell Street and Goswell Row.... The vast increase of London during the present century and the consequent demand for building ground affected very much the fortunes of Charterhouse School. Large blocks of houses were built up to the very walls of the playground, and the School was thus deprived of the advantages of a free and open site, which it had enjoyed for 200 years. This change in the character of its position naturally gave rise to suggestions for the abatement of the evil: as early as 1825 the question of its removal was mooted: but though from time to time the proposal was revived, it was hardly entertained in serious earnestness till the Public School Commissioners issued their report in 1864. That distinguished body, after the most careful inquiry, decided that in their opinion "the School" would thrive much better if removed to some eligible site in the country, and they recommended the subject of this removal to the serious consideration of the Governors.

In a similar way overcrowding and the spread of buildings also affected the semi-independent or proprietary schools, which were not so rich, either in historical associations or finance, as the public schools. This type of school was often compelled to accept State aid as well as, in some cases, to move from old sites because of deterioration in its catchment-area. Two well-known boys' schools, Haberdashers' Aske's and University College School, gave up the battle against a hostile environment before the First World War and migrated to what they hoped would be more suitable surroundings in Hampstead.

In later years a girls' school that keenly felt the loss of fee-payers was the North London Collegiate, which was founded by the celebrated Miss Frances Mary Buss in Camden Town in 1850 to educate the daughters, in Miss Buss's words, of that "large and influential part of Society known as the middle classes". The school grew successfully during the nineteenth century in what was then a fairly prosperous residential neighbourhood, and before the First World War, under the guidance of a series of able headmistresses, was one of the best-known girls' day schools in England. However, even such an old and firmly-established institution as the North London Collegiate School, well placed as it was for transport from all parts of north London, had to give way before the impact of social and economic change. Gradually, the number of London pupils diminished, and those from Middlesex increased. Eventually it was decided to move the school from what had become a noisy and congested site in Camden Town to a more congenial environment at Canons, a Georgian manor near Edgware. Canons had space, light, air, grace, and dignity—all the conditions so lacking in the overcrowded buildings in working-class St. Pancras—and most important of all from the point of view of the school's financial future, it was situated in a middle-class residential neighbourhood in Middlesex where the type of pupil envisaged by its founder was most likely to be discovered.

This is how the momentous decision to move to Edgware is described in the official history of the School:

> What was happening meanwhile in Camden Town? . . . the girls had to fight their way to school by crowded tube and bus and tram from more and more distant suburbs. As the neighbourhood changed its character, the houses in Camden Road, once the prim homes of Victorian families with their horses and carriages in the mews behind, were becoming tenements or even factories. Camden Road itself had become a thundering, vibrating artery linking the traffic of the Great North Road with London's markets and motor sale-rooms, and the Midland Railway boomed and puffed louder than ever beneath the school's very windows. Parents hesitated to send their children to brave the teeming streets and to breathe the murky air. Dimly the authorities began to perceive that unless Miss Drummond's hopes (to move to Edgware) materialized the school would die.[1]

The largest group of proprietary schools in London at this time were the eight schools owned by the Girls' Public Day Schools Trust—a non-profit-making foundation set up in 1872 with the object of providing a good secondary education for middle-class girls. These schools had expanded during the late nineteenth and early twentieth century (in the

[1] *The North London Collegiate School for Girls*, by various authors, pp. 102–103 (O.U.P., 1950).

provinces as well as in London), and flourished chiefly in districts where there was a well-to-do residential population and where local grammar schools were insufficient to cope with the demand for girls' secondary education. The London schools began to feel the financial strain after the First World War when many of their customary clientele moved into the suburbs, and competition from Council grammar schools became keener. In the late 1920s and even more so in the early 1930s, when the economic crisis was depressing most types of schools, they all suffered a steady loss of fee-paying pupils, with the exception of the South Hampstead High School for Girls, which was situated in a district that continued to have a high proportion of business and professional people among its population.

The Board of Education had given some financial aid to these schools from their earliest days, and, as a result, they took some scholarship entrants (about one in nine in the mid 1930s); but this proved insufficient to meet rising costs, and in 1937 the Trust applied to the London County Council for further aid.

The Trust's letter to the Council summarized briefly and succinctly those social and economic factors that so sharply affected London secondary schools between the two World Wars. Indeed the explanation given of the need for increased assistance might equally well apply to the aided and maintained grammar schools.

> The reasons for the increase in financial loss at the schools in question, where it occurs, are the falling off in numbers and the ever increasing cost of providing education. The falling off in numbers is due to a combination of various circumstances, namely (1) the decreasing birth-rate; (2) the growing tendency of parents whose business is in London to remove their homes from London to the outer suburbs and even further afield; (3) changes in the neighbourhood resulting in an influx of residents who cannot afford the fees of the Trust schools (for instance, at Clapham); (4) growing competition from your Council's secondary schools (for instance, at Blackheath).[1]

Two other Trust schools, Notting Hill High, which moved to Ealing in Middlesex in 1931, and Kensington High, which closed its senior department when it was bombed during the War, were affected more by site and building problems than by financial difficulties.

[1] "The Girl's Public Day Schools Trust", Report by the Higher Education Sub-Committee, London County Council Education Committee, Dec. 2, 1937.

Since the end of the Second World War the financial position of the Trust schools has considerably improved owing to increased State aid (as direct grant schools they now accept between 35 per cent. and 50 per cent. scholarship entrants, and in certain cases the Ministry of Education makes up the deficit where only partial fees are paid) and larger income from fees, which have increased from a pre-war average of about £30–£33 per annum to a post-war figure of £48. This keener demand for fee-paying places is a phenomenon that has been experienced by most well-known independent schools. It is probably due, among other things, to the closure of fee-paying places in aided and maintained schools.

Need for Further Research

Considering how sharply changing social conditions in London affected both grammar and independent schools, it is surprising to observe how little public reaction there has been to the developments described in this and previous chapters. Studies of population trends are confined almost exclusively to the problem of the post-war "bulge" in the birth-rate. The middle-class character of the grammar school is rarely discussed. Fee-paying was abolished almost without a murmur of approval or protest, and no major analysis of the effect of this decision upon the grammar schools has yet been published. Problems of urban planning in relation to schools seem to be left to architects and other specialists.

The reasons for this lack of response are not clear. It may be that administrators[1] are reluctant to commit themselves openly on matters likely to arouse political controversy, or that teachers are so harassed by their day-to-day duties that they have little time to consider wider

[1] Reports of the London County Council School Inspectors for various years provide some of the few comments known to the writer of the influence of changing social conditions upon the London grammar schools. Written in confidence for the benefit of County Hall, they often comment in a manner that is usually in sharp contrast to the platitudes or vague generalizations of more public reports. Extracts from some of these reports, describing the new conditions in different boroughs, are given below:

Islington (1905)—The better-class inhabitants are going farther afield.

Stepney (1905)—The numbers have rapidly decreased owing to its conversion into a Jewish and alien population.

Fulham (1927)—. . . the area from which the school draws its pupils is definitely poorer than formerly.

Westminster (1928)—Housing conditions are so crowded in the district that it was found that the children were often doing homework under impossible conditions . . .

(*footnote continued on p. 65*

organizational problems. Possibly matters of "social class" are not regarded as polite subjects for discussion at educational conferences, even though they may be warmly debated in the privacy of staff rooms and Governors' meetings. The traditional emphasis in training colleges and universities upon the psychological at the expense of the sociological aspects of education undoubtedly has its effects. So far as independent schools are concerned, they are usually reluctant to divulge information about the way in which they control their intake of pupils, their sources of income, and the social background of their pupils.

Nevertheless, even allowing for all these explanations, it is disturbing to find so little attention paid to those long-term historical forces that have done so much to shape our schools, both locally and on a national scale. Clearly, there is a need for educational research to be broadened in its scope and objectives. To ignore such matters as the changing relation of social classes or the influence of urbanization upon schools is to dismiss factors that are among the most vital in English education. The history of the London grammar schools only confirms this viewpoint.

---

footnote continued)
the immediate neighbourhood is ceasing to be residential, at any rate for the class of child for whom the school is intended. . . .

Chelsea (1935)—The character of the area which now supplies most of the boys has also changed owing to the migration of many families to the margins of London. These changes have meant that during recent years there have not been so many boys of outstanding ability as there were formerly.

Clapham (1935)—. . . the character of the school is gradually changing, and may be expected to change further, owing to the growing flow of fee-paying parents to suburban districts. . . .

Dulwich (1937)—The problem of recruitment at ——— is a difficult one. One must accept the situation that the neighbourhood from which the school draws has changed greatly during the last twenty years, and that the class of good fee-payers likely to remain on in the sixth form and then go on to the university or into one of the liberal professions has practically disappeared.

Chapter 4

SCHOLARSHIPS AND METHODS OF SELECTION

A few recent philosophers seem to have given their moral support to . . . lamentable verdicts by declaring that the intelligence of an individual is a fixed quantity which cannot be increased. We must protest and react against this brutal pessimism; we are going to try to prove that it is without foundation.—Alfred Binet.[1]

. . . in (the) rapid development of free secondary education during recent years two ideals have each played a part. On the one hand the English scholarship system has always borne the impress of a system designed primarily with the idea of offering to all children of exceptional ability among the less well-to-do classes opportunity of advancement in life. . . On the other hand there has been undoubtedly a growing conviction that the value of secondary education . . . is not limited to children of exceptional ability, nor is it to be estimated solely by the difference which it makes in their worldly prospects. . . . It is more generally felt that . . . the standards of mental and physical development which a good secondary school maintains, and the diffusion of those habits which are formed and strengthened by a corporate school life, are ends desirable in themselves.—Report of the Board of Education, 1911–12.

THE history of scholarships in London goes back many centuries. Originally, many grammar schools were founded with the main (or sometimes even the sole) object of providing a good secondary education for poor, ill-fed, sick, orphaned, or otherwise deprived children. Christ's Hospital, for example, the most famous of the charity schools, was founded in 1552 with the aim of taking off the streets all "fatherless children and other poor men's children that were not able to keep them".[2] Charterhouse, another famous early City foundation, debarred in 1613 children "whose parents have any estate of land", and admitted into the school "onlie the children of poor men that want

[1] *Les Idées Modernes sur les Enfants*, by Alfred Binet, p. 141 (Ernest Flammarion, Paris, 1911).
[2] *Christ's Hospital*, by R. Brimley Johnson, p. xii (George Allen, 1896).

means to bring them up".[1] Merchant Taylors' in its original statutes of 1561 required that 100 out of its 250 scholars be "poore men's sonnes" paying no fee.[2] When the Rev. Ralph Davenant, rector of St. Mary's, Whitechapel, bequeathed money in 1680 for the schools that afterwards bore his name, he specified that it should be spent on "40 poor boys . . . and 30 poor girls in the parish".[3] Similarly, Mrs. Prisca Coborn, who founded a school in Bow in 1701, specified that her legacy should be used to "teach and instruct the children, male and female, of such poor inhabitants of the said hamlet (St. Mary's, Stratford) not being able to give them sufficient learning and education at their own costs and charges . . .".[4] John Roan, a philanthropist of Greenwich, in his will dated 1644 was so far ahead of his time as to provide for maintenance grants as well as fees for pupils in the school he founded. His money was left to "bring up soe many poore towne-borne children" each of whom should have "fortie shillings per annum towards their clothing" until they reached the age of fifteen years.[5]

Many other examples could be given of legacies and charitable bequests that had as their prime object the provision of secondary schools for the "poor, but able" children of London.

But over a long period of time, in many cases, the original aims of the foundations were lost or obscured. Some grammar schools became public schools for the sons (and to a less extent, daughters) of the rich; others were taken over or developed by trusts or City Livery Companies, and took as pupils, with a few rare exceptions, the children of middle-class parents who wished their sons and daughters to have a secondary education but could not afford the high fees of boarding-schools. Alterations in the distribution and size of London's population, the spread of industry and commerce, and changes in social structure and the relation of classes had all created new educational circumstances very different from those envisaged by the original benefactors. Consequently, many anomalies and injustices persisted in the provision of scholarships despite the reforms of the Charity Commissioners between 1850 and 1900.

[1] *Charterhouse*, by E. M. Jameson, p. 10 (Blackie and Son, 1937).
[2] *Endowed Grammar Schools of England and Wales*, by Nicholas Carlisle, pp. 50–1 (Baldwin, Craddock and Joy, 1818).
[3] "Endowed Charities (County of London)", Return presented to House of Commons, Vol. 1, Aug. 4, 1897.
[4] "Endowed Charities (County of London)", Return presented to the House of Commons, Vol. 1, Aug. 4, 1897.
[5] *The History of the Roan Schools*, by J. W. Kirby, Appendix I (Blackheath Press, 1929).

Towards the end of the century it had become apparent that certain essential conditions must be fulfilled if a scholarship system was to be successful.[1]

The scholarship examination should be centrally controlled and administered over a wide area. It should be held in various centres at the same time, and the regulations should be uniform and as simple as possible. The tests given should be suited to elementary school children, and the value of the scholarships sufficient to make worth while the entry of very poor children. The awards should preferably help towards maintenance as well as school fees. It was particularly important that the public should be fully aware of procedure for entry and conditions of tenure of scholarships. Above all, the scholarships should be sufficient in number to meet the needs of the considerable proportion of intelligent children who were debarred from grammar-school education only by their inability to pay fees.

Inadequacy of Scholarship System in the 1890s

Not one of these conditions was fully complied with in London in the early 1890s. For example, in 1892 there were less than 1,000 scholarships available in London for about 500,000 children of secondary-school age, a mere "drop in the bucket" as Llewellyn Smith described it. A few years previously a witness at the Cross Commission (1885) had said:

[1] In 1892 Llewellyn Smith, Secretary of the Committee charged with investigating technical education in London, described the conditions that he considered essential for the successful working of a scholarship system. "It must be administered on a large scale and over a wide area", he said. "The conditions of candidature and tenure must be simple and well known, the examination uniform and well planned on lines suited to elementary school-children. The examinations should be conducted at many centres on the same day, and above all the scheme should be well before the public; advertisements pinned on Church doors or inserted in local papers will not suffice. The co-operation of the teachers and managers of the elementary schools and the School Board must be enlisted in making the scholarships widely known, and if practicable some inducement held out to teachers of elementary schools to overcome their natural reluctance to part with their best pupils at an early age. Lastly, the scholarship must be sufficient in amount to provide for maintenance as well as pay fees." (Report to L.C.C. Special Committee on Technical Education, by H. Llewellyn Smith, p. 79, 1892.)

Llewellyn Smith estimated the number of scholarship pupils attending public secondary schools in London in 1892 at 591 boys and 263 girls. He reckoned that the schools that made no returns brought the total to about 1,000. London, it should be pointed out, was no worse off than the rest of the country in respect of scholarships (indeed it was in some respects better off because of the City Livery Companies, ancient foundations, and other charitable bequests). Lowndes estimated in *The Silent Social Revolution* (O.U.P., 1937) that in 1895 there were less than 2,500 scholarships available for all secondary schools in England and Wales.

It would be next to expecting a boy out of a London Board School to take wings as to expect him to advance by his own efforts to the University.

There were many endowed or other publicly recognized secondary schools that took only a tiny proportion of scholarship entrants, and frequently the latter were so selected as to discriminate against very poor children. Apart from the inadequate number of scholarships, the organization of the awards was so chaotic and the anomalies so numerous that it was impossible to discover any coherent plan or principle in the methods used.

Scholarships are offered singly, or in twos and threes, by individual secondary schools, or obscure foundations possessing no adequate means of advertising them,

commented Llewellyn Smith. He continued,

There is no limit to the variety and complexity of conditions attached—conditions of attainment, of age, of locality, of residence, of parents' poverty, of attendance at particular schools, and the like. Many of the scholarships only cover fees, or even half fees, and there is often a want of cooperation between the teachers of elementary and secondary schools in the matter of sending in candidates ... scholarships are administered by more than a hundred distinct bodies of Governors under every variety of conditions of selection and tenure. Many of these scholarships are fettered with local restrictions, many are too small to be of real service to poor children, some are burdened with a poverty test, some are confined to attendance at Sunday school. The mere waste of power resulting from the minute division of management is incalculable.[1]

Reform of Scholarship System

In view of these deficiencies it was not surprising that there should arise a strong demand for the reform of the scholarship system. Llewellyn Smith was not alone in his criticisms, and both the London

[1] Report to L.C.C. Special Committee on Technical Education, by H. Llewellyn Smith, p. 79, 1892.

County Council and Board of Education were aware of the necessity for a wider and more comprehensive plan to enable a much greater number of working-class children to go on to secondary schools, and possibly the university. Indeed, the proposals to reorganize the scholarship system were seen as an integral part of the general movement to reform secondary education.

The demand for reform became irresistible when three streams of thought joined together in one powerful tide of opinion. First, there were individuals such as Sidney Webb, or organizations predominantly Socialist in character, such as the Fabian Society and Labour Party, that wanted a fairer deal for working-class children. Secondly, there were educational bodies such as the National Union of Teachers who disliked the inadequacies and disorganization of the old system, and wanted efficiency and order in secondary education. Many school governors and head teachers, concerned with financial difficulties of their schools, were also anxious to see an increased flow of State or locally aided scholars into the schools. Thirdly, there were the more far-sighted politicians and administrators (Morant being a typical example) who were not necessarily sympathetic to progressive political views, but who saw the urgent need to recruit from the widest possible sources talent and ability for the growing professional and commercial occupations.

Junior County Scholarships

The combined influence of these three groups, which often overlapped in their views, grew sufficiently powerful towards the end of the century to force the introduction of the Technical Instruction Act (1891) enabling county councils to incur expenditure on scholarships in secondary schools.

> In the year 1893 the (London County) Council recognized that one of the most pressing wants which had to be met was that of further inducements and facilities for the very poor to keep their children at some secondary or continuation school after leaving the elementary school,

reported the London County Council's Education Officer,[1] continuing,

[1] Report of the L.C.C. Education Officer, p. 74, 1905.

The bridge by which the children were to pass from the elementary school to the secondary school was at once erected: it took the form of the establishment of a system of county scholarships.

This bridge, though weak in relation to the load it was asked to bear, was stronger and broader than anything so far devised by an English local authority; and because in an expanded form it remained for fifty years the main pathway by which poorer children could move from the State elementary into the grammar schools, it is worth considering in some detail. Fundamentally, the new scheme consisted of the award of up to 600[1] scholarships each year, tenable at certain aided secondary schools in London. They were awarded to children under thirteen years of age, and consisted of free tuition (usually for two years) and maintenance grants of £8 for the first year, and £12 for subsequent years up to fourteen, with possible extension.

As well, there were 100 intermediate scholarships offered at 16+, and from twenty to forty scholarships offered at 18+ for study in a university. An upper income limit of £150 per annum was fixed for parents of Junior County Scholarship holders.

In 1904 when the London County Council took over responsibility for secondary education, this scheme was slightly modified, and in 1905 a more ambitious plan was introduced after a vigorous discussion in which Sidney Webb took a leading part. In the latter year there were 2,068 Junior County Scholarships held in about eighty secondary schools in London. This figure, though an improvement on the total of fifteen years previously, still represented less than one in ten of all grammar-school pupils.

The revised scheme visualized the annual award of 2,600 Junior County Scholarships with free education up to 14+ years, with the possibility of extension for another two years. A maintenance grant of £6, £10, or £15 was payable in certain circumstances. The number of intermediate scholarships was to remain at 100 but maintenance grants were to range from £20 to £35 per annum, and the upper limit for parents' income was raised to £400 per annum. There were also to be 800 probationer scholarships for potential teachers. An important new development (which was abandoned in 1908) was that two-thirds of the Junior County Scholarships were to be allotted to girls, presumably in order to encourage the training of women teachers who were then in great demand because of the expansion of elementary schools.

[1] Between 1893–1904 the number of awards fluctuated from year to year. In 1903, for example, 330 (191 boys, and 139 girls) awards were made.

71

During the next five years the London County Council consolidated the ground already won, a process that was assisted by the provisions of the 1907 Education Act. This Act made grant aid to secondary schools conditional upon the school offering a fixed proportion (usually one-quarter) of free places.[1]

By 1910 the proportion of scholarship holders had risen to over one-third in the case of aided and over one-half in the case of maintained secondary schools, or 7,880 pupils out of a total attendance of 18,977.[2]

Reactions of Schools to Influx of Scholarship Entrants

The reactions of schools to the influx of large numbers of scholarship entrants varied considerably. At first, there was a general mood of optimism and confidence in the new experiment, particularly among officials and administrators. Humanists such as Sidney Webb regarded the new scheme as a wonderful chance to open up opportunities for higher education to wider sections of the community. Headmasters and headmistresses were also glad to welcome into their schools boys and girls who could usually be relied upon to be hard working and intelligent, even if their manners and habits might be different from the fee-paying pupils. School governors, confronted with rising expenses and dwindling fee-paying resources, also appreciated the increased scholarship income from the London County Council. When in 1906 a questionnaire asking their opinion of the new scholarship entrants was circulated to various headmasters and headmistresses, most of the replies were favourable, as the following questions and answers show:

QUESTION I Do the scholars appear to be inferior, equal or superior to the average fee-paying pupils at your school in regard to (a) intelligence; (b) initiative; and (c) power of work?

[1] Regulation 20 of the 1907 Education Act stated: "In all fee-charging schools a proportion of free places must be open in each year to pupils entering from public elementary schools. This total will ordinarily be 25 per cent. of the total number of pupils admitted during the previous year, but may be reduced or varied by the Board on sufficient grounds in the case of any particular school, or any particular year".

[2] Volumes of *London Statistics* for 1909–10–11 give the following figures of scholarship holders:

Aided Schools		Maintained Schools	
Total Attendance	Non-fee-Payers	Total Attendance	Non-fee-Payers
(1910)	(1910)	(1909)	(1909)
14,786	5,182	4,191	2,698

ANSWER:

Intelligence:		Initiative:	
Inferior	6	Inferior	33
Equal	52	Equal	43
Superior	22	Superior	4

Power of Work:	
Inferior	4
Equal	48
Superior	28

QUESTION II Have you any special difficulty (i.e. greater than might be expected in a similar number of paying pupils) with regard to (*a*) conduct; (*b*) manners; (*c*) habits?

ANSWER:

	Conduct		Manners		Habits	
	Yes	*No*	*Yes*	*No*	*Yes*	*No*
	8	72	15	65	23	57

The general impression appears to be that the new system of awarding Junior County Scholarships is on the whole superior to the old, and that it is a distinct advantage that the scholars are sent to the secondary school at a younger age,

concluded the London County Council.[1]

Four or five years after the new scheme was introduced, however, certain doubts and hesitations were raised. The intellectual powers of the scholars were not queried so much as their moral, hygienic, and physical qualities. Bad home environment was particularly stressed as a factor that militated against success at school. As early as 1906 the Council admitted that a number of headmasters and headmistresses had pointed out that some of the scholars could not profit fully by the education given "on account of being insufficiently fed". Certain teachers also drew attention to the importance of securing that the scholars should be fitted "morally as well as intellectually for admission to the schools". They recommended that a certificate of good moral character for scholarship entrants be required from previous head-masters. In 1909 and again in 1912 further inquiries were made as to the

[1] Report of the Higher Education and Scholarships Sub-Committee, L.C.C., 1906.

influence of home conditions upon the scholars' progress at school. The Conference of Headmistresses of London Secondary Schools concluded that the girls selected were suitable under headings of intellect and character, but they felt that so far as health was concerned a minority of children was not up to the required standard. The Headmaster of St. Olave's and St. Saviour's School advocated that those pupils who "suffer irremediably from home surroundings above which they cannot rise, should, if given scholarships at all, be sent to boarding schools". One headmistress went so far as to claim that "children of very poor parents apart from drunkenness or disreputability, obtained little or no benefits from scholarships".[1] Several teachers wanted to see free or very cheap dinners provided for poor scholars.[2] The Council's Education Officer concluded in 1910 that:

> Broadly speaking, the reports show that the children selected are of a high average standard as regards character, but poor as regards physique.[3]

There was divergence of opinion as to whether scholars tended to improve or to deteriorate physically during the tenure of the scholarship. In some cases it appeared that the better food and clothing obtained in consequence of the maintenance grants, as well as the higher standards of personal hygiene insisted on in secondary schools, produced a marked improvement in the scholars' physique. In other cases it appeared that the strain of school work, combined with adverse home conditions, produced an actual physical deterioration during the tenure of the scholarship.

[1] Report of Higher Education Sub-Committee, L.C.C., page 5, 1912.

[2] "Considerable stress is laid by many of the headmasters and mistresses, especially headmistresses, on the fact that some of the scholars cannot profit fully by the education given on account of being insufficiently fed". (Report of Higher Education and Scholarships Sub-Committee, L.C.C., 1906.)

[3] "Several headmasters and headmistresses recommend that in the award of scholarships some account should be taken of the character of the homes from which the children come, and urge that, while no child should be excluded on the grounds of poverty, it is a waste of public money and of no benefit to the children themselves, to give scholarships to children of drunken and disreputable parents. The question is one of great difficulty, and the Council has not thought it advisable to take directly into account the character of the parents in selecting children for scholarships. It may, however, be pointed out that medical examination does, as a matter of fact, act to some extent as a test of the character of the parents. In this connection, it will no doubt be found that a rule which has recently been introduced by the Higher Education Sub-Committee, whereby a child is to be finally rejected if he or she has been found deficient in personal cleanliness on three separate occasions, will in practice have the effect of excluding children whose home conditions are such as to prevent them from deriving benefit from secondary education." (Report of L.C.C. Education Officer, 1910.)

In consequence of these criticisms the Council decided to terminate some of the scholarships held, and during the three years 1908–10, 443 out of approximately 5,100 scholarships were thus withdrawn. This decision to cancel some awards led to a difference of opinion with the Board of Education, as the Board's regulations required at least 25 per cent. of new entrants to aided and maintained grammar schools to be scholarship holders.

A delegation led by the Chairman of the Education Committee was appointed by the Council to discuss the matter, and in July 1909 it interviewed Mr. Runciman, President of the Board of Education.[1] The Council's attitude was that a higher standard of what it called "diligence and intelligence" should be expected from scholarship winners in contrast to fee-payers. It was argued that as the Council paid the fees (and was therefore somewhat *in loco parentis*) it should be allowed to withdraw scholarship pupils if it thought fit. The Chairman of the Education Committee declared that he thought in consequence of the Board's regulations that "children were being retained in secondary schools by means of scholarships, contrary to their own interests, and that in some cases the effect of the Board's requirements was to encourage a boy to become an inferior clerk rather than a good artisan".

The President of the Board of Education replied that the desire of the Council was contrary to the Board's regulation, which laid it down that no conditions as to "conduct, progress, or attendance may be attached to the tenure of the free places which do not apply equally to all pupils of the school". He suggested, however, that there was no legal obligation to pay maintenance grants as well as providing free tuition.

The Council's attitude all along had been that maintenance and free tuition went together (the report of the Council's Education Officer for 1910 speaks of "scholarship and maintenance allowances as inseparable"), but they now reversed this policy and accepted the President's suggestion.

In 1910, 1,570 scholars, in their third year, were treated as follows:

1,457 ("those likely to profit by further education") had their full scholarships continued;

98 ("those not likely to profit by further secondary education, but not so unsatisfactory as to be required to withdraw") were offered free places but no maintenance grant;

[1] A delegation led by the Chairman of the L.C.C. Education Committee met Mr. Runciman, President, Board of Education on July 27, 1909. See Report of L.C.C. Education Officer for 1910.

15 ("Those who were so unsatisfactory that they would have been required to withdraw if they had been fee-paying pupils") were required to withdraw.

In 1911 the Council reported that in large numbers of cases where maintenance grants had been withdrawn parents then withdrew their children, but continued:

In a few cases parents allow their children to remain beyond the third year, notwithstanding the withdrawal of the maintenance grant, and in such cases it is probable that where the scholar's deficiencies are due to idleness rather than stupidity, the withdrawal of the maintenance grant may have a bracing effect, and he may in the end derive advantage from further attendances.

First World War and the Fisher Act, 1918

During and immediately after the First World War the number of grammar-school places in London steadily increased. Many secondary schools, which had previously been independent, accepted State financial assistance and became recognized as aided grammar schools. Simultaneously, the number of scholarships increased, though not in proportion to the total number of new places. By 1920, the attendance at all assisted secondary schools in London was just over 35,000, of which a little under one-third did not pay fees.

ATTENDANCE AT LONDON SECONDARY SCHOOLS IN 1919–1920 [1]

Assisted		Maintained	
Total attendance	*Non-fee-payers*	*Total attendance*	*Non-fee-payers*
(1919)	*(1919)*	*(1920)*	*(1920)*
35,447	11,041	9,579	4,356

The mood of the immediate post-war period, so far as education was concerned, was one of optimism and dreams of expansion—soon to be shattered by the harsh realities of the economic situation. Arising out of the ruins of the War it was hoped to build a land fit for school-children, at least, to live in. The Fisher Act of 1918 promised, among

[1] Figures taken from volumes of *London Statistics* for 1920–21.

other things, that there would be an increase of scholarships, requiring that:

Children and young persons shall not be debarred from receiving the benefits of any forms of education by which they are capable of profiting through inability to pay fees.

The Board of Education also hinted about this time that free places in secondary schools might be increased from 25 to 40 per cent. if schools were to qualify for grant. As soon as the War was over the London County Council began to consider what plans should be made to increase the number of grammar- and central-school places.

The onset of severe trade depression in 1920–21 brought all these plans to a standstill. Instead of thinking of increasing the number of free places and cutting fees in secondary schools, the Council sought to economize on educational expenditure. In 1920, for example, the Council decided that:

Before giving a grant in addition to free education, it was only reasonable to require evidence that the community as well as the student himself would benefit from his admission to the particular type of education required.[1]

It therefore agreed that a maintenance grant would be awarded when the student:

Possessed ability above that indicated by mere capacity to profit, showed fitness for the teaching profession and was prepared to undertake to enter upon this work.

The Council also decided that, as well as introducing more stringent scholarship regulations, grammar-school fees should be raised wherever possible.[2]

During the mid 1920s the financial position improved somewhat and the number of Junior County Scholarship awards was again increased to nearly 2,000 a year, while the number of supplementary and intermediate awards was also increased. By 1925 the number of non-fee-payers in London secondary schools reached 12,500, and by 1930 nearly 15,000.

[1] Report on Scholarship Scheme, L.C.C. Higher Education Sub-Committee, p. 4, March 4, 1920.
[2] In 1921 average fees in London aided and maintained grammar schools were raised from about £8 8s. to about £14 per year.

Then began in 1931 that world-wide economic crisis that seriously reduced the financial expenditure of all local authorities in Britain. The London County Council reported the pressing need for economy occasioned by the national financial situation, and proposals were made for an immediate cut in the education services. In December 1931, the Council decided to reduce the number of new Junior County Scholarship awards to a maximum of 1,750.[1] Maintenance grants for new scholars were cut by 20 per cent. and for old scholars by 10 per cent. The standard of the intermediate examination was raised.

In 1932, on the advice of the Board of Education, it was decided also to raise fees in some grammar schools. This extra charge was confined to schools in wealthier districts because it was feared that if fees were raised in the poorer districts the number of new entrants would quickly decline.

In September 1932, the Board of Education issued new regulations to the effect that scholarships should only be granted if the parents' financial circumstances justified such aid. A kind of "means test" was visualized. The main change was that "free places" were superseded by "special places". Broadly speaking, this meant that the old so-called "free places" would have to be reconsidered or reduced. They were no longer to be regarded as automatically free. The London County Council proposed that those who were getting free places should either continue to have them free or else pay reduced admission fees. Those who were getting free places plus maintenance grants, i.e. full scholarships, should get free places without maintenance. Pupils who were most in need, however, would get the highest scale of grant.

The Education Officer's report for 1933–4 contains a table showing how the "special place" awards of 1933–4 differed from the "free place" awards of 1932. In 1932 there were 2,681 "free places" held—1,021 in maintained, and 1,660 in aided grammar schools. During the following two years the "special places" were split up as follows:

School	Full Fees 1933	1934	Partial Fees 1933	1934	Remission of Fees 1933	1934	Totals 1933	1934
Maintained	34	37	107	131	1,181	1,278	1,322	1,446
Aided	59	48	154	168	1,507	1,662	1,720	1,878
Totals	93	85	261	299	2,688	2,940	3,042	3,324

Analysing these figures it would appear that, out of a total of between

[1] This rule does not seem to have been observed, as the lowest number of Junior County awards after 1931 was 1,888 in 1934.

3,000 and 3,400 "special places" held in 1933–4, only about 350 to 400, or one in nine, were compelled to pay full or partial fees as a result of this new regulation. So far as was known no candidate declined a special place because he was requested to pay full or partial fees.[1]

Social and Economic Factors Causing Increase of Scholarships

But the economic depression passed after a few years, and as financial conditions improved so the Board of Education and the London County Council became willing once more to increase their expenditure on grammar schools. There were other economic and social factors affecting scholarships that proved more decisive in their long-term influence than the temporary fluctuations of the trade cycle. These factors, which had already shown themselves so powerful in their influence upon grammar schools at the beginning of the century, increased in significance as the years went by. Broadly speaking, they were three in number:

(1) The demand on democratic grounds, generally expressed in the slogan "secondary education for all" for wider educational opportunities for working-class children. Individuals such as Professor R. H. Tawney and organizations such as the Labour Party, Workers' Educational Association, and National Union of Teachers carried forward the campaign that had been initiated by Sidney Webb, the Fabians, and others before the First World War. This campaign reached its peak during the years immediately preceding the 1944 Act when the Council for Educational Advance was set up, comprising the National Union of Teachers, Workers' Educational Association, and the Trades Union Congress.

[1] In 1938, 2,550 Junior County Scholarships were awarded at the age of 11–12 years based on an examination in English and arithmetic with an intelligence test. The maximum value was free tuition at a grammar school with a maximum maintenance allowance of £9 rising to £14 per year at age of 14+. Sixteen hundred special places were awarded, usually to pupils who had just failed winning a Junior County award, on the basis of examinations in the grammar schools themselves. The maximum value of these was free tuition with no maintenance grant up to the age of 14+, when £13 per year was paid if annual parental income did not exceed £150, and there was one dependent child. Five hundred supplementary Junior County awards were made at the age of 13+ on the basis of examination in English arithmetic, history, and geography. About 65 per cent. of these were won by pupils already in grammar schools, 20 per cent. by pupils in central schools, and 15 per cent. in modern schools. The value was the same as Junior County awards. A smaller number of Intermediate and Senior County Scholarships were also awarded at the ages of 16 or 18 respectively.

(2) The ever-growing need for more trained and qualified "white-collar" workers compelled the authorities to expand the number of grammar-school places. It was realized that if the commercial, administrative, and professional occupations were to get the personnel they required then they must recruit from among the most intelligent working-class as well as middle-class children.

(3) As the cost of running the grammar schools rose steadily because of higher building standards, more expensive equipment, and improved pay for teachers, so the governing bodies were faced with the question of either increasing fee-paying income or else accepting more scholarship pupils. But in London especially, where the middle-class fee-paying population was falling gradually because of migration to the suburbs, it was difficult to attract more fee-payers into the grammar schools. Indeed, the problem was to maintain rather than to increase the number of fee-payers. So serious was the decline in fee-paying income in many of the grammar schools situated in the poorer central and East End boroughs that the London County Council decided to allow governors of certain schools to remit up to 75 per cent. of fees in what were termed "hard cases". Undoubtedly one of the reasons why the "special place" system was not extended as much as it might have been in 1931–3 was the fear that grammar schools in poor areas would be gravely depleted if the regulations were enforced too strictly.

In the long run the pressures making for the expansion of free secondary education proved stronger than those making for contraction, and gradually the number of scholarships was increased. By 1935 more than half of all the places in aided and maintained London grammar schools were held by scholarship pupils. The expansion in the number of scholarships may be seen in the following tables:

ATTENDANCE AT LONDON SECONDARY[1] SCHOOLS

	All Secondary Schools			Maintained Schools		
Year	Total Attend-ance	Non-fee-payers	Non-fee-payers as % of total	Total Attend-ance	Non-fee-payers	Non-fee-payers as % of total
1920	35,447 (1919)	11,041 (1919)	31	9,579	4,356	45·5
1925	42,832	12,548	29	9,587	4,090	43
1930	43,239	14,728	34	10,987	5,128	46·5
1935	43,842	18,818	43	12,139	7,025	58

[1] "Secondary" refers to schools of the grammar or independent type.

NUMBER OF JUNIOR COUNTY SCHOLARSHIPS HELD
IN LONDON GRAMMAR SCHOOLS[1]

Year	No.	Year	No.	Year	No.
1905	2,068	1916	6,725	1927	7,987
1906	3,929	1917	6,653	1928	8,182
1907	5,646	1918	6,897	1929	8,464
1908	6,876	1919	7,069	1930	8,757
1909	7,869	1920	7,300	1931	9,143
1910	7,675	1921	7,568	1932	9,085
1911	7,524	1922	7,708	1933	9,040
1912	7,378	1923	7,362	1934	8,847
1913	7,307	1924	7,263	1935	9,338
1914	7,291	1925	7,242	1936	9,708
1915	7,047	1926	7,757	1937	10,425

Abolition of Fees

During the Second World War the demand for a more democratic secondary-school system culminated in the 1944 Education Act, which abolished all fees in aided and maintained grammar schools, and thus represented the triumph of the "free place" idea.

The fact that the provisions of this Act were so easily adopted is an indication of how widely accepted the scholarship system had become by Members of Parliament and public as well as by teachers and administrators. Criticisms of the working of the free-place system there were in individual cases, but in broad outline, the reforms were generally recognized as necessary, and even inevitable. The innovation of earlier decades became the commonplace of the 1940s and 1950s.

The abolition of fees represented a fundamental change in attitude towards secondary education, but at the time the 1944 Act was passed not all its implications were fully understood. In particular, it was not really appreciated how the grammar schools, with their special historical, social, and vocational problems, would be affected. For example, would the introduction of the 100 per cent. free-place system simplify the question of selection? Would it alter the vocational aims of the grammar schools? How would it affect the different social classes in their efforts to get the secondary education to which they thought they were entitled? Was it to be assumed that the basic principle of scholarships was to enable children of very poor parents to get into the grammar schools? And if so, how far had this aim already been achieved?

[1] Figures are taken from volumes for various years of *London Statistics*.

To answer these questions (which are, of course, vital to the understanding of the whole idea of secondary education for all) it is necessary to describe how the State-scholarship system affected children of different social classes and to what extent environmental factors have influenced children's chances of winning scholarships.

Scholarships and Social Status

In the late 1880s, Charles Booth made a survey of the social class of scholarship winners in London grammar schools. His main conclusion was that the few scholarships that then existed were being won, not by the sons and daughters of the very poor, but by the children of the lower middle class, or else by what he called the "upper fringe of the working class".[1] Analysing the occupations of parents of 100 free scholars attending three east London secondary schools, he found that seventy could be broadly classified as middle class and thirty as working class. In a group of girls' high schools he found that out of fifty-six scholarship winners twenty-nine were middle class and twenty-seven working class.

As a result of his investigations, Booth concluded:

> . . . the elementary scholars, who as yet have found their way into London Secondary Schools, had been the aristocracy, no less socially than intellectually, of the schools from which they have been drawn . . . the social class of the majority of the boys selected by scholarships does not differ very greatly from that of the other pupils of secondary schools . . . boys who are successful in the competition for scholarships come from the richer homes, for by the age of eleven or twelve the influence of the home atmosphere has had time to tell to such a degree as to handicap severely the boys from rougher homes where there is little appreciation of education and little opportunity for quiet study.
>
> There seems good reason to believe that instead of the scholarship enabling working men to send their daughters to middle-class schools it rather encourages middle-class men to send their daughters to Board schools in the hope of obtaining a scholarship.

[1] *Life and Labour of the People in London,* by Charles Booth, First Series, Poverty (3), p. 277 (Macmillan, 1904).

Booth (or more properly Llewellyn Smith, who wrote the chapter on Education in Booth's famous survey of London) was, of course, writing of the period before there was any State or local authority system of scholarships. Nevertheless, later and more comprehensive evidence bears out the point that it was the children of skilled workers, clerks, shopkeepers, and the like who mainly benefited from the new London County Council schemes of 1893 and 1904.

It was not the Council's policy that these more socially privileged children should win most of the scholarships. On the contrary, it was the ablest and most talented children from the poorest homes that the Council hoped to get into the grammar schools. "In the year 1893 the Council recognized that one of the most pressing wants which had to be met was that of further inducements and facilities for the *very poor* [my italics] to keep their children at some secondary or continuation schools", says an early Council report.[1] Income limits for scholarships were introduced in order that "access to the scholarship ladder can be made really effective to the clever children of the *poorest homes*" [my italics].[2]

SOCIAL CLASS OF PARENTS OF JUNIOR COUNTY SCHOLARS 1904 AND 1905[3]

Social class[4]	Number		%	
	1904	1905	1904	1905
Middle	1	—	0·3	—
Lower middle	83	569	24·7	24·0
Skilled working	176	1,152	52·4	48·5
Unskilled working	63	594	18·7	25·0
Unclassified	13	60	3·9	2·5
Totals	336	2,375	100	100

[1] Report of the L.C.C. Education Officer, 1904–5.

[2] Report of the Scholarship Section of the Higher Education and Scholarship Sub-Committee of the L.C.C., p. 3, 1904. The L.C.C. Scholarship regulations of 1905 required that two-thirds of the Junior County Scholarships awarded that year must be to children of parents whose incomes did not exceed £160 per year. There was no upper income limit for parents whose children were at State elementary schools but the limit for other children was also to be £160 per year. In 1914, a similar proportion was fixed for children of parents with incomes up to £160. Again, there was no upper limit for children at State elementary schools, but this time the limit for privately educated children was £300 per year. Higher limits were fixed for Probationer, Intermediate, and Senior County Scholars.

[3] Report of Higher Education Sub-Committee, L.C.C. Education Committee, 1906.

[4] Details about these social classes are given in Chapter 3, "The Changing Social Structure of the Grammar Schools".

That the scholarships did not during the first decade of the century, in fact, mainly reach these "very poor" children is clear from the Council's own investigations. In 1904 and again in 1905, an analysis was made of the occupations of parents of over 2,500 Junior County Scholarship winners, which showed that less than 25 per cent. came from the unskilled and labouring class, about 50 per cent. from skilled workers, and the remaining 25 per cent. from clerical, commercial, and minor professional occupations. The results of this analysis are given in the table at the foot of p. 83.

The London County Council Education Officer made an income analysis for 1905–6 with the following results :

INCOMES OF PARENTS OF JUNIOR COUNTY SCHOLARS
SELECTED 1905-6

	1905		1906	
Income	*Number*	%	*Number*	%
Less than £160	2,080	87·6	1,667	84·2
£160 to £300	230	9·7	250	12·6
Over £300	65	2·7	64	3·2
Totals	2,375	100	1,981	100

What is surprising about these figures is not that four-fifths of the scholarships went to children of parents who earned less than £3 per week (one would expect that) but that some hundreds went to those in income groups £160 to £300 per year, and several score annually to those in income groups above £300 per year.

Pre-1914 an income of £6 per week put a person definitely into the middle class, and parents with that kind of income could easily have afforded the comparatively low fees payable at the aided London grammar schools. Such fees varied widely from school to school but were seldom above ten guineas a year.

During the first decade of this century the great majority of industrial workers were getting under £2 per week, and unskilled men were getting in the neighbourhood of 25s. or 30s. a week, or less. It would, therefore, have been more valuable from the point of view of the social historian if the above figures had been broken down to give further details. For example, what proportion of scholarship winners were in the under £100 or under £75 a year class?[1]

Social Status of Scholarship Winners During Inter-War Period

After the First World War the London County Council made a further analysis of the occupations and incomes of parents of scholarship winners, which showed that the position was much the same as it had been pre-1914. The children of skilled parents were winning most awards, those of the clerical and shopkeeping class were close behind, and children of unskilled and labouring parents were still relatively unsuccessful in their efforts to win scholarships. Indeed, in the immediate post-war period the lower middle class were doing slightly better, and the poorer working class slightly worse than pre-war.

SOCIAL CLASS OF PARENTS OF JUNIOR COUNTY SCHOLARSHIP
WINNERS IN LONDON 1921 AND 1922

Social Class	Number	%
Middle	—	—
Lower middle	1,320	42
Skilled working	1,276	41
Unskilled working	515	17
Totals	3,111	100

Allowing for the rise in prices that had occurred during the war, it can be seen from the table on p. 86 how less than one in five of the successful candidates had parents in the poorly paid category of under £3 a week, but nearly one in three was in the comparatively well-paid group earning over £5 a week.

[1] That the London County Council itself was not clear about the answer to this question is shown by the contradictory replies given by Council officials on different occasions. For example, early in 1911 the Education Officer reported that: "It would appear, from the returns supplied by parents, that the incomes of about 30 per cent. of the Junior County Scholars are not in excess of 30s. per week". (Report of the L.C.C. Education Officer, Nov. 3, 1911.) A few months later, however, a memorandum by the Chief Inspector concluded that: ". . . judging from the lists, not more than 10 per cent. of the present winners (of Junior County Scholarships) came from homes with less than 30s. weekly income". ("Award of Junior and Intermediate County Scholarships", p. 5. Report of L.C.C. Higher Education Sub-Committee, Mar. 21, 1912.)

INCOME OF PARENTS OF JUNIOR COUNTY SCHOLAR-
SHIP WINNERS IN LONDON 1921 AND 1922

Income	Number	%
Under £160	550	18
£160–£250	1,626	52
Over £250	935	30
Totals	3,111	100

Moreover, writing as late as 1926, another critic of the scholarship system could say:

... secondary education is outside the reach of the unskilled worker, except for between 2½ and 3 per cent. of the total entering secondary schools; this figure has been fairly constant for the last ten years ... the unskilled and lowly paid worker, the farm worker and the casual labourer, are as yet not really touched by the scholarship system. Individuals there undoubtedly are, but the mass remains unaffected.[1]

No further analysis of the social background of scholarship winners appears to have been made by the London County Council since 1922, but judging by the evidence given in previous chapters it would seem that increased numbers of poor working-class children (all of whom, it would be safe to assume, came in by means of scholarship) began to enter the grammar schools in the late 1920s and 1930s.

Scholarships Won in Different Boroughs

There was, however, another related social aspect of the scholarship problem with which the London County Council remained preoccupied for many years, and that was the question why certain boroughs (and elementary schools) in the metropolitan area won proportionately far more scholarships than others.

[1] *Social Progress and Educational Waste*, by Kenneth Lindsay, pp. 21 and 26 (Routledge, 1926).
  (1) About 40 per cent. of the parents, both in the early days of scholarships and equally today, are skilled workers, earning in 1905 and 1906 under £160 a year, and today earning between £3 and £5 a week.
  (2) About 35 per cent., both in the early days and now, come from official and clerical classes or professions.
  (3) About 10 per cent. can be classed as shopkeepers and assistants.
  (4) The remainder, 15 per cent. of whom about 5 per cent. in the earlier days and nearly 10 per cent. today are widows, belong to an unskilled class of worker". (Lindsay, p. 110.)

The wide variations between boroughs at various dates may be seen in the tables that follow. Analysis of the figures shows that such comparatively prosperous districts as Hampstead and Lewisham have consistently won several times as many Junior County Scholarships per head of population as such poor districts as Southwark and Shoreditch. To take some of the more extreme examples: in 1905 in Dulwich, 8·3 per thousand of the children in average attendance at elementary schools won Junior County Scholarships, but for North Lambeth the figure was only 0·5 per thousand. In 1914, the figure for Lewisham was 5·8, but in Mile End only 0·3 per thousand; in 1925 it was 8·2 for West Lewisham and 0·4 for South-West Bethnal Green and Finsbury; in 1935 it was 14·0 for Streatham and 1·3 for North Southwark. The inverse relationship between poverty and scholarship successes is brought out even more clearly when different electoral constituencies in the same borough are compared. Thus, the poorer constituency of West Islington consistently won fewer awards than the wealthier constituency of North Islington. Similarly, North St. Pancras remained superior intellectually as well as socially to South-West St. Pancras.

LONDON JUNIOR COUNTY SCHOLARSHIP AWARDS
1905 AND 1914

	Per 1,000[1]	
Electoral Constituency	*1905*	*1914*
Battersea	5·5	2·4
Bermondsey	2·3	1·3
Bethnal Green N.E.	2·2	1·8
„ „ S.W.	0·6	1·0
Bow and Bromley	1·7	1·6
Brixton	3·1	2·7
Camberwell N.	3·9	2·2
Chelsea	3·8	2·0
City of London	2·4	0·8
Clapham	6·5	4·0
Deptford	3·6	3·0
Dulwich	8·3	5·6
Finsbury Central	3·1	1·9
„ E.	0·5	0·4
Fulham	3·0	1·8
Greenwich	2·4	1·8
Hackney Central	7·3	6·8
„ N.	7·3	6·2
„ S.	5·1	3·2

[1] The figures refer to the number per thousand of pupils in attendance at L.C.C. elementary schools.

LONDON JUNIOR (cont'd)

Electoral Constituency	1905	Per 1,000[1] 1914
Haggerston	3·9	1·0
Hammersmith	5·0	1·2
Hampstead	9·5	5·1
Holborn	2·2	0·3
Hoxton	4·6	0·7
Islington E.	4·1	0·7
„ N.	3·3	3·3
„ S.	3·8	0·8
„ W.	1·8	1·1
Kennington	2·8	1·9
Kensington N.	2·7	0·7
„ S.	3·0	3·0
Lambeth N.	0·5	0·9
Lewisham	2·9	5·8
Limehouse	1·9	2·0
Marylebone E.	1·7	0·8
„ W.	3·0	0·5
Mile End	1·2	0·3
Newington W.	8·0	2·1
Norwood	3·1	2·9
Paddington N.	3·9	1·5
„ S.	2·6	2·0
Peckham	4·1	2·0
Poplar	1·9	2·2
Rotherhithe	3·0	1·9
St. George's, Hanover Square	1·8	2·0
St. George in the East	0·9	2·2
St. Pancras E.	2·6	2·2
„ N.	5·9	2·3
„ S.	1·1	1·7
„ W.	3·1	1·3
Southwark W.	1·5	0·7
Stepney	2·8	2·7
Strand	1·0	1·1
Walworth	3·7	2·1
Wandsworth	4·2	3·5
Westminster	3·2	1·4
Whitechapel	1·6	1·5
Woolwich	5·4	4·8
Averages	3·5	2·4

[1] The figures refer to the number per thousand of pupils in attendance at L.C.C. elementary schools.

LONDON JUNIOR COUNTY SCHOLARSHIP AWARDS
1925 AND 1935

Electoral Constituency	Per 1,000[1]	
	1925	*1935*
Abbey	1·4	2·5
Balham and Tooting	3·2	6·1
Battersea N.	3·1	3·5
„ S.	4·7	8·7
Bermondsey W.	2·1	4·3
Bethnal Green N.E.	2·0	2·8
„ S.W.	0·4	2·6
Bow and Bromley	1·9	6·2
Brixton	3·9	6·1
Camberwell N.	1·7	2·9
„ N.W.	3·2	6·1
Chelsea	4·9	7·0
City of London	4·1	3·6
Clapham	5·6	6·2
Deptford	2·7	8·4
Dulwich	6·1	11·6
Finsbury	0·4	1·4
Fulham E.	3·1	6·4
„ W.	3·0	8·8
Greenwich	2·7	4·6
Hackney Central	5·7	9·7
„ N.	6·2	13·2
„ S.	2·3	3·5
Hammersmith N.	2·8	4·5
„ S.	2·6	4·9
Hampstead	3·5	5·5
Holborn	0·8	0·9
Islington E.	4·1	7·4
„ N.	4·6	9·2
„ S.	1·3	3·5
„ W.	1·8	2·1
Kennington	1·6	4·1
Kensington N.	1·3	2·4
„ S.	3·2	5·4
Lambeth N.	0·5	2·2
Lewisham E.	7·5	9·8
„ W.	8·2	13·3
Limehouse	1·4	3·0
Mile End	2·6	3·0
Norwood	4·9	6·6

[1] The figures refer to the number per thousand of pupils in attendance at L.C.C. elementary schools.

LONDON JUNIOR (cont'd)

Electoral Constituency	Per 1,000[1]	
	1925	1935
Paddington N.	2·3	6·0
,, S.	0·8	2·2
Peckham	2·9	8·0
Poplar S.	2·2	2·6
Putney	6·4	6·8
Rotherhithe	0·8	2·9
St. George's	3·8	3·7
St. Marylebone	1·9	2·3
St. Pancras N.	5·1	11·4
,, S.E.	1·9	4·0
,, S.W.	1·3	3·7
Shoreditch	0·6	1·4
Southwark Central	2·1	2·4
,, N.	0·5	1·3
,, S.E.	1·9	1·3
Stoke Newington	2·9	10·0
Streatham	6·3	14·0
Wandsworth Central	5·5	10·1
Whitechapel and St. George's	1·5	2·6
Woolwich E.	3·4	8·6
,, W.	6·7	6·3
Averages	2·9	5·5

Council's Attitude to Problem

One of the earliest references to this problem was by Sidney Webb, who, writing in 1904 said:[2]

> It is often stated that the system of selecting children from London as a whole results unfairly to the children in the poorer districts, and that a proportionate quota of scholarships should be allocated to each district.

In spite of evidence to the contrary, Webb did not agree that there was an inverse relationship between the poverty of the district and the

---

[1] The figures refer to the number per thousand of pupils in attendance at L.C.C. elementary schools.

[2] Report by Sidney Webb, Chairman, L.C.C. Higher Education Committee, 1904.

number of scholarships won. He therefore rejected the idea that a certain number of scholarships should be allocated to each borough on the grounds that it would:

> diminish the keenness of the competition, lower the general average of quality, and result in the exclusion of able children in some districts by less able candidates from other districts.

In 1916[1] and 1924, the London County Council again returned to the subject, and on the latter occasion the variations in figures between different boroughs had become so striking as to lead the Council to publish a table showing the relationship between scholarship awards and overcrowding in London (see p. 92).

Nine years later Mr. Lewis Silkin and other Labour Councillors pressed for further investigations to be made, and asked that something be done to help poorer boroughs to win more scholarships. In the same year the Council's Education Officer presented a Report,[2] which agreed that:

> There is no doubt that the proportion of scholarships won by children in certain areas is very much higher than in other areas.

Junior County Scholarship winners in 1928–9 were analysed as follows:

	Average No. in elementary schools	Scholar-ships	Scholarships per 1,000 elementary school-children
Nine electoral areas in outer ring gaining high proportion of scholarships	69,500	986	7·1
Nine electoral areas in inner ring gaining low proportion of scholarships	71,500	220	1·5
County as a whole	540,000	3,818	3·6

[1] In 1916 the L.C.C. concluded that: ". . . there are probably schools in certain neighbourhoods where the home conditions of the children are such that it is hardly to be expected that any candidates could be found who would be capable of either winning or taking advantage of a scholarship". ("Method of Award of Junior County Scholarships", p. 6. Report by L.C.C. Higher Education Sub-Committee, 1916.)
[2] Report of the London County Council Education Committee, July 19, 1933.

TABLE TO SHOW THE RELATIONSHIP BETWEEN JUNIOR COUNTY
SCHOLARSHIP AWARDS AND OVERCROWDING IN LONDON[1]

Borough	(per 1,000 population)			Scholarship winners per 1,000 elementary school-children (1923)
	No. of living-rooms	Acres of parks, open spaces, etc.	Attendance at secondary schools (1919)	
Battersea	960	2·5	7·7	2·4
Bermondsey	750	0·6	2·7	1·1
Bethnal Green	680	0·8	2·2	1·4
Camberwell	960	0·9	9·4	2·6
Chelsea	1,170	0·08	5·6	3·5
City	1,020	0·3	9·7	1·8
Deptford	960	0·3	7·2	2·0
Finsbury	670	0·1	2·7	0·7
Fulham	960	0·4	6·0	3·5
Greenwich	990	4·6	7·9	1·8
Hackney	950	2·8	7·0	4·0
Hammersmith	960	2·2	6·0	3·0
Hampstead	1,410	3·8	14·5	3·7
Holborn	890	0·2	4·7	2·1
Islington	850	0·1	4·3	2·1
Kensington	1,230	0·3	5·2	1·4
Lambeth	980	0·9	5·3	2·3
Lewisham	1,240	2·0	18·8	7·9
Paddington	1,080	0·7	5·1	1·8
Poplar	760	0·5	3·3	1·8
St Marylebone	1,140	3·3	5·2	1·2
St. Pancras	820	1·6	3·7	3·0
Shoreditch	650	0·09	1·3	0·8
Southwark	730	0·07	2·3	1·3
Stepney	690	0·1	4·5	1·9
Stoke Newington	1,090	1·1	12·6	3·5
Wandsworth	1,190	3·5	15·7	5·1
Westminster	1,230	5·0	5·4	1·2
Woolwich	1,030	3·1	10·1	4·9

[1] Sidney Webb was insistent that there were other factors such as quality of schools, teachers, etc., that influenced the winning of scholarships, and no doubt in the early days of the scheme there was some truth in this point of view. For example, it was well known pre-1914, and even during the 1920s and 1930s, that Church primary schools consistently had poorer scholarship results than primary schools directly provided by the Council. In 1914 the average number of Junior County Scholarships per 1,000 elementary school-children won by Council schools was 2·7

(*footnote continued on p. 93*)

footnote continued)
but for Church schools was only 1·1. In 1925 Council exceeded Church schools by 3·3 to 1·4, and in 1935 by 6·4 to 2·4. This ratio of two or three to one in favour of Council schools affected local variations in scholarships because some boroughs had far more Church schools than others. In 1914 the City of London, E. Marylebone, and St. George's, Hanover Square, had *no* Council schools at all. In later years Whitechapel and St. George's, S.W. St. Pancras, St. Marylebone, St. George's, Hanover Square, N. Paddington, Limehouse, N. Kensington, W. Islington, Holborn, S. Hackney, the City of London, Brixton, and N. Battersea appear to have had their scholarship averages reduced by having an unduly large number of Church schools within their boundaries. Moreover, certain well-staffed and well-equipped primary schools may maintain high scholastic standards even though they may be situated in a poor neighbourhood. Bloomfield Rd. (Woolwich), and Hugh Myddelton (Finsbury) as Council schools, and the Jew's Free (Whitechapel) as a Church school were outstanding examples of such primary schools with long lists of scholarship successes to their credit.

Nevertheless, even allowing for all these circumstances, there can be no doubt that the *major* factors in determining which borough won the most scholarships over a long period of time were social and economic rather than purely educational. "... it has been conclusively proved that success in winning scholarships varies with almost monotonous regularity according to the quality of the social and economic environment ... one school in Lewisham wins as many scholarships as the whole of Bermondsey put together." (*Social Progress and Educational Waste*, by Kenneth Lindsay, p. 8, Routledge, 1926.)

In 1930 the *New Survey of London Life and Labour* (Vol. I. Chap. VIII), which was a sequel to Booth's *Survey* of 1890, made a detailed survey of the social background of primary and secondary education in London in the late 1920s.

Sir Hubert Llewellyn Smith, the survey's chief author and the same man who had assisted Booth in 1890, warned that the chief obstacle to more perfect coordination between primary and secondary schools was still poverty. "The children from the poorer homes", he says, "are not only less physically vigorous, but have less ample and quiet means of home study, while in addition their parents find greater difficulty in making the necessary sacrifice of their earnings to keep them longer at school. These are handicaps which have only been partially removed by maintenance scholarships. The point is illustrated by the following analysis of Junior County Scholarships awarded in 1927, classified according to the relative poverty and wealth of the area:

			No. of children in elementary schools	No. of scholarship winners	No. of scholarship winners per 1,000 children
Poor districts*	..	..	205,521	354	17
Other districts	..	..	445,922	1,560	35
Total London	..	..	651,443	1,914	29

It will be seen that in proportion to numbers the children in the poorer areas won less than half as many Junior County Scholarships as those in the rest of London. Nevertheless, the percentage of scholarship winners even in the poorest boroughs was considerably higher for London as a whole than when Charles Booth began his survey", concluded Llewellyn Smith.

A detailed study of backwardness among London school-children and its relation to environmental factors has been made by Professor Sir Cyril Burt in his book *The Backward Child* (Univ. of London Press, 3rd edition, 1950).

* ("Poor districts" included boroughs of Bermondsey, Bethnal Green, Deptford, Finsbury, Poplar, Shoreditch, Southwark, and Stepney.)

A further investigation was made in 1929 into certain specially selected primary schools, which showed that twelve "better-off" primary schools with 8,000 pupils won 102 Junior County Scholarships but that twelve other primary schools "attended by children of parents with small incomes" (8,500 children) won only eleven scholarships. The Report continues:

> The director of the New Survey of London kindly supplied figures regarding parental incomes of children attending schools in five metropolitan boroughs. These figures, when related to statistics concerning the incomes of parents of scholarship holders, indicated that the children of poor parents are less successful in winning scholarships than the children of better-off parents. This was most clearly evident when the children of parents with incomes of £2 a week or less were compared with children of parents with £5 a week or over.

Experiments made with intelligence tests only aggravated the trend towards richer children winning more scholarships, as is shown by the following figures:

	Poor electoral area	Better-off electoral area
Junior County Scholarships actually gained in 1929	35	74
Scholarships that would have been gained on basis of intelligence tests	26	78

The Report sums up by stating that children from poor areas, poor schools, and poor homes win proportionately fewer scholarships than children from richer areas, richer schools, and richer homes. The introduction of an intelligence test would not make much difference.

Having discussed the nature of the problem, the Report then goes on to mention three proposals that were advocated as remedies:

1. More scholarships for "poor" areas.
2. More marks for schools that have won consistently few scholarships.
3. Some scholarships to be restricted to children of very poor parents.

The second of these suggestions is favoured most, but the Report adds that:

> It should be realized that all these three proposals would involve the awarding of scholarships to children who, from the examination test used, are less able intellectually than others to whom the scholarships would be awarded.

In fact, nothing was done about any of these proposals, and the situation continued that the Council awarded scholarships to the metropolitan area as a whole. No attempt was made to restrict awards in any way to particular districts, schools, or sections of the community.

Council's Dilemma

It is easy to understand the London County Council's dilemma regarding the social status of scholarship pupils, particularly since the 1944 Education Act abolished all fees in grammar schools. The authorities have long realized that to try and assess fitness for free grammar-school education on any other basis than intellectual merit would at once lead to serious difficulties.

In the early days of the new scholarship scheme the Council had rightly rejected suggestions that scholars from very poor or disreputable homes should be deliberately excluded from grammar schools, the Council's view being that a pupil who could overcome the handicaps of environment and win a scholarship must have ability and character beyond the ordinary. It was also very properly doubted whether the "goodness" or "badness" of a scholar's home environment could be measured in a way that was generally satisfactory. Similarly, in more modern times it was felt that to weight the scholarship examination not against, but for, the socially under-privileged would be equally unsatisfactory in practice, whatever might be said for it in theory. In the first place, to adopt such a policy would lead to the exclusion from grammar schools of certain pupils who, on the basis of examinations, had proved themselves superior in ability. Secondly, it was again asked on what social grounds (housing, wages, standard of living?) would bonus marks be added or taken away in the selection examination.[1]

---

[1] In exceptional cases where home conditions are unusually difficult, pupils may be given the opportunity of going to the Council's own boarding-school in Suffolk.

H

In the prevailing circumstances the Council decided to stick to its policy of choosing grammar-school entrants solely on the basis of a written examination and a report from the primary school head teacher. Basically, there was little change in the examination up to 1954.

Methods of Selection

The history of the methods actually used in selecting the scholarship entrants provides an interesting example of the way in which psychological theory has been influenced by external social and administrative developments, and vice versa. In the 1890s, children who sought a free place in a London grammar school were examined in a wide range of subjects at varying ages and with different standards. The entrance tests differed widely in type, and also from school to school. The first official (i.e. publicly controlled) scholarship examination was in 1893 when about 1,000 candidates sat for 200 secondary-school places awarded by the Technical Education Board. This examination, which in the following year became known as the Junior County Scholarship Examination, consisted of preliminary papers in English and arithmetic followed by papers in French, algebra, and science. In 1905, after the number of scholarships had been substantially increased, the method of selecting Junior County Scholars was systematized. A specially selected Board of Examiners replaced the Headmasters' Association as examining body, and a chief examiner was appointed who held office for several years. Junior County Scholars were then chosen by an examination comprising ". . . arithmetic; common-sense problems with alternative questions; and an English composition, to test also writing, spelling, intelligence and powers of observation".[1]

Suggestions that a quota system, based either on the primary schools or on particular areas of London, were rejected on both theoretical and practical grounds. It was agreed that some weight should be given to the primary head teachers' recommendations, but that in no circumstances should these be the sole criteria.

Only minor changes were made in the examination until 1917 when it was decided, after an account had been given of marked differences in results caused by the varying ages of candidates,[2] that two examinations (in May and November) should be held annually. In later years it

[1] Report on Scholarships to L.C.C. Higher Education Sub-Committee, p. 1, 1926.
[2] For example, in 1914 it was found that children born in the first six-monthly age-group did on the average almost twice as well as those born in the second six-monthly age-group.

was decided that a better way of getting over the difficulty would be to hold one examination but to make allowances in marking for different ages. The question of age limits and their influence on standards, however, continued to be a matter for concern, and on several subsequent occasions the regulations were slightly modified. Generally speaking, the age of eleven was accepted within fairly rigid limits as the most suitable age for sitting the examination, in contrast to the public-school policy of taking their entrants at the age of thirteen or fourteen. For example, in 1905 it was stated: "We find an almost universal consensus of opinion among those engaged in education that the transfer from the elementary to the secondary school should normally take place at the age of between 11 and 12".[1] In 1916, the age limits for the November examination were ten years four months to eleven years three months. In 1926 the limits were ten years seven months to eleven years one month for the final examination, and three months less for the preliminary. In 1955, the limits for the January examination were ten years four months to eleven years four months, though "exceptionally talented children . . . specially recommended by the district inspector" might enter up to six months younger.[2]

Between the two World Wars the practice was continued of weeding out the less able pupils, and permitting only a proportion of pupils to sit for the final examination. In 1926, for example, out of 75,000 boys and girls in the appropriate age-group, 46,000 sat for the preliminary and 17,000 for the final examination. During recent years all pupils leaving primary schools, except the very backward, have been encouraged to sit the examination.

The most serious problem confronting the examiners was, of course, how to devise a selection technique that would be as accurate as possible in its prognostic powers. The aim was to set papers that would test those academic qualities supposedly mainly required in a grammar school, and great pains were taken to make the examination as "scientific" as possible in this respect by extensive research. Frequent discussions were held at County Hall in the 1920s and 1930s between examiners, psychologists, and inspectors for the purpose of setting and marking papers—indeed, it is probably true to say that more time was devoted to this problem than any other psychological aspect of secondary education.

[1] Report of L.C.C. Education Committee on New Scholarship Scheme, p. 4, Feb. 28, 1905.
[2] *L.C.C. Education Bulletin*, Nov. 3, 1954.

It was generally agreed that of the two subjects, English and arithmetic, which comprised the main part of the examination, the latter was the simplest to examine. An arithmetic paper could be fairly easily set that would test general ability as well as primary-school teaching. Moreover, it graded pupils fairly effectively, which was one of the chief objects of the examination. English, on the other hand, was a more difficult subject to assess, particularly with regard to essay questions. There was also danger of the English examination tending to distort the curricula of the primary schools. ". . . the problem of how to examine English is still far from solved", stated an official report in 1926. "English is a far more intractable subject (than mathematics) to deal with, both in school and examination; it is at once too easy and too difficult. The inspectors feel that in the past far too great weight has been given in this examination to essays."[1]

The question of testing "intelligence", as distinct from achievement, occupied the examiners from the beginning, and as early as 1905 the Chief Examiner expressed the hope that the Junior County Scholarship examination would discover the "presence or absence of intelligence in the candidates as distinct from an examination of the mere results of instruction".[2] "The examination has tested real intelligence as opposed to 'cram'," he concluded, though he wisely entered the caution (incidentally revealing some confusion of thought in doing so) that the examination "also no less tested how far that intelligence has been trained and put to use during the preceding school years". In 1920, an important Government consultative committee was set up to discuss "Psychological Tests of Educable Capacity", and in its report published four years later (and reprinted in 1932), it stated clearly and unambiguously that it was the opinion of its psychological advisers that the tests claimed to measure "inborn, all-round intellectual ability".[3]

In 1926, the London County Council examiners, who by this time had acquired a great deal of experience in mental testing, published a report that discussed in considerable detail the techniques used in selecting children for grammar-school education. This Report is of great interest because it expressed not only very similar hopes but also much the same reservations as were made by the Council's Chief Examiner twenty-one years previously. It was stated plainly that:

[1] Report on Scholarships to L.C.C. Higher Education Sub-Committee, p. 3, 1926.
[2] Report of Chief Examiner on Awards of Junior County Scholarships, L.C.C. Education Committee, p. 42, June 23, 1905.
[3] Report of the Consultative Committee on Psychological Capacity and its possible use in the public system of education. (H.M.S.O., 1924.)

The object of the (Junior County Scholarship) examination is to select children of ability with the least possible regard to achievement, so as to eliminate as far as possible the difference between school and school . . . it is intended that this examination, shall, as far as possible, be directed to the discovery of ability and not of acquirement, and that, therefore, the work done in the schools shall be ignored; but this last is almost impossible inasmuch as the subjects of examination are subjects of school instruction.[1]

The search for pure and uncontaminated mental ability had received a fillip in 1913 when Cyril Burt was appointed educational psychologist to the Council and began his official experiments with intelligence tests. For many years these tests have had a great vogue, partly because they were taken up so enthusiastically by prominent psychologists, and partly because they suited administrative convenience. For three or four decades the outlook of most educationists has been deeply coloured by the work of such men as Terman in America, and Burt, Thomson, and Cattell in Britain.[2] An enormous amount of research was devoted to the improvement of these tests, and great faith was placed in their reliability because of their apparent scientific objectivity. As has been pointed out, it was widely believed that they could measure innate as distinct from acquired ability. It was accepted by many authorities that the intelligence quotient, when once carefully measured, was fixed and unalterable, and could not be changed by teaching or environment. For some people, in fact, the I.Q. was a kind of magic talisman that might for ever open (or shut) the gates to the promised land of the grammar school. The 1944 Education Act, with its emphasis on the tripartite system and the necessity for selection at the age of eleven, temporarily gave intelligence testing a renewed impetus.[3]

During recent years it has become more widely appreciated, however, that teaching or other external environmental circumstances may affect

[1] Report on Scholarships to L.C.C. Higher Education Sub-Committee, pp. 2–3, 1926.

[2] Terman's book, *The Measurement of Intelligence*, published in 1916, makes it clear that the author believes that intelligence tests can measure inborn ability, and that children's I.Q.s remain fairly constant. In 1936 Cattell wrote: "It is the aim of the intelligence test to test natural inborn capacity as distinct from acquired abilities." (*A Guide to Mental Testing*, by R. B. Cattell, Univ. of London Press, 1936.) This reference had disappeared in the 1946 edition of the book.

[3] By far the most stimulating discussion of this subject is contained in *Intelligence Testing and the Comprehensive School*, by Brian Simon. (Lawrence and Wishart, 1953.)

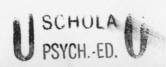

intelligence quotients in much the same way as they affect other examination subjects. This has long been suspected by practising teachers and others interested in the broader aspects of education, but was only forcibly brought to the public's attention in Britain as a result of the experiments of Prof. P. E. Vernon. The latter, who is an eminent authority on intelligence testing and a prominent psychologist in the University of London Institute of Education, came to the conclusion after a series of investigations with children who had been coached in intelligence tests that the children's I.Q.s were raised after practice by from nine to eighteen points—a substantial rise when it is realized that the alteration of a few points may make all the difference between getting into a grammar school or not.[1]

Dr. A. F. Watts, another prominent psychologist and senior research worker at the National Foundation for Educational Research, found in a large-scale series of experiments that: "Coaching raised the average scores of groups of children in intelligence tests by five to nine points of standardized score."[2]

Experiments conducted along similar lines in Manchester and Southampton showed that the average increase in scores was from five to eleven points.

It was the London County Council's realization, among other things, of the fallibility of the selection methods used that led directly to proposals for setting up a comprehensive system of secondary education. Now that these comprehensive schools are beginning to become a reality the Common Entrance test, which was planned mainly for the tripartite system, is being revised accordingly. In June 1954, an important new statement of policy regarding the eleven plus examination was placed before the Council's Education Committee, and accepted by the majority of members. The new scheme—which incidentally once again shows the influence of administrative developments upon the type of examination used, and vice versa—arose out of what the Council described as the "changing pattern of secondary education in London". It visualized that when comprehensive schools were widespread and fully in operation the selection examination at the age of eleven would disappear altogether. Meanwhile, so long as separate grammar, technical, central, and modern schools existed the old Common Entrance test would continue, but with much greater emphasis on parents' wishes

[1] "Intelligence Testing—After Practice and Coaching", by P. E. Vernon. Two articles in *The Times Educational Supplement*, Jan. 2, 1952 and Feb. 1, 1952.
[2] *Secondary School Entrance Examinations: Second Interim Report*, by A. F Watts, D. A. Pidgeon, and A. Yates, p. 15 (Newnes, 1952).

and the reports of primary school teachers.[1] In order to emphasize the examination's new role it was renamed the Junior Leaving Examination —the third change in nomenclature since 1904, each of which reflected important changes in the examination's function.

Poverty and Educational Opportunity

Surveying the history of free grammar-school education in London over a period of more than half a century, one is led irresistibly to the conclusion that the transformation of a small, patchy, and unsystematic provision of scholarships into a large centrally controlled plan of free places has brought immense benefits to the community as well as to the grammar schools themselves. Tens of thousands of intelligent boys and girls, who might otherwise have been debarred by their family circumstances from the benefits of higher education, have been enabled to go to good secondary schools, and in many cases to a university. Sources of talent and ability that were previously constricted by the harsh bonds of poverty have been opened up in a way that was hardly conceived possible by the pioneers of free education in the late nineteenth and early twentieth centuries. Grammar-school life in all its aspects, scholastic, cultural, and athletic, has been greatly enriched by the influx of children selected for their intellectual merit rather than for willingness to pay fees. Indeed, in view of the rising costs of school administration and the difficulty of increasing fee-paying income because of the relative decline in the number of middle-class people in London, it is certain that many secondary schools would have been in serious financial trouble without the steady flow of State-aided pupils. It is no exaggeration to state that the overwhelming majority of London

[1] "The new scheme of transfer is a definite step forward from the scheme of selection under which local selection committees determine the allocation of pupils to one of three categories to which some schools no longer correspond and which fewer schools will correspond in future. It gives the head teachers of primary schools a greater share in the process of determining the secondary school to which each pupil ought to be transferred; it is a move in the direction of changing the procedure from one of selection to one of educational guidance and of making the procedure more flexible: it will tend to enhance the importance of a pupil's achievement and progress in the junior school and to reduce the importance of what is now called the Common Entrance test. Decisions will be reached in collaboration with parents by a large number of head teachers each considering the needs of a small number of individuals whom they know, instead of by nine committees each considering a large number of names on the basis of information on paper." Minutes of London County Council Education Committee, June 2, 1954. Report of Primary and Secondary Schools Sub-Committee (No. 3).

grammar schools could not continue to exist if they were solely dependent upon fee-payers. It is also true that the recent expansion of London's commercial, administrative, and professional life would have been impossible without the greatly increased number of trained and qualified students coming from the grammar schools; and this increase had necessarily to come from working-class as well as middle-class sources.

Nevertheless, though the scholarship system has proved a great success and brought substantial social and educational benefits, it has not solved the problem of secondary-school selection. The attempt to replace an aristocracy of wealth by an aristocracy of talent in the grammar schools has not proved as simple as was hoped, and the new methods of allocation to secondary schools have raised almost as many problems as they have solved. In the first place, the number of grammar-school places has varied greatly in relation to child population, which has meant that the degree of competition in the Common Entrance examination has altered from year to year. Secondly, despite the reduction and eventual abolition of fee-paying, environmental and family circumstances still play a big part in influencing a child's chances of winning a place in a grammar school, as is shown by the wide variations in the number of scholarships won in different boroughs. Thirdly, it has proved impossible so far to devise really accurate means of measuring suitability for a grammar-school education. Great advances have been made in examination and testing techniques, but they are still very fallible instruments, as modern psychological research has shown.

The London County Council cannot, of course, be directly blamed for the social conditions that have handicapped the working of the scholarship system. It is not responsible for the fluctuations in population that complicate grammar-school selection, nor for the poor home environment that may so seriously hamper children at school. Moreover, by its decision to introduce comprehensive high schools the Council indicated that it recognizes the impossibility of devising a perfect selection technique at the age of eleven.

The history of the Council's scholarship scheme suggests that in the long run a further substantial increase in educational opportunity can only be achieved when slums, overcrowding, malnutrition, low wages, unemployment, and all those other social evils making for backwardness at school have been abolished, and a more flexible and all-embracing type of secondary-school system developed. Meanwhile, as a practical short-term measure to ease the financial burden on poorer homes, and to reduce premature leaving, the Council should increase its maintenance grants and impose a less strict means test. It is as true today as it ever was that in cases of acute poverty a free place in a grammar school is of little use without a maintenance grant, particularly for older pupils.

Rowntree   30% below poverty line
now 3%

Chapter 5

CAREERS OF GRAMMAR-SCHOOL LEAVERS[1]

Whatever administrators and teachers may think should be the aim of a grammar school, it has to be admitted that the grammar school in the eyes of parents and scholars is essentially a school with a vocational bias. The struggle to get into that type of school is determined by the fact that parents and pupils see in that type of education the door to certain types of vocation.—Report of the London County Council Education Committee, July 9, 1944.

Problem of Grammar-School Leavers

THE age at which pupils leave school, and the occupations that these pupils take up in adult life are clearly matters of the greatest importance to all grammar schools.[2] The first point touches upon several complicated organizational matters, including staffing ratios, the economical use of school accommodation, and the degree of

[1] Since this chapter was written the Central Advisory Council for Education (England) has published an important survey on the subject of *Early Leavers* (H.M.S.O., 1954). Based on an investigation of 120 representative grammar schools in England, this most valuable report broadly confirms the conclusions reached by the present writer as to the extent and causes of premature leaving.

The gravity of the problem is stressed, but at the same time it is very properly pointed out that the percentage of grammar-school pupils who leave school under the age of sixteen, or fail to go on to the sixth form when they would have been well advised to do so, is not increasing but diminishing. However, it is estimated that out of the 1946 grammar-school intake about 50 per cent. more boys and 70 per cent. more girls might have stayed in the sixth form than did in fact do so. The Report shows the very wide range (from 1·4 to 26·1 per cent.) in the proportion of sixth-form pupils to the grammar-school population as a whole in different parts of the country.

The reasons given for premature leaving are very similar to those advanced in this chapter. It is agreed that the problem is extremely complex. Nevertheless, a careful analysis is made of the most likely causes, social as well as more narrowly educational. Among the most important factors were:

    (i) Poor home background of certain pupils, including poverty, overcrowding, family discord, lack of facilities for homework, and ignorance as to the real advantages of a grammar-school education.

[footnotes continued on page 105

specialization possible in the sixth form—not forgetting the amount of the headmaster's salary! The second point is of even more fundamental importance because it concerns the question of the vocational role of the grammar school in modern society. Unfortunately, however, up to the present there has been little serious study of either of these problems. The authorities have only just begun to investigate the problem of premature leaving, and so far there has been no large-scale review of the vocational aspects of grammar-school education. The purpose of this chapter is to describe some of the main reasons why boys and girls leave school at particular ages, taking into account both psychological and sociological factors, and also to summarize such information as is available about the careers of leavers from schools in London and other parts of the country.

In theory, all children who enter grammar schools are expected eventually to sit for their General Certificate of Education examination soon after their sixteenth birthday, and a minority are expected to go on to the Advanced Level of this examination at the age of eighteen or nineteen. The whole grammar-school course is geared to this five- or seven-year time-sequence. Curriculum and time-table are based on it; and administratively the programme of work is planned on the assumption that few, if any, pupils will leave prematurely. Most local authorities stipulate that a child can only be accepted for a grammar-school course on the understanding that he or she will not be withdrawn before the proper time without good reason. In some counties a penalty is imposed (or attempted to be imposed, for it is legally difficult to enforce) on parents who remove their children from school without official permission.

Moreover, the sixth form is regarded as one of the most important features of the grammar school, distinguishing it from the other types

---

footnotes continued]
    (ii) Changing conditions in the juvenile labour market owing to shortage of labour in relation to demand, and the desire to get settled in work before call-up in the Armed Forces. Apprenticeship regulations are also discussed.
    (iii) Faulty selection techniques or variations in proportion of grammar-school intake between different areas, which lead to wrong allocation of pupils at the age of eleven.
    (iv) Discontent of pupils with discipline and methods of work in certain schools.

The Advisory Council Report—which must be regarded as a milestone in official Ministry publications because of its emphasis on social factors in education—concludes by recommending certain administrative actions that should be taken to encourage older pupils to stay at school, among the most important being a substantial increase in maintenance grants for pupils over sixteen.

[2] See two articles on "Problem of Early Leavers" in *The Times Educational Supplement* of Aug. 24 and Aug. 31, 1951.

of secondary school.[1] It is generally recognized that a large number of older boys or girls give a sense of solidity and purpose in a school. They give it a reputation for both academic and sports successes; they provide a stabilizing influence, and are of incalculable help to staff in all kinds of organizational ways; they are the leaders to whom the rest of the school looks for guidance; they form the bridge between adolescent and adult life, and link the schools to the universities and professions; they bring an atmosphere of maturity into a community that tends perpetually to lapse into childishness. From the teachers' point of view nothing gives more pride or pleasure than the knowledge that he has guided some boy or girl from the first tentative steps at the age of eleven or twelve to the triumph of an open scholarship, half a dozen Certificate distinctions, or an outstanding sports victory.

This idea of the five- or seven-year course is the theory of the grammar school. In practice, however, many pupils, who so eagerly began their five-year course at the age of eleven or twelve, never reach the first stage of the Certificate examination, and only a small minority stay on to the sixth form. In 1948–9, for example, 26 per cent. of the girls and 23·4 per cent. of the boys, and in 1949–50 25 per cent. of the girls and 22·4 per cent. of the boys, left State-aided grammar schools in England and Wales before the age of sixteen.[2] In London the position was worse, with 41·7 per cent. of the boys and 30 per cent. of the girls leaving grammar schools prematurely.[3] Less than one in twenty of the London grammar-school leavers went to a university.

The harmful consequences of this premature leaving are very plain. Teachers are frustrated in their efforts to build a balanced school programme, and administrators have their plans upset for the proper

[1] "The sixth form is indeed the most characteristic and most valuable feature in a grammar school in the training of character and a sense of responsibility, and on its existence depends all that is best in the grammar school tradition", says the Spens Report (p. 166). "Not only does it make possible that free and yet ordered self-government, which is the admiration and envy of educationists of other lands, and a national asset, but it acts as a perpetual stimulus to the work of both teachers and pupils, providing both with a new and wider horizon." The Report continues: "There is general agreement that much of what is most valuable in the grammar school tradition depends on the existence of a sixth form" (p. xx Introduction), and concludes: "We have already expressed our opinion as to the supreme importance of cultivating sixth forms, both for their effect upon the corporate life and internal affairs of a school, and for their effect upon the length of school life and after careers of individual pupils. This opinion is upheld by evidence from Teachers' Associations and other witnesses". (Report of Consultative Committee on Secondary Education, p. 333, H.M.S.O., 1938.)

[2] Figures given in House of Commons on May 10, 1951.

[3] Report by Ministry of Education on Premature Leavers from Maintained Grammar Schools in England, 1949–50.

allocation of school places. The time and energy of numerous officials are wasted, and parents are disappointed that the high hopes that they held about their children's future are dashed. Perhaps worst of all, the children themselves leave school in an atmosphere of failure and disapproval, where there should have been a sense of progress and achievement.[1] So far as the schools themselves are concerned, too few senior pupils make it hard to organize prefects and sports teams, which are so essential for the creation of a healthy corporate spirit. There is a lowering of academic standards, and inability to specialize owing to staffing difficulties. For the community as a whole the loss is equally serious, because the adult world needs the more highly trained and adult products of the sixth form. In view of the fact that the grammar schools, together with the public schools, are supposed to supply the bulk of the leaders in the professions, commerce, science, and industry, a total of 27,500 pupils aged seventeen years and over in attendance at such schools can hardly be considered adequate in a population of forty-five millions.[2]

Official Concern at Problem

That the authorities are aware of the gravity of the problem is shown by the numerous recent discussions on the subject. Official investigations of premature leaving (admittedly on a limited scale) have been made during the last four years by the Ministry of Education, the Association of Education Committees, and the Incorporated Association of Head-masters.[3] The specialist press has devoted some attention to it, and so has the National Union of Teachers. During a recent debate in the House of Commons the Parliamentary Under-Secretary for Education

[1] This heart-cry from the headmaster of ——— School in reply to the I.A.H.M. questionnaire illustrates the point: "I am very glad that some action is contemplated to bring to the notice of the Ministry the seriousness of this problem. This district has been hit particularly hard by premature leaving as there are such lucrative jobs available for juveniles—a girl can be earning up to £4 per week within six months. You will readily see that the magnitude of the problem (in 1947–8, 27 out of 82; in 1948–9, 26 out of 67; and in 1949–50, 24 out of 60 leavers left prematurely) is such that the whole school organization has been undermined. On several occasions staff have left, and I have been refused permission to replace them. Hence several subjects have had to be dropped from the curriculum. . . . Also it has been necessary to make all the pre-School Certificate forms follow the same or very similar curricula, since I know that next year coalescing of forms will be inevitable. . . . Premature leaving has also had a very unsettling and depressing effect on the staff."

[2] Mr. D. R. Hardman in the House of Commons, July 24, 1951.

[3] In 1950 the Incorporated Association of Headmasters sent a questionnaire about premature leavers to the headmasters of boys' grammar schools in England and Wales. At least three hundred replies were received.

spoke of the wastage of fifteen-year olds as "this extremely important crisis which faces the grammar schools".[1]

But while all educationists are agreed about the gravity of the problem there is controversy as to both cause and cure. Indeed, most public discussions of the subject have only served to emphasize that the problem has only just begun to be scientifically studied. Fifteen years ago all the Spens Committee could report was: "There is no general factor which determines the age at which a pupil leaves the grammar school."[2] A further example of official vagueness was given during the Commons debate referred to above when the Parliamentary Under-Secretary for Education, who might be expected to have all the latest information available on the subject, appealed to other M.P.s for advice, saying: "I do not know of any solution to this problem except the patient missionary work of the schools".[3]

Some critics have blamed faulty selection techniques at the Common Entrance examination for premature leaving. Intelligence tests are not yet sufficiently accurate, these critics argue, to distinguish between the academic and non-academic types, with the result that too many unsuitable boys and girls are admitted to the grammar schools. The number of grammar-school places in proportion to local child population varies considerably from area to area, so that one county may have 40 per cent. of the age-group in such places and another 10 per cent. In the former case it is not surprising that a large number of entrants leave school before reaching their sixteenth birthday.[4] This theme is strongly developed in many of the replies to a questionnaire sent out by the Incorporated Association of Headmasters.[5] Typical of the comments made by headmasters in various parts of the country were:

Lack of interest and ambition. (Glamorgan.)
We always get a small residue of entrants who are not really fitted for academic education. (Norfolk.)

[1] Mr. D. R. Hardman in the House of Commons, July 24, 1951.
[2] Report of the Consultative Committee on Secondary Education, p. 167 (H.M.S.O., 1938).
[3] Mr. D. R. Hardman in the House of Commons, July 24, 1951.
[4] The percentage of grammar-school entrants in England who leave school before reaching the age of sixteen varies greatly from county to county. During 1949–50 for example, 41·7 per cent. of the boys in London and 41·3 per cent. of the girls in Gloucestershire left prematurely as compared with 7·8 per cent. of the boys in Northumberland, and 7·1 per cent. of the girls in East Sussex.
[5] One hundred and twenty-four out of 300 replies mentioned wrong selection of pupils as a major (but not the only cause) of premature leaving.

Inability to cope with a grammar-school course. In the years 1945-7 many boys were admitted who were quite unsuitable for an academic education. (Berkshire.)

The Westmorland Authority admits between 45 per cent. and 50 per cent. of the age-group to its grammar schools. Some of the unsuitable material thus accepted fails to stay the course. (Westmorland.)

Selection puts the stress on quick wit, and little or none on staying-power characteristics. (Northumberland.)

Lack of real ability to profit. (Bedford.)

Other students of the problem have suggested that the personality of individual teachers, more especially head teachers, or the atmosphere of particular schools, determine to some extent the child's attitude towards early or late leaving. Even if the pupils are not doing exceptionally well academically there may be other circumstances, such as games or clubs, that give children the opportunity to develop their personalities in a way that persuades them to stay longer at school than they would otherwise have done.

In a study[1] of 107 boys who left a north London grammar school before the age of sixteen[2] during the years 1948-51, it was found, as might be expected, that those who did badly in school often left earlier than those who did well, but there was no irrefutable proof that backwardness in school work owing to lack of intelligence was highly correlated with premature leaving. On the one hand, comparatively few boys (13 out of 115, excluding sixth formers) left out of the upper, or "A", streams, and of these more than half (8) migrated from the district. Furthermore, phrases such as "poor", "weak", "fair", "below average", "poor quality", or "low standard" were frequently appended to the report cards of early leavers. On the other hand, a more careful analysis of examination records showed that on 54 occasions early leavers came in the first ten, 54 in positions 11 to 20, and 67 below 20 (there are usually about 30 boys in each class).

In other words, the tendency was for early leavers to be slightly below average, but not overwhelmingly so, in school examinations.

What was even more remarkable in this survey was the very high

---

[1] See "The Changing Environment of the London Grammar School 1900-50" by F. C. Campbell (Ph.D. thesis, University of London, 1953).

[2] Another eight boys aged 16-18 left before completing their sixth form course.

proportion of leavers who came from broken homes. Divorce, separation, marital discord, father away from home, widowhood, and neurotic parents were often mentioned as causes of early leaving, confirming the psychologists' conclusions that emotional instability and lack of a secure and happy home life are major causes of restlessness and failure to make steady progress at school. Remarks written in these cases by form masters on report cards such as "apathetic", "restless", "clowning", "erratic", "introspective", "sulky and resentful", "unhappy boy", "tendency to sulk", "no ambition", "nervous and easily discouraged", "talkative and restless", "insolent", "deceitful", "evasive", and "temperamentally unstable" were made with such disturbing frequency as to suggest something more fundamentally at fault than the usual laziness or variability of temperament expected in the adolescent.

Correlated with this record of unstable home life was a poor report of achievement in school work. Out of twenty-six boys whose homes were in some way unsatisfactory only eight secured an average or above-average report. There was also frequently an account of numerous absences from school, suggesting that low morale and parental irresponsibility often went hand in hand with ill health.

Social Factors in Premature Leaving

It would be a mistake, however, to try to explain all the causes of premature leaving in terms of bad selection methods, low intelligence, emotional difficulties, unsympathetic schools and teachers, or other predominantly psychological influences. Individual boys or girls might leave before their proper time because they were wrongly chosen, and proved unable to cope with the academic curriculum. There may even be special circumstances such as broken homes or family bereavements that unsettle children at school or compel them to seek work at an early age. But all the evidence available suggests that the problem cannot be understood in narrowly psychological terms alone; the social status of the schools and the environment of the pupils must also be taken into account. In other words, just as such educational questions as the Common Entrance examination and curriculum should be considered in relation to local population trends, class structure, housing conditions, and occupations, so also should the question of the age of leavers.

So far as these environmental factors are concerned it is convenient to treat them under two broad headings:

1. Status of school, and environment of catchment-area during pupil's school career.
2. State of the labour market and vocational opportunities at the time when a pupil is contemplating leaving school.

The social status of a school is often an elusive and imponderable affair, depending in varying degrees upon traditions, income of parents, buildings, examination results, and sports successes. Nevertheless, it is one of the most distinctive characteristics of any educational establishment, deciding, among other things, the average length of school life. Up to about thirty years ago it was a common practice to "grade" schools according to their social status. In 1864, for example, the Schools Inquiry Commission divided secondary schools into three types:

a. First-grade, providing education up to 18 or 19.
b. Second-grade, providing education up to 16.
c. Third-grade, providing education up to 14.

The Royal Commission on Secondary Education, reporting in 1895, stated that in their opinion conditions had so changed during the previous thirty years that the classification should be changed as follows:

a. First-grade, providing education up to 19 years.
b. Second-grade, providing education up to 18 years.
c. Third-grade, providing education up to 16 years.[1]

This classification of schools on the basis of leaving age was also to a great degree a social classification, the "first-grade" schools catering mainly for the upper classes, and the "second-grade" mainly for the middle and lower middle classes. The "third-grade" schools

---

[1] This conception of sixteen as the "critical age" was adopted in 1909 when the Board of Education Regulations laid it down that "an adequate proportion of the pupils remain in the school up to and beyond the age of sixteen" if the school was to be recognized as a secondary school (exceptions were made in cases of small towns and rural areas).

corresponded more to elementary schools, and were intended primarily for working-class children.[1]

The London County Council did not officially attempt after 1919 to grade the secondary schools under its control, but sufficient data is available from the 1920s and 1930s to show how closely correlated was the age of leaving with such social factors as fees, relative proportion of fee-payers and scholarship entrants, and entrants from State primary or private preparatory schools. In the following tables various London secondary schools have been divided into broad categories on the basis suggested above. The first category concerns independent public schools, which have high fees, few, if any, scholarship entrants (and these drawn mainly from the upper classes), and take practically no children at all from State primary schools, drawing upon the well-to-do for the overwhelming majority of their pupils. The second category covers State-aided grammar schools with moderate fees, taking about half to two-thirds of their entrants from State primary schools, usually more than half as fee-payers, and drawing predominantly from middle-class residential areas in the suburbs. The third division covers the poorer grammar schools of the East End, with eight or nine-tenths of their entrants from State primary schools, and less than half (sometimes as few as one quarter) paying fees.

[1] In 1877 Mr. T. H. Green, referring to the grading of secondary education, wrote: "It embarrasses all schemes. Such and such a course of study is settled on logical grounds, the best adapted for boys who are being educated for a certain kind of life—the education of a gentleman; second-grade being less gentleman-like, and so on—the education significance being a social one". Mr. Sidney Webb, writing in 1904 when he was Chairman of the L.C.C. Higher Education Committee, accepted the idea of grading schools according to the ages to which pupils were retained and their later occupation in life, but denied—and in this respect most contemporary educationists would have disagreed with him—that this grading on an age basis was also a grading of education merit. He wrote: "Taking as the marks of a 'first-grade' secondary school that it retains a fair number of its pupils until 18, prepares them generally to proceed to university courses, and wins open scholarships at the universities, London seems to be fortunate in possessing about fifteen such schools, of which half-a-dozen are for girls. Most of the rest represent different types of the 'second-grade' secondary school, retaining few scholars after 17, preparing hardly any for university courses, and passing most of their boys (and many of their girls) into business life, the Civil Service, or the teaching profession, at the age of 16 or 17. In about a dozen cases the usual leaving age is at present lower and these schools may be said to represent various modern and experimental types of what formerly would have been classed as a 'third-grade' secondary school. It is perhaps desirable to state, clearly and emphatically, that this grading of the schools has no relation whatsoever to their efficiency. By a second-grade school we do not mean a second-rate school. It may, on the contrary, be a school of the very highest efficiency; all that is meant is that its pupils leave at 16 or 17." (Report of the L.C.C. Higher Education Committee on Secondary Education, 1904.)

CORRELATION OF SOCIAL STATUS AND PERCENTAGE OF PUPILS OVER SIXTEEN IN LONDON SECONDARY SCHOOLS, 1926

SCHOOLS		Total	% over 16
Upper Division:			
A	(b)	679	37·5
B	(g)	441	34·7
C	(b)	707	19·5
D	(b)	489	19·2
E	· (b)	715	17·9
F	(b)	893	25·0
Middle Division:			
G	(b)	693	16·3
H	(b)	784	16·3
I	(b)	656	13·7
J	(g)	581	17·9
K	(g)	590	19·3
Lower Division:			
L	(mixed)	317	9·4
M	(b)	425	11·3
N	(b)	360	7·8
O	(g)	319	7·8
P	(b)	359	5·0

The relationship of premature leaving to the changing social environment of London, particularly the fall in child population, migration of the middle class to the suburbs, and the impoverished state of many catchment-areas, is emphasized by many London County Council Inspectors.

... it is probable that the neighbourhood is on the down-grade.
It is noteworthy that some of the best children in the lower school do not proceed to the upper as their parents leave London and go across the border into Essex.
In cases where early leaving means the end of daytime education, the main causes are difficult economic circumstances at home, and the ease with which young girls can now obtain suitable employment,

CORRELATION OF SOCIAL STATUS AND AVERAGE LEAVING AGE IN
CERTAIN LONDON SECONDARY SCHOOLS, 1933-6[1]

School		Total	PUPILS % from elementary schools	% of fee-payers	Average age of leavers over 14
Higher Social Status (Fees over £10)					years months
I	(b)	696	59·5	63·9	17 0
II	(b)	529	54·6	60·4	16 10
III	(g)	627	64·4	46·6	17 4
IV	(b)	616	38·2	72·7	17 2
V	(g)	501	77·4	47·1	17 2
VI	(g)	474	37·5	61·0	16 9
VII	(g)	243	51·4	58·8	17 3
Lower Social Status (Fees under £10)					
VIII	(g)	377	79·9	33·2	16 3
IX	(b)	505	93·9	28·7	16 3
X	(mixed)	282		12·0	16 4 (b) 16 0 (g)
XI	(b)	303	99·0	39·3	15 10
XII	(b)	416	91·8	44·5	16 4
XIII[2]	(g)	327	78·9	48·3	15 11

are characteristic comments on a girls' school situated in a predominantly working-class London borough.[3]

In the poorer central and East End boroughs such as Finsbury, Southwark, Bethnal Green, Stepney, and Poplar, where the population has long been of an unskilled working-class character and where overcrowding is acute, the Inspectors[4] frequently drew attention to the connection between falling school rolls and the poverty of the neighbourhood. For example, it was reported of —— School for Girls (Poplar):

> The average leaving age during this period (1933–6) is below the average for all London girls' schools on the Board's lists. . . . The main causes of early leaving are difficult economic circumstances at home and the ease with which young girls can obtain employment.

[1] Figures are taken from L.C.C. Inspectors' Reports for various years.
[2] Figures apply to years 1929–30, and to pupils over 12.
[3] Reports by L.C.C. Inspectors on —— Girls' School, 1927 and 1936.
[4] Quotations are from London County Council Inspectors' Reports for various years.

The high rate of wastage from —— Girls' School in Southwark was explained by the "poor neighbourhood", which made it difficult to "ensure that pupils stay for the full secondary course unless they have some form of assistance".

—— Girls' School in Finsbury had suffered a reduction of fifty-six girls in the senior school, there was an "unduly large leakage before the completion of the school course", and the "intellectual quality of the girls had depreciated". This was due to the fact that the "school is becoming definitely more local in character" and to the "changed character of the neighbourhood". In —— Boys' School in Stepney "difficulty was experienced in retaining boys beyond the general school age" because many came from homes where "social conditions were adverse".

—— Boys' School in Bethnal Green had lost 56 per cent. of its boys between the ages of fourteen and sixteen during the years 1925–33. ". . . there seems little room for doubt that the social conditions of the homes from which the boys come are largely responsible for this premature leaving" comment the Inspectors.

—— School in Poplar suffered from various disadvantages of environment. Its premises were "noisy", its site was "restricted", and most of its pupils came from homes where "poor circumstances prevail". It was not surprising therefore that the leaving age was "comparatively low", that the sixth form had "tended to shrink", and that examination results were "not quite as good as they were a few years back".

Information collected by the Incorporated Association of Headmasters confirms that the social circumstances of the home are the most important single factor in determining the age of school-leavers. The pressure of poverty upon the family and the resultant necessity for children to begin earning as soon as possible was the cause most frequently mentioned by headmasters (131 times in 300 replies) for premature leaving. Various aspects of these social and economic factors are emphasized in the following comments:

> The reason is nearly always economic. The boy's parents want him to start earning money. — Grammar School (Lancashire).
> The economic position in the home . . . the boy's own desire to give financial help. — Grammar School (Dorset).
> Several parents were quite frank in stating that they required financial help from their children. — Grammar School (Yorkshire).
> Straitened home circumstances. — High School (Yorkshire).

Financial difficulties at home. — Grammar School (Glamorgan).

Rising cost of living. — High School (Yorkshire).

This is the centre of a large and important agricultural area in East Anglia. The inducement to go out to work on the land at fifteen for high wages is naturally very strong. There is always the opportunity here. Boys in large families find their parents anxious for them to get out as soon as possible, as they cannot maintain several at school at once. — Grammar School (Norfolk).

Envy of the earning capacity of friends formerly at modern secondary schools was stressed by several headmasters. For example, the Headmaster of —— Grammar School mentioned a boy's "dislike at not earning himself when friends of his own age . . . are earning". The Headmaster of —— Grammar School referred to "parents who weakly fall in with boys' desire to leave—a phase which many boys go through when their pals leave school at fifteen". The Headmaster of —— Boys' School spoke of: "The draw of 'growing up' and getting into the world, especially marked when there are friends leaving modern schools at fifteen plus".

The Headmaster of the —— Grammar School, Sheffield, attributed early leaving partly to the fact that: ". . . the boy's friends near his home are working. They have no homework but plenty of money, and the pupils want to be in the same position".

The influence of home environment is also apparent in the survey made of early leavers from a north London grammar school during 1948–51:

PREMATURE LEAVERS FROM —— SCHOOL, 1948–51

	Total	Forms 1–5	Form 6
Leavers	115	107	8

	Social class of their parents		
Social class	No.	%	% of all entrants 1945–9
1–2	2	1·7	1·0
3–4	27	23·5	19·1
5	36	31·3	53·8
6–7	43	37·4	21·2
Unclassified	7	6·1	4·9
Totals	115	100·0	100·0

Causes of premature leaving

Broken homes	26
Parents moved from district	
Classes 1–4	11
Class 5	12
Classes 6–7	4
Compulsory transfers	19
Upper or "A" stream boys (excluding sixth formers) who left prematurely	13
Upper stream boys who moved from district	8

It will be seen from the above table that wastage is markedly worse among the poorer pupils. For example, the rate of wastage among social classes six and seven (the poorest) was nearly twice as high (37·4 per cent.) as the normal distribution of those social classes among the entrants for 1945–9. On first impression it might appear that the wastage is also higher than expected (23·5 per cent. as compared with normal distribution of 19·1 per cent.) among social classes three and four (broadly speaking, the lower middle classes); but a more careful analysis shows that out of a total of 27 boys in classes three and four who left prematurely, 11 migrated from the neighbourhood whereas out of 43 leavers in classes six and seven only 4 left the neighbourhood. In other words, the lower-middle-class parents are tending to leave the catchment-area (mainly Islington and St. Pancras) at a greater rate than the unskilled workers. It should be noted that there has been a general tendency for population to fall over most of the catchment-area, particularly Islington. The relative stability among class five (skilled workers) is significant. It suggests that where financial pressure is not so great (as in classes six and seven), or the urge to migrate less pronounced (as in classes one to four), the tendency to withdraw the pupil prematurely from school is not so marked.

Similarly, when a team of research workers from the London School of Economics and Political Science investigated the age at which 350 pupils attending grammar schools in the Home Counties and London preferred to leave school they found a significant difference between pupils from middle-class as compared with working-class homes. "The middle-class group felt that their parents would like them to leave school at 16·8 years, while for the working-class group the comparable age was 16·3 years", concluded the report of this investigation.[1] It was also found that, in general, pupils from large families wanted to leave sooner than those from small families.

The most recent, abundant, and possibly most convincing set of statistics on the leaving age of London schoolchildren is that in the report of the 1951 Census of Population. In this report the population is divided into five social classes and the various ages at which persons in these social classes left school. When the two categories are compared we find an extremely high correlation between the percentage of the population broadly classified as middle class and the number of people who have stayed in full-time education beyond the age of sixteen years.[2] The figures in the table on page 119 illustrate the point with remarkable clarity.

Juvenile Labour Market

The second important factor affecting the age of leaving is the child's relation to the juvenile labour market. Boys and girls contemplating leaving school are not, of course, solely influenced by the success or failure of their academic studies or by the environment of their home and neighbourhood. They are also concerned about their impending transfer to the adult world, where jobs and careers are of the first importance. Children do not normally think very seriously about their future occupation until they are fourteen or fifteen years old, but when they come near to the school leaving age the question of employment begins to weigh heavily upon their minds. It is during this phase (roughly the fourth and fifth years in the grammar school) that vague ideas about their future status in life begin to crystallize into more definite vocational aspirations. At such a stage the two questions of school and career, which previously had tended to be regarded separately, become associated with each other. For the potential leaver it becomes, not merely a matter of escaping from school circumstances, which may be boring or distasteful, but also of getting a job and earning a living. Automatically, therefore, the leaver is forced to consider the whole question of his school progress and family circumstances in relation to his hopes and ambitions in the world at large.

[1] "Selection for Secondary Education and Achievement in Four Grammar Schools", by A. H. Halsey and L. Gardner, pp. 66–8. *British Journal of Sociology*, Vol. IV. No. 1. March, 1953.
[2] See *Census of Population 1951*, County of London Volume (H.M.S.O.).

TABLE SHOWING RELATION OF SOCIAL CLASSES TO SECONDARY
SCHOOL LEAVING AGE IN LONDON

Area	Social classes 1–2 (per 1,000)	Area	Terminal education age 16-19 (per 100)
Hampstead	381	Hampstead	35
St. Marylebone	371	Chelsea	28
Kensington	330	Holborn	25
Chelsea	329	St. Marylebone	24
Westminster	277	Kensington	24
City	259	City	19
Holborn	245	Wandsworth	18
Paddington	223	Lewisham	15
Wandsworth	221	Westminster	13
Lewisham	194	Stoke Newington	13
Woolwich	169	Hackney	12
Stoke Newington	164	Fulham	12
Fulham	152	Lambeth	11
Greenwich	149	Paddington	11
St. Pancras	139	St. Pancras	10
Lambeth	136	Woolwich	10
Camberwell	135	Camberwell	10
Battersea	133	Deptford	9
Hackney	126	Battersea	9
Hammersmith	122	Hammersmith	8
Deptford	120	Greenwich	8
Islington	104	Islington	7
Finsbury	90	Finsbury	6
Bermondsey	88	Stepney	6
Stepney	84	Southwark	5
Poplar	75	Bermondsey	4
Bethnal Green	69	Poplar	4
Southwark	68	Shoreditch	3
Shoreditch	55	Bethnal Green	3

Coefficient of correlation	+ 0·93

Parental influence is strong during this critical period, and so in-creasingly is that of the Youth Employment Service, but whoever exerts most pressure, family, officials, or teachers, the pupil has two main points to consider. First, the general state of the labour market (and more particularly juvenile wage rates and the degree of unemploy-ment), and secondly the opportunities available in specific occupations.

Regarding the first point, there is good evidence to suggest that the age of leaving is related to some extent to the movements of the trade cycle. During the "boom" period of the cycle, when jobs are easy to obtain, there is a strong impulse to leave as soon as legally possible. Rising prices affect parents' willingness to keep their children at school. This particularly affects poorer parents, who will also probably be those who least understand the implications of a grammar-school education. Employers also may not be so fussy during this phase about the qualifications of those young people to whom they offer jobs.

During the depression phase, on the other hand, jobs are hard to get, and employers like to choose carefully from the many applicants for work. Parents may feel that their sons or daughters might as well stay longer at school and become better qualified rather than risk a long period of unemployment after they leave school.[1]

Before the Second World War the Spens Report published some significant statistics on this matter, showing how the average age of grammar-school children rose during times of economic depression, and fell again when economic conditions improved somewhat in the late 1930s.[2]

TABLE TO SHOW CHANGES IN NUMBER OF OLDER PUPILS IN STATE-AIDED GRAMMAR SCHOOLS CORRESPONDING TO MOVEMENTS OF THE TRADE CYCLE (England and Wales)

Age	1925	1928	1931	1932	1936	1937
11–16:	290,010	314,277	339,144	351,236	387,976	389,336
16 and over	37,531	38,396	48,780	51,747	45,924	46,082
Older pupils as % of total	12·9	12·2	14·4	14·7	11·8	11·8

[1] On the other hand, if economic conditions got very bad, and there was acute poverty in the home, then some parents might tell their children to try to get work as soon as possible.

[2] The year 1925 was one of depression; 1928 of partial recovery; 1931–2 of severe depression; and 1936–7 of recovery. London County Council Inspectors confirm these conclusions of the Spens Report. For example, the Report on ———— County Secondary School for Girls states (1935): "In the first two years of this period (1929–30) girls left most frequently between the ages of 17 and 18, but in the next two years owing to the difficulty in finding posts that then prevailed, the pupils stayed longer at school, and the largest number left between 18 and 19. The improved conditions of employment that have marked the last year (1934) are reflected in a return of the figures to a state similar to that obtaining in 1929, 1930, and 1931." The Report on ———— School for 1935 said: "In 1934, both these figures (average age of leavers and duration of school life) fell by about three months, owing to the improvement in the conditions of employment, which caused many boys to remain at school longer than they would otherwise have done". As early as 1914 the Education Officer reported: "The improvement in the length of tenure (of Junior County scholars) is probably due to the slight decrease in commercial prosperity experienced during the earlier part of 1914, and the consequent shortage of openings for boys and girls". (Report of L.C.C. Education Officer, 1914.)

Post-war Shortage of Juvenile Labour

Since the end of the Second World War there has been an almost continuous inflationary boom lasting nearly a decade and this has naturally affected the juvenile labour market.

This shortage of labour as compared with pre-war has been aggravated by the raising of the school leaving age to fifteen and the increase of the conscription period to two years. Moreover, there has been a temporary sharp decline in numbers of young people in the age-group 15–19 because of the low birth-rate of the 1930s.

The diminishing proportion of the total population in this age-group, and the fact that the number of such youths and girls has fallen absolutely by about one million between 1939 and 1951 may be seen in the following table:

POPULATION OF THE U.K. (*in thousands*)

| Year | Total | Number aged 15–19 years | | |
		Males	Females	Total
1931	46,038	1,987	2,002	3,989
1939	47,762	2,105	2,093	4,198
1951	50,287	1,559	1,628	3,187

The economic boom has, of course, been accompanied by rising prices, and these have pressed hard upon parents of large families, who have found the cost of feeding and clothing their rapidly growing children a severe drain upon their budgets. The special maintenance allowances, which are supposed partially to compensate poorer families for the expense of keeping children at school beyond the statutory leaving-age, have not kept pace with the rising cost of living—resulting in economic hardship for some parents. These maintenance allowances have always been fairly small and awarded only after a strict means test. During the last few years the London County Council has become increasingly aware of their inadequacy, and in 1953 proposed to raise them slightly, but permission to do this was refused by the Ministry of Education, except for the poorest pupils. The Council's original post-war scales, its 1953 proposals, and the plan accepted by the Minister are set out in the table on the next page:

LONDON COUNTY COUNCIL ANNUAL MAINTENANCE GRANTS FOR
PUPILS[1] (*aged 15 and over*)

Parental Income	Original grant		March, 1953 proposal		March, 1954 proposal	
	Up to 16 +	Up to 18 +	Up to 16 +	Up to 18 +	Up to 16 +	Up to 18 +
£	£	£	£	£	£	£
150	24	45	30	51	30	51
175	21	42	27	48	30	51
200	18	39	24	45	24	45
225	15	36	21	42	18	39
250	12	33	18	39	12	33
275	9	30	15	36	9	30
300	6	27	12	33	6	27
325		24	9	30		24
350		21	6	27		21
375		18		24		18
400		15		21		15
425		12		18		12
450		9		15		9
475				12		
500				9		

Problem of the Leaving Age

As may be seen therefore, the problem of the grammar-school leaving age is both difficult and complex. The remedy for premature leaving is not merely a matter of devising more efficient selection tests or of choosing the right schools for the right pupils: it is part of a much larger social problem. On the one hand, the leaving age depends upon the statutory age fixed by authority, which in turn depends upon the general economic situation and the importance accorded to education by the Government. On the other hand, the length of school life beyond the legal leaving age is to a large degree determined by the comparative wealth of parents, and their ability (or willingness) to make financial sacrifices to keep their children at school. The stability and happiness of the family is an important but subsidiary factor so far as home environment is concerned.

Furthermore, the vocational requirements of the community must be taken into account, particularly the type of training demanded by the professions and higher administrative and technical ranks of industry and commerce. Movements of the trade cycle and consequent fluctuations in employment are part of this vocational aspect of the grammar schools.

[1] Minutes of London County Council Education Committee, March 3, 1954.

Thus, it may be concluded that any substantial rise in the average leaving age will depend upon long-term economic and political developments.[1]

Occupations of Leavers

The problem of the actual occupations taken up by grammar-school leavers is, of course, of fundamental importance to the whole study of the function and role of secondary education. There was a time not so long ago when such vocational considerations were dismissed as irrelevant. Nowadays, however, owing to the country's economic difficulties and to the temporary shortage of juvenile labour, it is more widely appreciated that the ultimate careers of secondary-school leavers should be of keen concern to everyone, Government, professions, commerce, industry, and trade unions alike. Moreover, it is being increasingly realized that no arbitrary line can fairly be drawn between academic and technical education. The origins of the liberal versus vocational controversy, and the way in which vocational training for a special group of occupations have influenced grammar-school curricula in the past, are discussed more fully in the chapter on Curriculum. Meanwhile, as a background to this debate, it will be useful to give some figures relating to grammar-school leavers, as well as to discuss briefly the relations between secondary education and social mobility.

Accurate and detailed information on these points is not as abundant as one might wish, but there is sufficient statistical material available broadly to confirm the truth of the argument that the grammar school trained pupils (as someone aptly expressed it) for the "black-coated rather than the black-handed" occupations. During the inter-war

---

[1] Conscription is a new circumstance that did not affect boys before the War. Although the influence of the call-up upon the school-leaving age has not been investigated, it is believed by some authorities (see certain replies to the Incorporated Association of Headmasters questionnaire on premature leavers) that it may discourage boys from staying in the sixth form because of their desire to get established in a career before conscription. Employers may not be keen, especially if it involves training, to offer a boy of 17 or 18 a job if they know he will be called up within a few months.

Craft apprenticeship regulations, which require a boy to become articled before the age of 16, may also encourage boys to leave grammar school prematurely. This applies particularly to schools situated in industrial areas. The student apprenticeship scheme, which accepts older boys for training, may help to counteract this tendency.

123

period commerce, banking, accountancy, insurance, teaching, and the Civil Service absorbed the great majority of pupils leaving school between the ages of sixteen and eighteen. Comparatively few boys or girls possessing a "School Cert." or "Matric." qualification went into the "black-handed" jobs. This was particularly true of London where so many administrative, commercial, and professional occupations are concentrated.

Ministry of Education figures extending back to the First World War show that grammar-school boys seeking "white-collar" or clerical careers outnumbered those entering manual or technical jobs by at least two to one, or even more for the earlier period.[1] As late as the mid 1930s, the ratio for girls was nearly ten to one.

The Spens Report, also covering the country as a whole, stated that of those pupils going directly into employment for which it had information, 75 per cent. of the boys and 92 per cent. of the girls in 1925-6, and 67 per cent. of the boys and 90 per cent. of the girls in 1935-6 went into clerical or minor professional occupations. "It will be seen that what are popularly called the black-coated occupations still absorb the great majority of pupils—both boys and girls—from the Secondary Schools", concluded the Report.[2]

The Headmasters' Employment Committee, which operated mainly in London and the Home Counties before the Second World War, points out that of the boys aged 16–19 years it placed in work at various times, 91 per cent. in 1925, 81 per cent. in 1932, and 88 per cent. in 1938 went into similar types of occupation.

[1] ". . . until the 1939–45 war almost half the boys leaving the secondary schools entered professional or clerical work straight from school, while a further number entered after a period in a university or training college. The position in this respect changed very little between 1909 and 1938", says Dr. O. Banks in her recent study of the grammar school "Concept and Nature of the Grammar School in relation to the development of Secondary Education since 1902". (Ph.D. thesis, University of London, 1953.)

[2] Report of the Consultative Committee on Secondary Education, p. 101 (H.M.S.O., 1938).

The Ministry of Education figures on which the Spens Report is presumably based, suffer from the disadvantage that they only group the leavers in very broad categories. There is also reason to suspect that when the original information was collected from schools there was a good deal of guesswork involved. Headmasters or headmistresses, harassed by other duties at the end of the summer term, have not always the time or inclination to investigate adequately what their pupils do when they leave school. Quite often such pupils do not establish themselves in a permanent career for some time. This is particularly true since conscription was introduced. It is to be hoped that now that the local authorities have taken over responsibility for vocational guidance for grammar-school leavers the material will be more systematically collected.

More detailed figures are given in the following tables:

OCCUPATIONS TAKEN UP BY GRAMMAR-SCHOOL LEAVERS—SPENS REPORT

Occupations	Boys 38,184 %	1925–6 Girls 32,026 %	Total 70,210 %	Boys 45,904 %	1935–6 Girls 38,623 %	Total 84,527 %
Universities U.T.D.	5·9	4·4	5·2	5·4	2·9	4·2
Other education	10·3	28·0	18·5	7·6	25·5	15·7
Professional, commercial, or clerical	47·5	30·2	39·5	46·1	43·9	45·1
Industrial or manual	16·3	2·8	9·9	22·9	4·7	14·6
Others	20·0	34·6	26·9	18·0	23·0	20·4
	100	100	100	100	100	100

—HEADMASTERS' EMPLOYMENT COMMITTEE REPORTS

Occupations	1925 No.	%	1932 No.	%	1938 No.	%
Professional or semi-professional	108	12·0	59	7.0	219	16.0
Banking, insurance, finance	171	19·0	72	8·0	333	24·0
Shipping and merchanting	151	17·0	66	7·5	169	12·0
Transport (clerical)	8	1·0	2	—	18	1·5
Civil and municipal service, etc.	28	3·0	46	5.0	94	7·0
Manufacturing and engineering (clerical)	158	17·5	307	35·0	293	21·0
Retail and wholesale trade	194	21·5	158	18·0	85	6·0
Technical and manual	75	8·0	144	16·5	137	10·0
Others and unclassified	12	1·0	28	3·0	32	2·5
Totals	905	100·0	882	100·0	1,380	100·0

Records kept by many London grammar schools confirm for individual schools what has been deduced from surveys made on a wider scale. The two following examples are fairly typical:

—— BOYS' SCHOOL (WANDSWORTH)

Occupations chosen by 241 boys who left 1932–5

Occupation	No. of Boys
Further education	49
Civil Service and Local Government	12
Commerce, banking, insurance	33
Distribution, wholesale and retail	13
General clerical	50
Manual industry, engineering	26
Unclassified	58

―――― *SCHOOL FOR GIRLS (FULHAM)*

Occupations chosen by 66 girls who left in 1934	
Occupation	*No. of Girls*
Further education	14
Civil Service, clerical	31
Shop assistants	6
Nursing	3
Other occupations	12

Swing to Science and Technology

Among grammar-school leavers during the last ten or fifteen years there has been a certain swing away from the clerical occupations towards science and technology, even towards skilled manual occupations. This has been due partly to the general change in status of the technical-manual jobs, and partly to the larger numbers and more working-class composition of the children now entering the grammar schools.

These schools, like other higher educational institutions including the universities, have been influenced by the changing economic and technological circumstances of the post-war period. The War gave increased emphasis to science, and also brought about a rearrangement of occupational priorities. Scientists were given first claim upon money, manpower, and resources, and acquired great social prestige as well as financial reward. In the popular imagination the designers of the Spitfire came second only to the pilots themselves, and the discoverers of atomic energy acquired an almost magical reputation. Technicians and specialist engineering workers were deferred from military service and, on a lower social scale, miners and farm labourers were no longer regarded as a depressed class, but were classified as "essential workers". Clerks, shop assistants, and minor professional people, who had been accustomed to a higher social status before the war, suddenly found themselves classified as "inessential" and unceremoniously drafted into the Armed Forces.

The emphasis upon heavy industry and the productive processes of manufacture rather than distribution and exchange has been continued in the period of the post-war boom, and has naturally affected recruitment of juvenile labour.

As foreign competition has become keener and the long-term difficulties of British trade become more apparent, so economists and industrialists have stressed the necessity for cheaper as well as higher productivity. The key to this greater productivity is seen to be a more advanced technology. Industrial techniques have become more complex, and so all kinds of new skills are required. More intensive and specialist technical education is seen as one means of developing those skills, not only at the higher levels of pure science in universities and research establishments, but also at lower occupational levels, such as works managers, junior technicians, supervisors, and foremen.

The trend towards manual-technical jobs has naturally affected the occupations of grammar-school leavers. The last Ministry of Education statement on the careers of these leavers showed that in 1946–7, 27.1 per cent. of the boys entering directly into employment got jobs in industry, agriculture, or transport as compared with 26·7 per cent. in the clerical-professional group. This was the first time in which the "white-collar" category was exceeded in this way. The Headmasters' Employment Committee hardly considered manual jobs worth a separate mention in the early days of its activities, and in the mid 1930s less than one in ten of the Committee's placings were classified as "Apprentices and Learners". However, just before the Second World War the Committee reported:

> ... the technical occupations continued their tendency to attract a bigger share of the supply of boys, accounting for 10 per cent. of the placings in 1938 as compared with 8 per cent. in 1937.[1]

The percentage going into this type of job steadily increased during the War, and in 1948 comprised 35.42 per cent. and in 1950 33.91 per cent. of the total number of placings by the Committee. In the former year the Committee reported:

> ... the technical group of occupations continues to attract more candidates than any other group.... As regards individual occupations, engineering apprenticeships are leading all the rest in popularity, closely followed by banking and insurance (18·6 per cent.) and scientific laboratory work (8·7 per cent.) ... shipping and merchanting took 13·8 per cent.[2]

[1] Report of H.E.C., 1938.
[2] Report of H.E.C., 1948.

Girls were much less affected by these developments than boys. According to the Ministry of Education figures for 1946–7 only 6 per cent. of the girls leaving grammar schools in England and Wales went into industry. Out of 5,359 girls placed in jobs by the Headmistresses' Employment Committee during 1949–51 only 1,222 (or 23 per cent.) took up some kind of manual, including domestic, work.

In London also, the trend towards manual or technical jobs has been much less marked than in the rest of the country. Twenty years ago when the London County Council investigated the problem, just under 50 per cent. of all boys leaving grammar schools (including transfers, boys going to further education, etc.) went into clerical posts as compared with 8 per cent. into industry. The latest figures provided by the Council show that at least three-quarters of all boys and over four-fifths of all girls from grammar schools placed by the Youth Employment Service went into "white-collar" or minor professional jobs, whereas only about 8 per cent. of boys (much less for girls) went into science or engineering.

The very low proportion of pupils from London grammar schools going into technical employment (which probably can be best explained by the predominance of commercial occupations in the metropolis) may be seen in the following table:

GRAMMAR-SCHOOL PUPILS PLACED IN JOBS BY THE YOUTH EMPLOYMENT SERVICE, LONDON COUNTY COUNCIL, 1953–4

Boys		*Girls*	
Insurance	289	Insurance	202
Banking	74	Banking	141
Merchants	117	Shorthand-	
Shipping	146	typists	190
Accountancy	128	Distribution	89
Other clerical	543	Other clerical	420
Total clerical	1,297	Total clerical	1,042
Engineering	73	Laboratories	50
Science	61		
Others	253	Others	177
Total	1,684	Total	1,269

It is important to note that the above figures do not include pupils who go on to higher education or sit for Civil Service examinations. They do include, however, pupils from out-county grammar schools who are helped to find jobs in London, and also London pupils who are placed in employment outside the County.

Social Mobility and the Grammar School

The controversy about whether the grammar schools do, in practice, bias their leavers towards a particular group of professions should not blind us to the general social or vocational role of these schools. The fact that one of the main purposes of a grammar-school education is to train pupils for a particular social status in life has long been recognized,[1] but perhaps it has not been appreciated as widely as it should how this role of developing a social and educational *élite* has been given increased importance by recent political and economic developments.

During the nineteenth and early twentieth centuries, a certain number of able, ambitious, and hard-working persons might have expected to rise from humble origins, regardless of how they were formally educated as children. In a period of expanding, competitive capitalism personal qualities of drive and energy might often have compensated for lack of early schooling, particularly in commerce and industry. During recent years, however, the self-educated and self-made man who is boss of his own business has increasingly been replaced by the trained executive or technician possessing formal educational qualifications and employed by a large-scale enterprise, either joint-stock or Government. School certificates, university degrees or other examination qualifications have always been a necessity for a professional career. To a growing extent this is the case for business and commercial careers also. The 1944 Education Act, by abolishing fees in grammar schools and opening wider the door of educational opportunity to working-class children, gave increased impetus to this trend; and so also have developments in

[1] Lord Eustace Percy, a Conservative former President of the Board of Education, expressed this point of view perfectly in 1933 when he said: ". . . the main function of the secondary (grammar) school . . . should be . . . that of a lift or stairway to the higher stories of the social structure". (*Hansard*, July 7, 1933.) Mr. Ramsbotham, formerly Parliamentary Secretary to the Board of Education, stressed the importance of recruiting children from the working class for this purpose, when he said: ". . . the aim of a sound system of secondary (grammar) education should be to secure an adequate amount of the best brains of the country from all the social strata of the community, and cultivate these with the greatest possible care". (*Education*, Oct. 7, 1932.) See also the chapter on Curriculum for further discussion of this topic.

the social structure itself. The growth of monopoly and consequent squeezing out of small business, the increased bureaucratization and spread of "white-collar" jobs, and the growing complexity of technical processes have all been responsible for the greater importance that is nowadays attached to formal educational qualifications. The grammar school, by making it possible for poorer children to win many of these qualifications, is thus a key factor in the matter of social mobility.

Dr. Olive Banks emphasizes this point in her recent study of the grammar-school curriculum:[1]

> With the foundation of a public system of secondary education the secondary schools ceased to be regarded as educating exclusively or even predominantly the sons and daughters of the middle classes. Yet the traditional association with the occupations offering higher economic reward and social prestige was still retained. As the social composition of the schools changed, greater emphasis was laid upon their selective role as agencies by which the able children of the poor were raised a step or two in the social and occupational scale. This selective aspect of secondary education has been further emphasized by changes within the occupational structure itself. The narrowing of opportunities for advancement in business on the basis of the accumulation of capital; the rise of the salaried professional and administrative middle classes, and the consequent importance of formal educational qualifications as distinct from native intelligence and strength of character, have combined to render the secondary school the most important avenue of social mobility. Increasingly throughout the twentieth century the secondary school has offered to the children of the working class the only opportunity of rising into the ranks of the middle class salariat. It is no wonder, therefore, that the driving force in the demand for secondary education has been the desire for "status rather than for education as such", and that parental ambition sees in the educational ladder "steps not to Parnassus but to a secure job and a villa in Suburbia".

Unfortunately, despite the growing interest in, and greater information about, the social background of secondary education, there are

---

[1] "Concept and Nature of the Grammar School in relation to the development of Secondary Education since 1902", by O. L. Banks. (Ph.D. thesis, University of London, 1953.) The "Parnassus" quotation is from *Education and Social Change*, by Sir Fred Clarke, p. 32.

still many gaps in our knowledge about the precise way in which the grammar schools act as an agency of social selection. We still know very little, for example, about the social origins of grammar school pupils in different parts of the country, and there are large gaps in our knowledge about the ambitions and ultimate careers of grammar-school leavers. The forthcoming volume on *Education and Social Mobility*, edited by Mrs. Jean Floud of the Institute of Education, University of London, which is based on extensive sociological research in London, Hertfordshire, and Middlesbrough, should be extremely useful in this connection.

Chapter 6

CURRICULUM

. . . in reality much of the education described as "liberal" or "general" was itself vocational education for the "liberal" professions.—Spens Report.[1]

THE planning and arrangement of grammar-school curricula touch deep springs in English social life and culture. Superficially, there may appear to be a remarkable resemblance in the syllabuses of various types of secondary school—there is almost invariably a common core of English, mathematics, science, history, geography, music, art, and physical training—but, in fact, these likenesses only mask wide differences of approach and outlook. Paradoxically, the choice of curriculum (the word being here used in its broadest sense to include the way in which subjects are taught, the standards of work reached, as well as the actual proportion of time allocated to each subject in the time-table) is one of a school's most distinctive characteristics, measuring, among other things, its social status, intellectual reputation, and record for leadership in the community. Historically, the subjects taught in school have been influenced by deep-seated political and economic trends, while philosophically there are vital educational issues involved. So far as the psychology of individual children is concerned, difficult questions of abilities and aptitudes arise. The relation of social classes is affected, and so are the vocational needs of society. Complex administrative and organizational matters are involved because of the tripartite division of secondary education.

Particularly is this true of the grammar schools, which in many cases have their origins in the distant past, and have been closely associated with the public schools in the creating of an educational *élite*. So many influences, philosophical and vocational, psychological as well as cultural, have been brought to bear upon the grammar-school syllabus,

[1] Report of the Consultative Committee on Secondary Education, p. 67 (H.M.S.O., 1938).

132

that it is very difficult to disentangle one factor from another. As the Spens Report says:[1]

> The history of the traditional curriculum bears witness to the unending struggle between rival philosophies of life and widely divergent theories of education and human development. These find expression in varying forms in succeeding generations in the controversies which centre round this or that aspect of education and training; for instance, the rival claims of a classical and a modern education; of the humanities and the sciences; of a general and specific (technical) education. . . . Curricula for higher schools, if they be carefully examined over any considerable period, will be found to reflect and reveal in a remarkable way the interplay of deep-seated forces in the national life.

During the nineteenth century the "deep-seated forces" to which the Spens Report refers took various forms such as the movement to encourage science teaching in secondary schools or the influence exerted by old-established public schools upon the endowed grammar schools; but before considering these influences in detail it will be useful to give a general picture of the subjects that were actually taught in some London grammar schools at the end of last century.

Curricula of Various London Grammar Schools in 1892

The curricula of the English grammar schools in the 1880s and 1890s were not regulated in any way by the State, except for the provision that a certain minimum amount of science had to be taught if State financial aid was required. In contrast to the experience of similar schools in France and Germany, where the subjects of the time-table were strictly defined by central authority, the headmasters and head-mistresses of secondary schools in this country could, in theory at any rate, arrange their syllabuses in any way they thought fit. This freedom to experiment naturally led to a certain amount of variety in school time-tables, but generally speaking the curricula of most grammar schools were rather alike because they were affected by much the same social and educational influences. In practice, of course, they were limited

---

[1] Report of the Consultative Committee on Secondary Education, p. 2 (H.M.S.O., 1938).

by the wishes of parents and Governors, and the traditions of the particular school with which they were concerned. Such differences as existed largely arose from the varying historical origins, social backgrounds, and financial circumstances of the schools, the poorer ones being compelled to teach more science in order to qualify for outside financial assistance, the richer ones being freer to continue their emphasis on classical and literary subjects.

In 1892, an investigation was made by a special committee of the London County Council into the curricula of sixty-eight (thirty-eight boys' and thirty girls') secondary schools situated in the County of London.[1] This showed that *religious knowledge* was given an important place in the time-table, and was taught on an average for about two hours per week in all but two of the sixty-eight schools investigated.

Classics and *ancient history* were the most important subjects in the grammar schools at that period, though the amount of time devoted to them varied considerably from school to school. Generally speaking, the higher the social status of the school and the less dependent upon State aid, the greater the emphasis upon Latin and Greek. Thus Alleyn's School, which had a large endowment and substantial income from fees, taught in the upper forms almost twice as many hours of classics as it did of science, whereas in the poorer school of Parmiter's the ratio was reversed. On the classical sides of Godolphin and University College Schools as many as eighteen to twenty hours per week in the fifth and sixth forms were devoted to Greek and Latin.

In contrast to this strong bias in the boys' schools, the girls' schools taught comparatively little Latin or Greek. Only one-third of all the girls' schools took classics right through from the first to the sixth forms. Occasionally, in a few forms, they devoted as little as one period a week to these subjects. This lack of interest by the girls' schools can probably be explained by the comparatively modern origins of girls' education, and the fact that the universities had been closed to women students.

Mathematics occupied on the average five to six hours of the time-table. Some schools taught as little as four hours, but others as much as nine hours. Girls usually did less mathematics than boys. The teaching of *science* had been encouraged by the money made available by the Arts and Science grants and also by various Acts, and was widely

[1] Report to the Special Committee on Technical Education to the L.C.C. by H. Llewellyn Smith, 1892.

taught in both boys' and girls' schools.[1] The methods of instruction used were, however, mainly theoretical. Practical chemistry was taught in twenty-two boys' schools, but almost invariably only in the fifth and sixth forms. Not a single school taught practical physics, though it was reported of the science side of St. Paul's School that it was taught "out of school hours". Nine girls' schools did practical work in natural science, but only one (North London Collegiate School) did it right through the school from first to sixth year.

English, which nowadays would be regarded as the key subject of the curriculum, held a peculiar status. Some schools taught as much as eight hours weekly, but others taught none at all in some forms.[2] Certainly, it was considered less important than classics or mathematics, and there seems to have been a marked tendency for the number of hours devoted to it to decrease as the pupil rose higher in the school. Thus, for example, Haberdashers' Aske's Boys' School taught eleven hours English per week in the first and second forms, decreasing to four hours in the sixth form; Emanuel School taught eight hours in the first form, but only one and a half hours in the sixth form; Battersea Grammar School taught eight hours in the first form, but only one hour in the fifth and sixth forms. The small importance given to English in the higher forms of the City of London School may be deduced from the fact that in the classical sixth form only one hour was devoted to English as compared with twelve hours to Latin and Greek and eight hours to mathematics. Judging by these figures, it would seem that much of the contemporary criticism of the teaching of English was abundantly justified. It is not possible from the information available in the 1892 Report to say precisely what aspects of English were stressed in the schools during that period, but on the basis of internal evidence and accounts given elsewhere, it is likely that much of the English taught in the lower school consisted of reading, writing, punctuation, and spelling. Literary appreciation and composition, particularly in the higher forms, were probably sadly neglected.

History and *geography* were taught in practically all schools, with periods averaging one to three hours devoted to them. Girls, in general, did noticeably less geography than boys.

Foreign languages had a considerable amount of time allocated to them. *French*, for example, was taught in practically every form in all

[1] Acts of 1889 and 1891, and the Local Taxation (Customs and Excise) Act of 1890.
[2] The Grocers' School in Hackney (now Hackney Downs School) for example, taught no English in the first, third and fourth forms, and only a little in others.

CURRICULA IN LONDON SECONDARY SCHOOLS, 1892

Number of minutes devoted to each subject per week

Form	Religious Knowledge	Classics	English	History	Geography	Mathematics	Science	French	German	Drill Singing	Art	Crafts
Alleyn's (boys)												
I	150	—	420	120	180	360	60	—	—	—	120	—
II	120	—	420	120	120	360	120	180	—	—	120	—
III	120	—	405	90	120	240	120	150	—	—	120	—
IV	120	—	240	120	120	360	180	240	120	—	120	—
V	120	240	240	120	60	360	180	240	120	—	120	—
VI	120	330	180	60	60	360	180	240	210	—	180	—
William Ellis (boys)												
I	—	120	210	90	90	240	60	120	—	90	120	60
II	—	120	210	90	90	240	60	120	—	90	120	90
III	—	120	210	90	90	240	120	120	—	90	120	90
IV	—	120	180	90	90	300	210	120	—	90	120	90
V	—	180	120	60	60	300	390	120	120	90	195	90
VI	—	180	120	60	60	300	390	120	120	90	195	90
Parmiter's (boys)												
I	60	—	480	120	120	420	—	—	—	180	120	—
II	60	—	480	120	120	300	—	120	—	180	120	—
III	60	—	480	120	120	300	120	180	—	60	120	—
IV	60	180	300	120	180	360	270	180	180	—	120	—
V	60	180	120	120	120	360	330	180	180	—	120	—
VI	60	180	120	120	120	360	330	180	180	—	120	—

CURRICULA IN LONDON SECONDARY SCHOOLS, 1892

Number of minutes devoted to each subject per week

Form	Religious Knowledge	Classics	English	History	Geography	Mathematics	Science	French	German	Drill Singing	Art	Crafts
North London Collegiate (girls)												
I	150	210	90	90	60	240	135	90	150	—	—	—
II	105	120	105	90	45	165	45	165	120	—	—	—
III	120	195	105	60	60	240	90	120	195	—	—	—
IV	105	225	45	75	—	330	90	120	225	—	—	—
V	120	210	165	105	45	225	45	90	195	—	—	—
VI	60	150	45	105	—	450	105	105	105	—	—	—
Owen's (girls)												
I	90	—	90	—	—	180	—	225	90	—	135	—
II	90	—	90	45	45	180	45	225	90	—	90	90
III	90	—	90	45	45	180	45	180	90	—	90	135
IV	90	—	90	90	90	180	45	180	90	—	90	45
V	90	180	90	90	90	180	45	180	90	—	90	—
VI	90	480	45	45	—	225	90	225	90	—	90	—
Coborn (girls)												
I	90	—	90	90	135	345	—	135	—	—	90	120
II	90	—	135	120	120	345	—	135	120	—	90	120
III	90	—	120	90	120	225	—	165	120	—	120	120
IV	90	—	90	90	180	225	—	195	120	—	120	120
V	120	120	180	150	180	420	—	120	120	—	120	—
VI	120	240	120	120	120	420	—	180	120	—	120	—

137

schools, the time devoted to it varying from one and three-quarters to four and a half hours. Three hours was about the average. *German* was taught to a less, but still considerable extent; no other foreign language was mentioned.

The remainder of the time-table was usually devoted to drawing, shorthand (which was taught in twenty-two boys', but, curiously enough, in only five girls' schools), book-keeping, singing, and drill. There was very little opportunity for acquiring manual skill, practical science was rare, as we have seen, and such subjects as manual instruction for boys, and cookery and domestic economy for girls were taken only in a few schools. Needlework for girls was, however, fairly common.

Details of the number of minutes devoted to various subjects in six typical London secondary schools are given in the table on pp. 136–7. The schools have been chosen for their representative nature, Alleyn's being a large, old-established school situated in the prosperous neighbourhood of Dulwich; William Ellis being a nineteenth-century foundation in St. Pancras; and Parmiter's situated in the poor East End borough of Bethnal Green. North London Collegiate School was a large and flourishing upper-class school for girls in St. Pancras; Owen's an old Tudor foundation in Finsbury; and Coborn a smaller and poorer school in Poplar.

Influence of Public and Old-established Grammar Schools

During the crucial years 1895–1904, when the curriculum for the State-aided and maintained schools was taking shape, the authorities were naturally influenced by the curricula of the existing public, old-established grammar, and organized science schools. Broadly speaking, these schools represented different approaches to the question of vocational education and the needs of society, and also to some extent different social classes.

The most powerful influence upon the new State grammar schools was undoubtedly that of the public and old-established grammar schools.[1] The public schools had a reputation surpassing any other

[1] "The new regulations (issued for secondary schools in 1904) were based wholly on the tradition of the grammar schools and public schools", stated the Spens report. "As will be seen from the detailed account of the Regulations of 1904 . . . the Board (of Education) took the existing public schools and grammar schools as their general cadre or archetype for secondary schools of all kinds. The further development of post-primary schools with traditions somewhat different from those of the grammar schools such as the higher grade schools, the organized science schools and the day technical schools which had sprung into existence in the last quarter of

[*footnote continued on p.* 139

type of secondary school. They had high social prestige and the tradition of providing the kind of leadership in social and political affairs that suited an era of great commercial and imperial expansion. They encouraged a code of morals and behaviour of which the upper and middle classes approved. The religion they propagated was strongly Christian without being awkwardly denominational or over-theological in spirit (this was important during a period when the religious issue rankled in other spheres of education). Their emphasis on games and on the house and prefect systems inculcated loyalty and courage at a time when military valour was given extreme prominence among the national virtues. So far as scholarship was concerned, they were content to bring the majority of their pupils to a certain average level, while at the same time cramming a minority of brilliant pupils to the high standards of an open scholarship at Oxford or Cambridge. Their curricula were almost invariably strongly classical in emphasis, and over-weighted according to the "faculty" theory of psychology.

The old-established grammar schools resembled the public schools in many respects. They did not cater for so socially exclusive a class, nor draw their pupils from such a wide area (the typical public school was generally a boarding-school), but they were nevertheless largely middle class in social composition, and in certain cases had even longer traditions than some of the public schools. In numerous ways, such as classical bias in curriculum, importance of house and prefect systems, and emphasis on games, they closely imitated their richer rivals. They also encouraged that non-denominational religious service and study of the Bible vaguely described as "scripture".

Furthermore, during the period when the new grammar schools were being developed, the old-established grammar schools were brought by financial pressure into much closer contact with the wholly Council-maintained schools. As their need for State aid increased, so they came more and more under the control of the local authorities, and thus into more direct association with the maintained schools.[1]

---

footnote continued]
the nineteenth century, was definitely discouraged and new secondary schools were in effect compelled to take as their model the curriculum of the existing public schools and grammar schools." (Report of the Consultative Committee on Secondary Education, pp. 66–73, H.M.S.O., 1938.)

[1] "The tendency of secondary schools maintained or aided by local education authorities to imitate the public schools and grammar schools has since 1902 been considerably accentuated by the fact that economic difficulties have forced many of the old, endowed schools to accept financial aid from public funds and thus become an integral part of the public system of education." (Report of the Consultative Committee on Secondary Education, pp. 72–3, H.M.S.O., 1938.)

In view of the immense social and educational prestige of the traditional forms of secondary school, it was not surprising that the new maintained schools should try to imitate them. The old pattern was greatly liked and respected, so when the authorities tried to design a new pattern, they made it resemble the old one as much as possible. The only other models on which the innovators might have tried to base their ideas were comparatively new and had not yet acquired much reputation.

Science and Higher Grade Schools

During the last quarter of the nineteenth century there had grown up a new type of secondary school, which differed considerably from the conventional pattern. These schools took various forms, such as the higher grade departments of State elementary schools, and the organized science and day technical schools, but they had much in common (and in these respects were unlike the grammar schools) in so far as they were financed to a large extent by the State and were biased in their curriculum more towards science and technology than towards literature and the classics. They were also unlike the traditional secondary schools because they were not so directly associated with middle-class status and values.[1] For example, in a comparison made between a number of higher grade and ordinary secondary schools in 1897 the social class of parents of children attending these schools was given as tabulated at the top of page 141.

[1] The contrasting status of secondary and higher grade schools is emphasized in a Board of Education report of 1906 quoted in a recent biography of Sir Ernest Sadler. "... The two types of school", says the Report, "prepare for different walks of life—the one for the lower ranks of industry and commerce, the other for the higher ranks and for the liberal professions ... the home conditions of the two kinds of schools are different and while, in the case of the secondary school, the home life may be expected to supplement and strengthen the school instruction, or at least not to hamper it, in the case of the higher elementary school the home conditions, at best, do little to favour the ends of school education and at worse are antagonistic." *Achievement in Education: The work of Michael Ernest Sadler 1885–1935*, by Lynda Grier, p. 143 (Constable, 1952).

The following figures relating to the class-structure of grammar as compared with higher grade schools are quoted in "Concept and Nature of the Grammar School in relation to the development of Secondary Education since 1902", by O. L. Banks, Ph.D. thesis, University of London, 1953. The return covered forty-three higher grade schools and forty-three public secondary schools claimed to be "fairly representative of the general average of those public secondary schools throughout the country which are of a purely local character and located in large towns".

[*footnote continued on next page*

	Secondary %	*Higher grade* %
Middle class	42·1	12·4
Lower middle class	48·8	47·6
Working class	9·1	40·0

Originally, these schools had been developed because of the need to improve the quality of scientific and technical education and to provide British industry with sufficient trained and skilled personnel. In the 1870s and 1880s there had been widespread public alarm at the rapid growth of German competition, and fear that British industrial technique was lagging behind that of Europe and America.[1] In 1880, a Royal Commission on Technical Instruction had been set up to "inquire into the instruction of the industrial classes of certain foreign countries", and three years later a group of eminent scientists and educationists, led by T. H. Huxley, had set up the National Association for the Promotion of Technical and Secondary Education. In 1889, the Technical Instruction Act was passed, enabling County Councils to aid technical education. Simultaneously, the Science and Arts department of the Board of Trade was increasing its grants to secondary and *footnote continued*]

Occupations of parents of all pupils who have been in the schools during the twelve months ending June 1, 1897

	Sec. Schools %	*H.G. Schools* %
Persons of independent means ..	4·9	1·6
Professional men	16·9	3·4
Teachers	3·2	1·4
Manufacturers, wholesale dealers, merchants (heads of firms) ..	17·1	6·0
Ditto (managers)	6·0	4·8
Farmers	1·8	1·2
Retail traders, etc.	15·5	15·1
Commercial travellers, etc. ..	4·3	4·1
Salesmen, shop assistants ..	1·7	2·5
Clerks, etc.	11·0	9·4
Subordinate public officials ..	3·1	3·5
Foremen	2·3	5·9
Skilled workers	5·8	26·8
Unskilled workers	1·0	7·3
Others	4·2	6·2
Unclassified	1·2	1·0

[1] Report of the Consultative Committee on Secondary Education, pp. 52–4 (H.M.S.O., 1938).

higher grade schools on condition that they taught a certain minimum amount of science.

Secondary-School Regulations of 1904

Modern educationists would find much to criticize in the curricula of both groups of schools, and condemn the exaggerated emphasis of the conflicting classical versus scientific viewpoints. In the public and grammar schools there was too much classics and too little science taught; in the higher grade and organized science schools there was a failure to appreciate the importance of English and foreign languages. In both types of school cultural subjects such as music and art were neglected; physical training was too formal, and physics and chemistry too theoretical.[1] Girls were not given equal facilities with boys in certain subjects. Psychologists would disapprove of the emphasis on "faculties", i.e. that subjects should be taught for their supposed advantage in developing certain faculties, irrespective of the intrinsic value or interest of the subject.

In the late 1890s, however, and more particularly during the first decade of this century, the attack on the prevailing curriculum was mainly concentrated on one issue—namely, that there was too much science and too little English being taught in the secondary schools. It was largely because of this pressure, and also because of the desire to coordinate and systematize the curricula that the famous secondary school regulations were introduced by the Board of Education in 1904. These required that a minimum of $4\frac{1}{2}$ hours per week should be devoted to English, geography, and history; not less than $3\frac{1}{2}$ hours to a foreign language, or 6 hours to two foreign languages; not less than $7\frac{1}{2}$ hours to science and mathematics, of which 3 hours were to be for science. If two foreign languages were taken Latin must be one, unless permission were granted for an exception.

Although the regulations were repealed in 1907, and grammar

[1] During the decade 1895–1905 many new science laboratories were opened in London secondary schools, and as a result substantial progress was made in the practical teaching of physics and chemistry. An official report of 1906–7 pointed out that the number of secondary-school pupils doing practical work in physics rose from 420 in 1893 to 1,954 in 1896, and the number of those doing practical chemistry rose from 971 to 2,220. "At the present time the percentage of those taking practical work in experimental science is considerably over 90 per cent. of those receiving instruction in this subject", concluded the Report. (Report by Chief Inspector on Secondary Schools Aided by the Council. L.C.C. Higher Education Sub-Committee, 1906–7.)

schools again became theoretically free to arrange their own curricula, most headmasters and headmistresses were content to follow the path pointed out to them by the Board. The tentative steps that had been taken in the direction of technical or vocational curricula were reversed, and henceforward the road taken by both aided and maintained grammar schools was definitely academic and liberal in direction.

Morant and the Idea of an "Educational Elite"

This trend from a scientific towards a more literary education (or more properly the confirming in new circumstances of a situation which had existed for centuries) has been conventionally attributed to Sir Robert Morant, who entered the Civil Service in 1895 and was later a dominant personality among those officials who sponsored the 1902 Education Act, the 1904 secondary school regulations, the expansion of the scholarship system, and subsequent developments affecting the grammar schools up to 1914.

Morant, with his definite ideas and forceful personality, undoubtedly played an important part in shaping the new secondary schools during the crucial period 1900–10. At a time when other educationists were looking for a formula to fit the new circumstances he vigorously put forward his own clear-cut conceptions of what the new system of State secondary education should be.

But to attribute the subsequent development of the grammar schools to Morant alone, as some historians have done, and to suggest that one man or a small group of men were solely responsible for biasing so effectively the grammar-school curriculum in a particular direction, seems a gross over-simplification of a complex problem. It exaggerates the power of the individual to influence such an important political development, and underestimates the influence of other more fundamentally significant social factors. Morant may have been a vigorous personality, and may have "sold" his ideas at a time when other possible reformers were too vague, uncertain, or ineffectual in their views; but he was not solely responsible for the decisions of 1902 and 1904.

The most significant of these influences, as we have seen, was undoubtedly that of the already existing secondary schools. They were important in their educational influence because they were relatively efficient, and were almost the only model upon which the new maintained

L   143

schools could base themselves. But they were also very important in their social influence, and in this respect Morant's ideas were not only his own individual theories but were also, to a very large extent, the ideas of the socially dominant upper and middle classes. The public schools, as has been pointed out, were institutions run for children of the aristocracy, wealthy professional people, manufacturers, and businessmen. Though Morant did not himself come from the hereditary ruling class (his father was a decorative painter who died young, leaving his family in poor circumstances) he was educated by means of scholarships at a famous public school (Winchester) and an ancient university (Oxford). In educational background he therefore resembled most of the other high officials of the Board of Education.[1]

The great majority of inspectors and headmasters came from either the public schools or old-established grammar schools, and many had also been to Oxford and Cambridge. The House of Commons was also dominated by the wealthier classes, and it is significant that the President of the Board of Education in 1902 was the Duke of Devonshire, a traditional Tory aristocrat of the old style. Thus, directly, or indirectly, the ideas, traditions, and values of the upper and middle classes were paramount in education at that time, and the voice of the Labour movement and the more radical wing of the Liberals and Nonconformists, though growing in volume, was not yet very powerful. Fabians, such as Sidney Webb and Graham Wallas, had a certain influence in London but were still in a small minority on the London County Council. Such influence as they had was in the realm of ideas rather than in direct legislative power. The general body of the trade unions, with the exception of the National Union of Teachers, which, of course, took an active interest in all aspects of education, had so far not clearly formulated their ideas about the role of the new secondary schools. Even the teachers' own professional associations had not broken away from the narrow class-status view of education. For

---

[1] "There have been recent attempts to make Morant the villain and Sadler the hero of technical education. But, up to a point, their views coincided. Both thought that all education should humanize. Both, possibly Sadler rather more than Morant, at one time feared that technical should dominate secondary education. But they differed in their views about secondary education, and Sadler had the most intense respect for technical education given that it was founded on a sound secondary education. Morant's vision of education does not appear to have gone beyond the conventional grammar school ideas which Winchester had given him. Anything else was to be thrust into the limbo of elementary education if it were for children under fifteen and into a segregated limbo of technical education if it were for those over fifteen." *Achievement in Education: The Work of Michael Ernest Sadler*, by Lynda Grier, pp. 138–9 (Constable, 1952).

example, the President of the Incorporated Association of Head-masters, speaking in 1898 said:

> I need not go over again the facts which compel us to recognize a distinction between the educational needs of the wage-earning class and those of the mercantile or professional class.[1]

In the same year the President of the National Union of Teachers (who might have been expected to have a more democratic outlook) said:

> We have to deal with large masses of the working population, we have to deal in our great centres of industry with those who will become artisans and foremen and leaders of labour. The needs of this class are outside what I conceive to be secondary education.[2]

Scholarship Entrants and Teachers

The introduction in 1905 by the London County Council of a comprehensive scholarship system was seen by the progressive members of the Council as a scheme to enable the more intelligent children of those "large masses of the working population" (who were so despised by the President of the N.U.T.) to get into grammar schools. It was widely felt that opportunities for higher education should be open to everyone capable of benefiting from it, irrespective of income. But though the scholarship entrants were welcomed in most schools, and the new scheme was generally regarded as a success, yet there was fear that the flood of new boys and girls might threaten middle-class standards and values in the schools.[3] The new scholars, coming as they did from working-class or lower middle-class homes, would not have the same cultural background as the fee-paying entrants, and therefore, they must be "civilized". This "civilizing" process was thought of in terms of a liberal, humanistic education, with particular emphasis on English, both spoken and written.[4]

[1] Annual General Meeting of I.A.H.M., 1898.

[2] Reported in the *Schoolmaster*, Jan. 15, 1898.

[3] In 1906 it was estimated that during the following five years between 10,000–11,000 Junior County, Probationer, and Intermediate Scholarship children would enter the L.C.C. grammar schools.

[4] "English is the essential foundation" for the more advanced work of Junior County Scholars in "language, literary and history". (Report of L.C.C. Chief Inspector on Secondary Schools Aided by the Council, p. 4, 1909–10.)
"A little more English is being introduced into the curriculum; this is wise, looking to the large proportion of county scholars in the school." (Report by L.C.C. Divisional Inspector of Education on ——— School for Girls, Poplar, 1906–7.)

When the scholarship system was instituted five years ago, one of
the chief problems which it produced was that of the literary
training of the large numbers of Junior County scholars, who though
clever and intelligent, were for the most part necessarily destitute of
general culture,

said the Council's Chief Inspector of Secondary Schools in 1909–10.

The secondary schools are now, to an unprecedented degree, fed
by pupils drawn from elementary schools, and in a number of
London schools such pupils form at present the majority of the
attendance. It should be noticed that the junior scholars are of
varied intellectual and social types, and in certain districts they
approximate much more nearly to the average secondary school
student than in others. But, speaking in general terms, the lack of
general culture is the chief obstacle in the way of the advantage
offered to them, and this general culture must, in the earlier stages
of their career at any rate, be derived through the medium of
English.[1]

This theme of the importance of encouraging written and spoken
English for those with "cockney accents" or "slurred and slovenly
articulation" is developed in an official Council memorandum circulated after the First World War. In 1926, Dr. F. S. Boas wrote:

Many of the new London (grammar school) foundations have been
natural centres of the revived study of the mother tongue and of our
national literature, which has been so marked a feature of educational progress in recent years. This has involved increased
attention to speech training. The average standard of speech in
London secondary schools, both as regards enunciation and
pronunciation, still leaves much to be desired. Slovenly and slurred
articulation and a cockney accent are enemies within the gate. But
by careful training in reading and recitation, by phonetic drill and by
dramatic performances, real and steady advance has been made.
And the love of good literature has been encouraged not only by
a careful choice of text-books for class study, but by the circulation
of lists of books for home reading, to which heads of schools and
English specialists have devoted infinite pains.[2]

[1] Report of Chief Inspector on Secondary Schools Aided by the Council, 1906–7,
p. 2, L.C.C. Higher Education Sub-Committee.
[2] Memorandum by Dr. F. S. Boas, quoted in the *London Education Service*, p. 91,
L.C.C., 1927.

Greater emphasis on the English language was also seen as the most suitable means of raising the general cultural level of intending teachers. In 1907 it was estimated that between 1,400 and 1,500 newly trained and certificated teachers would be needed in the London service every year, and most of these were expected to come from the secondary schools as the old pupil-teacher centres had been abolished.[1] The increased appreciation of English grammar, literature, and elocution was perceived as an important vocational aim of the grammar schools.

> . . . the important change in educational policy by which pupil teachers are being sent to secondary schools, instead of to special "centres" has given increased importance to English teaching in the upper forms of schools,

said the Council's Chief Inspector of Schools in 1907.

> The training of speech and of elocution in the widest sense of the term, has become more vitally important than ever in secondary schools owing to the influx of pupils who are preparing to become teachers,

says a Report a few years later,[2] and continues,

> It is frequently the case that it is these pupils even towards the end of their school life, whose articulation both in speaking and in reading or reciting is most unsatisfactory . . . a number of secondary schools, especially schools for boys, which used to specialize in their higher forms in science and technology, are extending considerably the teaching of languages, literature and history. . . . This movement towards an equal balance of studies in the upper forms of secondary schools has been accelerated by the new regulations under which bursars have for the most part replaced pupil teachers. . . . The curriculum that they have to follow is, though diversified, mainly of a literary character, and the schools of which they are pupils must therefore make their literary teaching as efficient as possible.

[1] Memo of Chairman of L.C.C. Higher Education Sub-Committee on Training College and Secondary School Accommodation, Sept. 5, 1907.
[2] Report of the Chief Inspector of Secondary Schools Aided by the L.C.C., pp. 4–5, 1909–10.

Minor Changes in Curricula

Grammar schools have undergone major social and organizational changes since the days of Morant, student-teachers, and the early scholarship entrants. They now take about one in five instead of one in twenty of the eleven to sixteen age-group. A large proportion of their entrants are now from the working class, and their old middle-class status has been seriously undermined. All fees have been abolished except in a few direct-grant schools. Entry can now be secured only on the basis of winning a competitive examination. In the outside world vast changes have occurred in science and technology, in the structure of business enterprise, and in the organization of government.

In these circumstances it might have been expected that the grammar-school curricula would have been modified to meet the new social and technological conditions. Subjects such as engineering, for example, might have been introduced for pupils entering industry, or a simpler syllabus devised for the large number of pupils (over 30 per cent. in the London area, and about 25 per cent. for the country as a whole) who leave school before sixteen years of age. In fact, surprisingly few changes have taken place in the choice and arrangement of the time-table. The bias remains liberal and academic, there is roughly the same balance of subjects, and the same emphasis on literary rather than technical ability. When the curricula for 1952 of several representative London grammar schools (pages 150–3) are compared with those of 1892 (pages 136–7), the most striking feature is not so much the differences as the similarities. Apart from the *methods* of teaching (which are discussed later) such changes as have occurred have been of a minor character. There is now greater uniformity of curricula in the London grammar schools because of increased centralization of control and wider official agreement about the role of the grammar school;[1] but so

---

[1] ". . . the curriculum of the London grammar school is not the result of impulse or of official pressure, formal or informal. It is the result of a long period of development accompanied, no doubt, by the process of trial and error. . . . Freedom in the secondary school leads to uniformity rather than variety of curriculum; and this is because, if a large number of able, intelligent people (and this is a fair, if inadequate, description of the heads as a whole) consider the premises which their task inevitably presents to them, they will in general arrive at one and the same conclusion . . . if an education which is to include what teachers think right, what inspectors, governing bodies, education authorities and the appropriate Government department also, in general, approve, and what educated parents (and most of the others) tolerate, and might, as to a majority of subjects, even demand, then it is inevitable that the number of subjects taken (until certain other powerful forces begin to operate) cannot fall far short of twelve . . . Scripture, Art, Craft, Physical Education, English,

[*footnote continued on next page*

far as individual subjects are concerned, the alterations have been more changes of emphasis than changes in the choice of subjects themselves.

Religious knowledge is now compulsory under the terms of the 1944 Education Act, and is usually taught for one period a week in all schools. Greek has generally disappeared from the curriculum, except for a few specialists in fifth and sixth forms. Latin (or alternatively German) is almost invariably taught only to the top "streams". English, which is nowadays regarded as the key subject in the time-table, is taught approximately the same number of periods per week as Latin (for top "streams") or French, namely four or five periods. Theoretically, English studies should be given greater prominence in the curriculum; but there is constant pressure for other subjects, such as French, to have the amount of time allocated to them increased because of the difficulty of getting pupils, especially the slower ones, up to the required examination standard. Similarly, teachers of mathematics frequently complain that they cannot cover the advanced syllabus in less than four or five periods per week. Science teachers also often find the time allocated to them insufficient because of the growing complexity of their subject. Incidentally, there is much more emphasis on practical work in chemistry and physics than there was fifty years ago.

In general, the remainder of the time-table is occupied by music and art (two periods each), physical training (two periods) and possibly a handicraft such as woodwork or domestic science for one or two periods. One afternoon a week is devoted to organized games in almost every school. Boys and girls do not differ so much in their curricula as they did at the end of last century, though girls still do slightly less mathematics, physics, and chemistry, and slightly more physical training and biology than boys.

Influence of External Examinations

The lack of flexibility in curricula, and more particularly the persistence in providing advanced academic work for the less able pupils who will leave school at sixteen or even earlier has been blamed by some educationists on the General Certificate and university examinations. The latter, it is said, have helped to "freeze" the curriculum in a mould

footnote continued]
History, Geography, French, Arithmetic, Elementary Mathematics, and Science." (Curriculum of Secondary Schools. Report by Chief Inspector to L.C.C. Higher Education Sub-Committee, 1933.)

CURRICULA OF LONDON GRAMMAR SCHOOLS, 1952

Number of minutes devoted to each subject per week

Owen's (boys)

Form	Eng.	Hist.	Geog.	Fr.	Lat.	Maths	Writ.	Science	Phy.	Bio.	Mus.	Art	Crafts	Dom.Sc.	P.T.	R.K.
								(Gen. Sc.)								
Ia*	280	80	80	—	160	200	40	80	—	—	120	80	—	—	80	40
Ib	280	80	80	—	160	200	40	80	—	—	120	80	—	—	80	40
Ic	280	80	80	—	160	200	40	80	—	—	120	80	—	—	80	40
IIa	240	80	80	160	120	200	—	80	—	—	40	80	80	—	40	40
IIb	240	80	80	160	120	200	—	80	—	—	40	80	80	—	40	40
IIc	240	80	80	160	120	200	—	80	—	—	40	80	80	—	40	40
								(Chem.)								
IIIa	160	80	80	160	160	200	—	80	80	—	40	80	80	—	40	40
IIIb	200	80	80	160	160	200	—	80	80	—	40	80	80	—	40	40
IIIc	200	80	80	160	160	200	—	80	80	—	40	80	80	—	40	40
IVa	200	80	80	160	160	200	—	120	120	—	40	40	40	—	40	40
IVb	200	80	80	160	80	200	—	120	120	—	40	40	40	—	40	40
IVc	200	80	80	160	80	200	—	120	120	—	40	40	40	—	40	40
Va	200	160	160	160	160	240	—	160	160	—	—	—	—	—	40	40
Vb	200	160	160	160	160	240	—	160	160	—	—	—	—	—	40	40
Vc	200	160	160	160	160	240	—	160	160	—	—	—	—	—	40	40

* Forms are "streamed" a, b, and c.

CURRICULA OF LONDON GRAMMAR SCHOOLS, 1952

Number of minutes devoted to each subject per week

Holloway (boys)

Form	Eng.	Hist.	Geog.	Fr.	Lat.	Maths	Ger.	Chem.	Phy.	Bio.	Music	Art	Crafts	Dom. Sc.	P.T.	R.K.
Ia*	220	145	75	185	—	255	—	75 (75)	70	—	40	70	—	—	70	35
Ib	215	105	105	140	—	180	—	80 (75)	70	—	70	70	—	—	70	35
Ic	215	145	110	180	—	215	—	70 (75)	80	—	105	120	—	—	70	35
IIa	180	75	70	175	225	185	—	105	105	—	40	80	—	—	70	40
IIb	190	115	115	190	—	195	40 (Project)	110	110	—	80	110	—	—	70	40
IIc	220	105	110	185	—	180	—	115	105	—	75	70	—	—	110	40
IIIa	200	75	75	185	180	195	—	110	115	—	40	80	—	—	80	35
IIIb	230	105	105	145	—	180	—	115	105	—	80	70	—	—	105	40
IIIc	215	105	105	180	—	175	—	105	105	—	70	70	—	—	110	35
IVa	175	180	105	210	230	215	195 (Germ.)	175	70	—	35	40	—	—	40	35
IVb	175	150	105	180	40	215	40 (Civics)	105	195	—	70	35	—	—	40	35
IVc	180	70	75	180	—	215	—	155	115	—	75	70	—	—	75	35
Va	180	70	145	220	230	180	230 (Germ.)	145	140	—	35	70	—	—	70	35
Vb	220	180	185	215	—	220	—	—	185	—	80	70	—	—	110	35
Vc	210	180	180	220	—	220	—	190	—	—	75	80	—	—	105	35

* Forms are "streamed" a, b, and c. Numbers in brackets represent extra time spent on various subjects by those who do not take up Latin.

CURRICULA OF LONDON GRAMMAR SCHOOLS, *1952*

Number of minutes devoted to each subject per week

Highbury Hill (girls)

Form	R.K.	Eng.	Hist.	Geog.	Fr.	Latin	Maths	Hobbies	Chem.	Phys.	Bio.	Music	Art	Crafts	Dom. Sc.	P.T.
IIIa*	60	200	80	80	200	—	200	60	—	120	—	40	80	—	80	120
IIIb	60	200	80	80	200	—	200	60	—	120	—	40	80	—	80	120
IIIc	60	200	80	80	200	—	200	60	—	120	—	40	80	—	80	120
IVa	40	160	80	80	160	160	200	—	—	120	—	40	80	—	80	120
IVb	40	160 (80)	80	80	160 (40)	160	200	—	—	120	—	40 (40)	80	—	80	120
IVc	40	160 (40)	80	80	160 (40)	160	200	—	—	120	—	40 (40)	80	—	80	120
Up. IVa	40	160	80	80	160	160 (Germ.)	160	60	—	120	—	40	80	—	120	120
Up. IVb	40	160 (40)	80	80 (40)	160 (40)	160	160	60	—	120	—	40 (40)	80	—	120	120
Up. IVc	40	160 (40)	80	80 (40)	160 (40)	160	160	60	—	120	—	40 (40)	80	—	120	120
Va	40	160	120	120	160	160	200	60	—	120	120	120	80	—	120	120
Vb	40	200	120	120	160	—	160	60	—	—	120	40	80	—	120	120
Vc	40	200	120	120	160	—	(40)	60	—	—	120	40	80	—	120	120

* Stream a is top form—b and c are parallel. Numbers in brackets represent extra time spent on various subjects by those who do not take up Latin.

CURRICULA OF LONDON GRAMMAR SCHOOLS, *1952*

Number of minutes devoted to each subject per week

Mary Datchelor's (girls)

Form	R.K.	Eng.	Hist.	Geog.	Fr.	Latin	Maths	Chem.	Phys.	Bio.	Music	Art	Crafts	Dom. Sc.	P.T.
Ia*	80	200	80	80	200	—	200	—	80	—	80	80	—	80	160
Ib	80	200	80	80	200	160	200	—	80	—	80	80	—	80	160
Ic	80	200	80	80	200	160	200	—	80	—	80	80	—	80	160
IIa	80	160	80	80	160	160	200	—	80	—	80	80	—	80	120
IIb	80	160	80	80	160	160	200	—	80	—	80	80	—	80	120
IIc	80	160	80	80	160	160	200	—	80	—	80	80	—	80	120
IIIa	80	160	80	80	160	160	160	—	120	—	80	80	—	120	120
IIIb	80	160	80	80	160	160	160	—	120	—	80	80	—	120	120
IIIc	80	160	80	80	160	160	160	—	120	—	80	80	—	120	120
IVa	80	160	80	80	160	120	200	—	240	—	80	80	—	200	120
IVb	80	160	80	80	160	120	200	—	240	—	80	80	—	200	120
IVc	80	160	80	80	160	120	200	—	240	—	80	80	—	200	120
Va	40 (120)	160	40 (120)	(120)	(160)	(200)	—	—	(120)	—	40 (120)	40 (120)	—	(200)	—
Vb	40 (120)	160	40 (120)	(120)	(160)	(200)	—	—	(120)	—	40 (120)	40 (120)	—	(200)	—
Vc	40 (120)	160	40 (120)	(120)	(160)	(200)	—	—	(120)	—	40 (120)	40 (120)	—	(200)	—

153

* Forms are parallel in each year—no "streaming" in school.

that has proved exceedingly difficult to break. External examinations, it has been argued with considerable justification, largely determine the choice of subjects and the amount of time allotted to them. Headmasters and headmistresses when considering the composition of their time-tables for the year think too often of the requirements of these examinations, and are too prone to assess their year's work solely in terms of the number of Certificates achieved or Open or County Major Scholarships won.

Certainly, the authorities, both national and local, agree as to the powerful influence exerted by external examinations, just as they are concerned at the possible harmful character of that influence:

> One of the main defects to which secondary schools have been liable has been the tendency to shape the whole curriculum of the school according to the requirements of a small number of pupils at the top and to sacrifice the many to the welfare of the few,

says the Spens Report.[1]

> In too many of the older public schools it has been the practice to pay too much attention to the standard required for university scholarships and to frame the work of the bulk of the school with a view to securing the success of a few picked boys, with the result that many a boy who has no likelihood of ever reaching scholarship standard has spent time over grammatical and linguistic details which might far better have been spent on subjects for which he had an aptitude. A similar course of action has too frequently been adopted in the newer secondary schools, though there the dominating force has been not so much a scholarship competition as some less advanced external examination.

> There is some truth in the criticism that a "university objective" is tacitly assumed throughout the course in secondary schools,

says a London County Council Officer.[2]

[1] Report of Consultative Committee on Secondary Education, p. 5 (H.M.S.O., 1938).

[2] "There is nothing wrong in schools having a 'university objective' for the pupils who mean to go to the university. The harm lies in the tendency to press too many pupils into this mould because it is convenient and economical of staff. . . . The university influence is strongly marked in the oldest established school subjects, classics and mathematics. . . . In science . . . the reform of practice still proceeds slowly. In history, also, university influence on both subject matter and teaching is strong. In English, the bias towards the study of texts and insufficient cultivation of the use of English as a tool may be ascribed to a similar cause. In modern languages, too, the influence of the university examinations is evident." (Report of Board of Education on Curriculum and Examinations in Secondary Schools, 1942.)

Education for Social Status

But the General Certificate and university entrance examinations cannot, of course, be held solely responsible for keeping the curricula biased in a particular direction. External examinations, in the last resort, only reflect, and do not determine, the course of study laid down for students to follow. If it were strongly felt that the subjects taught should be altered then there can be no doubt that in time the examinations themselves would be reformed to meet the new circumstances.[1]

Fundamentally, there would appear to be a number of other factors involved in maintaining the balance of the time-table unchanged for so long; and although it is difficult to disentangle the various philosophical, social, and psychological issues concerned, it would seem that there have been two main influences that have effectively prevented the introduction of more technical or "practical" instruction into the grammar schools.

In the first instance, there is a well-organized body of opinion, strongly entrenched in the higher ranks of education, that still holds firmly to the idea of an "educational *élite*" as laid down by Morant and others half a century ago. The primary purpose of the grammar schools, it is argued, is to accept only the most intelligent children, to give them a special education that will prepare them for the universities or other higher institutions, and thus train them ultimately to become leaders in industry, the professions, and administration. For such gifted children, carefully selected by means of elaborate tests at the age of eleven or twelve years, the hard work, painstaking accuracy, and strict mental discipline of the traditional academic curriculum are most suitable. This viewpoint, which was openly adopted in the Norwood Report, and is implicit in the conception of a "grammar-school type" and in the tripartite division of secondary education, accepts that the main aim of the grammar school is to educate children, not basically for cultural or democratic purposes, but for social status. It also implies indirectly that one of the chief aims of the curriculum is to preserve middle-class values. Professor Kandel makes this point succinctly in his important Appendix to the Spens Report:

[1] A striking example of the way in which an examination may be changed to meet new conditions in the schools and outside world is provided by the proposal in July, 1954, to introduce a new examining body for the General Certificate of Education. Designed to meet the needs of pupils taking technical and commercial courses, the new body, known as the Associated Examining Board, will examine in such subjects as building, engineering, electronics, surveying, home management, laundry-work, and laws of commerce.

Secondary (grammar) education as it is generally conceived in the popular mind has come to be regarded as education of the privileged few, as education for status.[1]

People of a more democratic outlook, who sincerely believe in "secondary education for all", have also occasionally allowed themselves to be so influenced by the grammar-school tradition that they automatically think of a bookish, academic education as the best possible. Welcoming enthusiastically the extension of grammar-school facilities to wider sections of the child population, they wish to see what they regard as most valuable in higher education—humane values, appreciation of literature, art, and music, and high intellectual standards—available to everyone. They reject proposals to make the curriculum practical or vocational because of their fear that the syllabus might be diluted or "watered down".

The Trades Union Congress indirectly adopted this point of view when in 1937 it stated:

> School time used for vocational training not only gives a bias to study but takes up valuable time and effort better employed in a wider and more useful field. Moreover, it stamps at an early and impressionable age, the idea of class and inferior status on the scholar, which it is the aim of a noble education to avoid.[2]

Problem of Working-Class Children

To both these groups the influx of larger numbers of working-class children presents a special problem. The advocates of "secondary education for all" warmly welcome the widening of educational opportunities formerly closed to the poorer sections of the community. Even the supporters of the *élite* theory accept that wider sources of talent and ability must be tapped if society is to get the trained administrators, scientists, and "white-collar" workers it needs. Both groups, however, still to a large extent display the old attitude towards scholarship entrants that was so characteristic of the late nineteenth and early twentieth centuries.

[1] Appendix II, Report of the Consultative Committee on Secondary Education, p. 418 (H.M.S.O., 1938).
[2] "Education and Democracy", T.U.C. pamphlet, 1937.

Fifty years ago it was widely feared that the poverty of the homes and the lack of general cultural background of poorer boys and girls would harm traditional grammar-school standards. This attitude was openly expressed before the First World War, and though the scholarship scheme has long since proved a resounding success, and more democratic views prevail about providing grammar-school places for all who can benefit from them, irrespective of income, yet the old class-conscious ideas still linger in many quarters. They may not be so crudely expressed as they were fifty years ago, and are sometimes held unconsciously by persons who pride themselves on their freedom from snobbery; but they undeniably exist, as anyone who has had experience of a modern grammar-school staff-room will agree.

So far as curriculum is concerned, such a viewpoint implies that intelligent middle-class children need an academic education mainly to develop their minds and character, but working-class children, no matter how intelligent, need also to be taught those social refinements that they are not supposed to learn at home. Boys and girls from well-to-do homes may come to school with a certain veneer of culture, but the sons and daughters of manual workers do not, it is argued, have these advantages. It is therefore one of the main tasks of a liberal education to compensate poorer pupils for what they lack at home. In particular, they must learn the social virtues—how to speak nicely, to be well mannered, to wear sober clothes, and to play gentlemanly games such as cricket and Rugby football with proper spirit and enthusiasm. Like the middle-class Philistines of Matthew Arnold's day they need "sweetness and light" as well as material progress in their lives. The poorer their family origins and the greater the talent they show in school the more important it is that they acquire that additional "polish" needed to equip them as future leaders and administrators. They must, in brief, be trained to rise out of their impoverished environment to a higher social class and wider intellectual horizons.

Grammar-school teachers themselves, by reason of their own training and position in society, often help to perpetuate these ideas. Educated mainly in the same type of school as the one in which they teach, and later at a university, and naturally tending to regard the education they received there as a highly desirable one, they frequently see little outside their own narrow sphere of work. Although they may not necessarily have been born into the middle class, they aspire to middle-class cultural values as well as to material comforts. Moulded in the liberal, academic tradition, they have little interest in other more specialized and directly vocational forms of education. They are often ignorant of, and indeed may be unsympathetic to, technical schools. As their own professional progress has been won by passing a series of examinations they regard that as a high form of achievement. They sometimes encourage pupils who might be better suited elsewhere to go to a university because that is the path they know best; and, like the headmasters and headmistresses mentioned earlier, they regard success in the General Certificate or university scholarship examinations as the best proof of the value of their work. In other words, they impose on the children they teach the standards and values of their own occupational and social status.[1]

Briefly to sum up, therefore, it may be said that the traditional nineteenth-century conception of a liberal secondary education, with its stress on academic, particularly literary, training, which was considered most suitable for the small number of children, mainly of middle-class origin, who then went into the grammar schools, has been carried forward almost unchanged into the new circumstances of the twentieth century in which a far larger number of children, including a much higher proportion from the working class, enter these schools.

Norwood and the 1944 Act

The 1944 Education Act, by adopting the Norwood Committee's recommendation of the tripartite system of secondary schools, carried the *élite* theory a stage further.[2] For the first time in English educational history it was officially claimed by a Government advisory committee that the nation's children could be divided into three distinct intellectual categories, and that these could be fairly strictly defined. In the first

---

[1] Mrs. Jean Floud, Reader in the Sociology of Education in the University of London Institute of Education, in a contribution to the volume *Social Mobility in Britain*, writes: ". . . the increasing intake, between the wars, of children from the lower status (working class) categories into the schools which, whatever their exact social composition (this of course varied widely from area to area), traditionally served mainly middle-class social groups, grew up with a distinctive middle-class tradition and were staffed largely by teachers of corresponding outlook and aspirations, presents a fascinating problem in the study of social mobility and assimilation." "Educational Experience of the Adult Population", by J. Floud, p. 108, *Social Mobility in Britain*. (Routledge and Kegan Paul, 1954.)

[2] Professor D. V. Glass, who is one of the greatest authorities in Britain on the subject of social class-structure, says "the 1944 Act . . . so far as social stratification is concerned, is probably the most important measure of the last century". (Introduction to *Social Mobility in Britain*, edited by D. V. Glass, Routledge and Kegan Paul, 1954.)

group was the mentally gifted child, who (in an oft-quoted phrase) is

> ... interested in learning for its own sake, who can grasp an argument or follow a piece of connected reasoning, who is interested in causes whether on the level of human volition or in the material world, who cares to know how things came to be as well as how they are, who is sensitive to language as an expression of thought ... is interested in the relatedness of related things, in development, in structure, in a coherent body of knowledge ... (who) can take a long view and hold his mind in suspense ... (and) will have some capacity to enjoy, from an aesthetic point of view, the aptness of a phrase or the neatness of a proof.[1]

For this admirable academic type, comprising possibly one in six of the population, the traditional grammar-school curriculum, with its emphasis on book-learning, was the most suitable. Ranked below these "high fliers" and separated into two distinct psychological groups were the other five-sixths of the country's children, presumed to be of lower intelligence or of different tastes and aptitudes. For them, the potential hewers of wood and drawers of water, a more technical or practically biased syllabus was regarded as best.

The weaknesses of the Norwood Committee's analysis are manifold, but for the moment we may concentrate on two main defects—renewed emphasis was given to the measuring, grading, and selective aspects of the work of educational psychologists, and the social and vocational implications of the tripartite system were avoided. It is to these two aspects of the curriculum that we must now turn our attention.

Psychological Aspects of the Curriculum

Child psychology is a science that has made striking advances during the last half century.

Intensive research has been conducted into the nature of learning processes, and substantial progress made in improving the techniques and methods of teaching. Schools have become more child-centred, activity methods and "learning by doing" have superseded rote-learning, and class-rooms have become places of creative experience and

[1] *Curriculum and Examinations in Secondary Schools*, p. 2. H.M.S.O., 1943.

purposeful work in a way that was undreamt of in the nineteenth century. The Montessoris and McMillans, Burts and Deweys, Isaacs and Vernons, can pride themselves that children today are not only much happier at school than were their parents and grandparents but are also keener scholars and better balanced human beings.

In secondary schools progress has also been considerable, though not perhaps on such a substantial scale as in primary schools. Formal class teaching may still be the most common method of instruction, but there is an increasing number of teachers who prefer to encourage the initiative of boys and girls. For example, pupils may be persuaded to make their own notes from text-books or library sources rather than to copy direct from the blackboard. In English essay-writing imagination and freedom of expression are encouraged more than formerly. Practical work in chemistry and physics has been greatly developed, the teaching of art and music is less conventional, and there is now more project work in geography and history. The intrinsic value and interest of subjects are stressed, and there is less emphasis on routine and mechanical repetition. Old-fashioned ideas that certain subjects have a special value mainly because of the mental exercise involved are not held so strongly as they were at the beginning of the century.

But despite the deeper understanding of the way in which children's minds grow and develop that has resulted from all these years of research and experiment, further developments in educational psychology as applied to older children have been hindered by the tripartite organization of secondary schools.

So much time has been spent in trying to measure intelligence, and to distinguish between various types of ability in children, that the true functions of child psychology have become obscured. Psychologists have in many cases allowed themselves to be diverted into the blind alley of intelligence testing when they might have been better employed studying the intellectual and emotional growth of children against their environmental background.

Not only has much wasted research been devoted to labelling and cataloguing children into modern, technical, and grammar-school types to suit administrative convenience, but teachers have also been encouraged to think in narrow, compartmental terms.

Moreover, inside the grammar schools teachers have been at great pains further to subdivide and separate pupils into "sets" and "streams". It might have been expected that the grammar schools—being already highly selective—would not need to make allowances for wide differences in intelligence, but this has not proved to be the case. Experience has shown that even within the category of the "grammar-school type" a fairly wide range of attainment exists. This applies particularly to districts that take a high percentage of grammar-school entrants, and also to districts where social conditions vary considerably.

To meet these difficulties, headmasters and headmistresses have evolved the devices of "streaming" and "setting". The usual practice has been to select the top "stream" in the first year on the basis of the Common Entrance examination. Occasionally this grouping into classes of rather similar ability is left until the second year, by which time new entrants should have settled down and their aptitudes become more clearly recognizable. In some schools there may be no "streaming" at all, but generally this can only be done when there has already been an exceptionally rigorous weeding-out at the point of entry, and consequently the great majority of pupils are of a very high standard. Only those schools for which there is a very keen demand for places can afford to be so selective in their choice of pupils.

In most schools in the third, fourth, and fifth years there is frequently the further complication of "setting"; that is, the pupils are again subdivided for special subjects. For example, a girl may be generally good at most subjects, but weak at mathematics, in which case she will be kept in the top "stream" of her year but placed in the bottom "set" for mathematics; or a boy may be weak at most subjects, but have a flair for languages, in which case he goes into the bottom "stream" for general work, but the top "set" for French or German. "Setting" is usually only carried out in those subjects, such as languages and mathematics, that are considered particularly difficult, or in which the speed of progress varies considerably. In the fifth year there is the added complication of the General Certificate examination. It is usual at this stage for pupils to concentrate on a limited number of subjects, and to reduce the number in which a substantial effort is made to seven or eight, or even less. Since the new Certificate regulations have been introduced, enabling pupils to take as many subjects as they like in the examination, there may be a further reduction in the number of subjects studied in the fifth year.

The fact that "sets" cut across "streams" seriously complicates the time-table. Why, then, do headmasters and headmistresses create extra work for themselves in this way? The answer appears to lie partly in a genuine desire to help pupils find the school group whose working pace will most suit them, and partly in the conscious or unconscious belief—arising directly out of the tripartite system and current psychological practice—that the selection, classifying, and labelling of children is somehow good in itself. In other words, the "streaming" that goes on inside a grammar school is merely a continuation of the process that was begun in the primary school and given its most obvious expression in grading the results of the Common Entrance examination.

Undoubtedly, it is the idea of a carefully selected academic "type" or educational *élite* (the "stream" being merely an extension of this theory) that has been a major factor in discouraging plans for broadening the grammar-school curricula.

Vocational Training for "White-Collar" Jobs

Another important factor that has helped to keep the grammar-school bias literary and academic rather than technical or practical has been the need to provide vocational training for a specific group of occupations. Traditionally, of course, the grammar schools gave vocational training for the universities and professions. Their classical and humanistic curriculum was regarded as preparation for the Church, law, medicine, Army, Navy, and Civil Service. That important function has been continued in the present century, and it is expected that most boys and girls who stay at school until they are eighteen or nineteen years of age will go on to a university. Eventually, these advanced pupils hope to get a higher post in the professions, industry, or public administration.

The majority of grammar-school pupils, as pointed out in a previous chapter, do not have such lofty ambitions. After five moderately successful years at school, they are content to leave at sixteen[1] (many, in fact, leave before then) with a sufficient number of passes in their certificate examination to enable them to get reasonably well-paid jobs in a clerical, commercial, or minor professional occupation. At least three-quarters of all grammar-school leavers finish school before the age of seventeen, and the overwhelming majority (the proportion being

[1] The predominance of the 16-year-old leavers may be seen in the following table based on records kept of pupils placed in employment by the Headmasters' (1951) and Headmistresses' (1950) Employment Committees:

Age of pupils taking up employment

			16	17	18 or over	Total
Boys ..	..	..	1,049	333	109	1,491
Girls ..	..	..	1,035	488	336	1,859

even higher among girls than boys) go into "white-collar" jobs. It is the vocational training of the latter group that is one of the main functions of the grammar school, and to which special attention must be paid.

It is surprising, in view of all the evidence to the contrary, to find as late as 1931 such a shrewd observer of the English scene as Professor I. L. Kandel writing:

> The curriculum of the English secondary school is thus determined by the aims and purposes of a general, liberal education, to the exclusion of any consideration of vocational preparation. On this point every class in English society, lay and professional, employers and workers, is agreed.[1]

Six years later, however, the vocational aspects had become so striking that the Spens Report could state:

> ... in reality much of the education described as "liberal" or "general" was itself vocational education for the "liberal" professions.[2]

More recently the London County Council has spoken of the School Certificate course as a "qualification which has been accepted by employers in many black-coated occupations as a sufficient guarantee of suitability for certain types of employment".[3]

Growth of "White-Collar" Occupations

The growth of a wide range of minor clerical, supervisory, administrative, and professional jobs (broadly classified as "white-collar" or "black-coated") has been one of the most remarkable features of the British economy during the last half century.

Commerce has expanded enormously since the 1890s, creating a multiplicity of new jobs as well as a great increase in the number of old ones. Bank clerks were needed in their thousands to deal with the expansion of business caused by the export of capital overseas and by the growth of the City as the centre of the sterling area; shipping

---

[1] *History of Secondary Education*, by I. L. Kandel, p. 363 (Harrap, 1931).
[2] Report of the Consultative Committee on Secondary Education, pp. 66–67 (H.M.S.O., 1938).
[3] Secondary schools—some interim developments. Report of the Higher Education Sub-Committee of the L.C.C., 1947.

agents were needed to handle the huge import and export trade of the Port of London; insurance men were required in large numbers as British insurance companies extended their business all over the world; accountants, buyers, salesmen, typists, clerical supervisors, and office managers were all demanded in ever-growing numbers by the expanding merchant houses, multiple shops, and other enterprises of the great metropolis. Moreover, as Government controls became more numerous with the development of the Welfare State, so an army of officials was recruited for civil and municipal service; and as the number of those who wrote in ledgers, handled correspondence, totalled columns of figures, bought and sold goods, or administered the affairs of State increased, so also multiplied the ranks of those who ministered to their needs in various ways—doctors, solicitors, actors, journalists, pharmacists, estate agents, advertisers, and other professional and semi-professional people.

London, as political capital and centre of the sterling area, was the chief magnet for this accumulation of black-coated occupations.

London stands alone as the greatest commercial centre in the world, and as the heart of the British Empire,

stated a London County Council report on commercial education published in 1899.[1]

London has not only a larger population of "clerks" than any other city in the world, it has probably also a larger proportion of clerks to the whole population than most other cities. Everything which affects British trade must affect London in a special degree, and it is only fitting that any measures which are taken for the defence of our commercial supremacy should be put forward in the first instance by the merchants and citizens of London.

That report was written nearly sixty years ago at a time when the vast proliferation of "white-collar" jobs had not reached its full extent. During this century the trend became accelerated, and by 1931 there were 1,426,000 clerks in England and Wales, of whom 544,000 lived in Greater London.

[1] Report of Special Sub-Committee on Commercial Education. Technical Education Board. Feb. 20, 1899.

It is interesting to note that clerks comprise 13 per cent. of the total occupied population of Greater London, compared with only 7 per cent. for the whole country. A clear result of the concentration in the capital of the main administrative centres for Government departments as well as the head offices of the most important British commercial enterprises,

says Gollan.[1]

The most interesting point in examining this question is the phenomenal growth in the amount of clerical labour for Greater London. The total occupied population for London has increased between the years 1891 and 1931 by 50 per cent., whereas the total number of clerks employed has increased over the same period by no less than 255 per cent.

In 1931, there were nearly five million people out of a total of approximately twenty-one millions occupied in Great Britain who were classified under the headings of commercial, financial, clerical, and professional occupations. London's figures for these occupations were well above the average for England and Wales, as the following table shows:

OCCUPATIONS (MALES) IN 1931 (per 1,000)[2]

	Clerks	Commerce, etc.	Public Administration	Professions
County of London	81	124	13	29
England and Wales	54	100	7	24

It was not only the large number and variety of "white-collar" jobs that appealed to the average boy or girl leaving the London grammar schools. There were also considerable advantages associated with these jobs. Wages, for example, were generally higher than could be earned either by unskilled youth in industry or even by apprentices to a skilled trade. The money that could be earned was usually higher at the starting-point, and prospects were better in the older age-groups. In 1925 the

[1] *Youth in British Industry*, by John Gollan, p. 144 (Gollancz, 1937).
[2] It has already been pointed out that during the last fifteen or twenty years the position has altered somewhat in the central area owing to the migration of the middle and lower middle classes into the suburbs. In practice, however, these developments have not yet affected the grammar-school curriculum to any noticeable extent.

165

average salary of boys leaving London grammar schools at the age of 16–17 (and obtaining employment through the Headmasters' Employment Committee) was £53 per annum, and for ages 18–19 it was £90 per annum. In 1938, the figures were £60 and £86 per annum respectively.[1] These figures compare with the £30–£45 per annum earned by the typical leaver aged 14–15 from elementary or central schools in the 1920s. Women shorthand-typists and clerks (many of whom were recruited from grammar schools) earned in 1931 an average of 50*s.* per week in public services, and 55*s.* in banking and insurance, as compared with the 25*s.* to 35*s.* that was the most that women factory workers could hope to earn.

There was also greater security in "white-collar" employment. In contrast to the chronic unemployment experienced in many industrial jobs, the "white-collar" occupations were expanding. There was some cyclical unemployment in the City of London, but nothing in the way of the structural unemployment of, for example, South Wales coal-mining, Lancashire cotton, or Durham shipbuilding. In the early 1930s, when the great depression was at its worst phase, London (and more particularly the middle-class suburbs in Kent, Surrey, Middlesex, Herts, and Essex) had a lower rate of unemployment than the country as a whole.[2]

The non-manual jobs usually also had better working conditions in the way of shorter hours, holidays with pay, more comfortable and hygienic offices, and improved recreational facilities. The consequence of all these advantages was an increased social status for the non-manual jobs. A secondary consequence was the higher social status of the grammar schools, which were the main path of entry for these occupations. Indeed, for poorer parents who were ambitious for their

---

[1] Reports of Headmasters' Employment Committee for various years.

[2] Non-manual occupations also had lower records of unemployment than manual occupations as may be seen from the following figures:

PERCENTAGE OF MALES OVER 14 UNEMPLOYED IN 1931
(ENGLAND AND WALES)

Non-manual		*Manual*	
Commerce and finance	7·2	Shipbuilding	41·7
Public admin., etc.	8·3	Mining	17·9
Professions, etc.	3·3	Steel	26·6

In July 1936 the percentage of persons unemployed in London and S.E. England was approx. 6 per cent. as compared with an average of approx. 13 per cent. for the U.K. *The Condition of Britain*, by G. D. H. and M. Cole, p. 224 (Gollancz, 1937).

sons and daughters to move to a "higher station in life" the grammar schools were almost the only means by which they could achieve this ambition.

Vocational Aspects in the 1890s

The vocational aspects of the grammar-school curriculum were widely recognized at the turn of the century when the new State-controlled system of secondary school was taking shape. For example, in 1897 the Incorporated Association of Headmasters stated:

> The aim of secondary schools is to provide more extended courses of study (*a*) adapted to higher commercial, scientific or professional requirements; (*b*) varying according as they are planned to terminate normally at seventeen or nineteen.[1]

In the same year the Assistant Masters' Association unanimously agreed, at their general meeting, that secondary schools should provide "curricula adapted to professional, scientific, mercantile and higher industrial requirements, or those of the public services".

In 1899 the London County Council Education Committee received a report that is of great significance, because it stated in the plainest possible manner the close connection that existed between the established secondary schools, education for commerce, and the necessity of meeting foreign business competition. In the 1870s and 1880s informed opinion had regarded *technical* education as one of the best means of meeting foreign competition, but in the 1890s the emphasis had apparently shifted to commercial education.[2] The Report stated:

> The great increase of foreign competition which has been felt by those engaged in almost every branch of commerce and manufacture has aroused a widespread feeling of alarm in the community. . .
>
> It is becoming more and more clear that among the principal causes which are threatening us with a grave diminution of international trade must be placed the better education enjoyed by our competitors . . . the German nation is aroused . . . widely and

---

[1] Scheme for the organization of Secondary Education, I.A.H.M., 1897.
[2] This was probably a reflection of the general change in economic emphasis from industry to trade.

energetically . . . to the necessity of commercial education as an important factor in their newly developed competition with other trading nations. . . .[1]

In view of the importance given to commercial education by the London County Council at this time, the decision of the Council to reject decisively the idea of setting up separate secondary commercial schools (as had been proposed) and to include commercial education in the ordinary grammar-school curriculum was of exceptional importance. It showed that the Council henceforward regarded the grammar school as the best type of school to train large numbers of efficient clerks, salesmen, and accountants, who were needed for commerce. Thus, only a few years before the 1904 regulations, which were supposed to "liberalize" the grammar-school curriculum and divert it from dangerous tendencies towards technical and scientific education, a definite vocational bias towards commercial occupations was given.

It was equally significant that in the voluminous evidence given to the Council at this time the teaching of subjects that were considered necessary for success in commerce were precisely those encouraged by the 1904 regulations.[2]

A large number of witnesses, representing a variety of occupations in London, were called to give evidence before the Committee reporting on commercial education. They were almost all unanimous in the type of education they required in their non-manual employees.[3]

For example, a building contractor reported:

The best type of boy for a business such as this was one who had been well-grounded in reading, writing, and arithmetic, was quick at figures and could write a grammatical letter. . . .

An engineering Company suggested that:

The most important subjects for those intending to enter upon the engineering trade were—mathematics (quick figuring, especially decimals), drawing, shorthand and typewriting, book-keeping, commercial geography, French, German, letter composition.

---

[1] Report of Special Sub-Committee on Commercial Education, p. 11 (Technical Education Board, 1899).

[2] ". . . the demands made upon the secondary schools were for clerks and school teachers rather than artisans or even technologists".—Dr. O. Banks in "Concept and Nature of the Grammar School in relation to the development of Secondary Education since 1902", Ph.D. thesis, University of London, 1953.

[3] Report of Special Sub-Committee on Commercial Education. (Technical Education Board, 1899.)

The P. & O. Shipping Co. said that what was required of those entering the service was:

> Good writing and spelling, figuring and composition. Shorthand, foreign languages, practical arithmetic, general principles of book-keeping and commercial geography.

A City accountant required:

> ... the essentials of good education, viz. spelling, writing, short-hand, arithmetic (especially quick costing and decimals) book-keeping, commercial geography, German, French, elementary Latin and shorthand as a training in correspondence.

An insurance company said:

> For practical commercial business life, what was wanted was that a boy should write well and rapidly, be well grounded in arithmetic, and be quick at figures, and if possible know foreign languages.

In other words, the London business community (which was then very strongly represented on the Council) was quite clear about what it required in its "white-collar" employees—the capacity to write neatly, spell, punctuate, and compose grammatical letters, to be quick and accurate at figures, possibly to be able to correspond in a foreign language, and also to be conscientious and well behaved.

Mr. Hoare, the banker, summed it up when he said:

> ... all that is required of clerks is reading, writing, arithmetic, and some manners and a little intelligence.

Vocational Requirements in Character and Personality

The conception of the grammar-school curriculum propounded by Morant and his associates in the first decade of the twentieth century was, as has been already pointed out, on an altogether loftier plane. Vulgar commercial and vocational ideas were as vehemently rejected as narrow technical considerations. Emphasis was put on higher intellectual matters, the training of character, and the development of personality.

Traditionally, of course, the grammar schools, like the public schools, had always prided themselves that they taught other values as well as the ordinary subjects of the curriculum. The inculcation of good manners, the building of character, training in speech, encouragement of initiative, development of self-discipline, honesty, loyalty, and team spirit—these were the virtues that the grammar schools consciously set out to foster. It was more than coincidental that those virtues suited so exactly the vocational requirements of the professional, administrative, and commercial world during the opening years of this century.

An official Council Report[1] of a slightly later period (1917) so clearly and unambiguously develops this theme that it is worth quoting at length. It concerns girls of fifteen to sixteen years about to leave grammar schools, but it might just as well apply to boys placed in a similar situation.

Take a girl of fifteen who does not desire to enter the teaching profession or to take up any other profession or career which calls for continued study after the matriculation stage . . .

The parents of this girl would probably like to keep her at the secondary school where she is gaining benefit from the life, is making friends and rising to a position of responsibility. But they may feel that they are bound to make some provision for preparing her for earning her living in the commercial world, and as matters stand at present, they frequently are led to cut short her school life and send her to an institution which avowedly sets itself, not to develop character, social responsibility and all-round growth, but to produce definite results in the individual pupil within a definite time.

The experience of the school cited above shows that it is possible to satisfy parents such as those referred to, by giving the girls preparation for livelihood and yet at the same time to keep them under the influences of their own school, which aims at giving them preparation for life. The girl can combine a study of shorthand with a place in her hockey team, and practice in typewriting with the duties of a school prefect . . .

It should be borne in mind that the intensive courses here proposed are avowedly suggested for the purpose of meeting a definite need in the business world, viz. the need for shorthand-typists. Recent experience has shown how great this need is. What

[1] Draft report by the Education Officer to the Higher Education Sub-Committee of the I..C.C., 1917, pp. 16–17.

the head of an office usually looks for is an assistant who can, from the first day of entering the office, take down correspondence and type it clearly and intelligently, who will have good manners, be dignified in behaviour and will fit in readily with office discipline. In this branch of work employers are not looking for assistants with a general knowledge of the commercial world, or of the particular organization of one part of it; they are not seeking for assistants who will rise to superior and responsible positions. These should, as a rule, be looked for in the ranks of the secondary school pupils who stay at school till eighteen years of age, or who go to the university or some higher commercial college. The shorthand-typist may rise to a position of confidential clerk or of foreign correspondence officer, especially if possessed of a good working knowledge of foreign languages. But, speaking generally, the main demand is for ordinary shorthand and typewriting and the qualities looked for are those referred to above. Few will deny that the wider outlook, the sense of corporate life and disciplined responsibility are more likely to be found in those who have had the full benefit of life at a secondary school, and that, if to these qualities can be added (as has already been proved possible) the technical aptitudes that the business world demands, the result will be better both for the community at large and for the individual employer.

Could anything be clearer than the qualities required in this Report? The virtues of "wider outlook, the sense of corporate life and disciplined responsibility" are taught in grammar schools, and are also invaluable in commerce. As for specific subjects: " . . . the girl can combine a study of shorthand with a place in her hockey team, and practice in typewriting with the duties of a school prefect". To succeed in the office the employee must be able to take down correspondence and type it clearly and intelligently, and also possess "good manners, be dignified in behaviour . . . and fit in readily with office discipline". In other words, the very qualities that the grammar schools fostered and commercial enterprise required were not unlike.

Industry and the Curriculum

The way in which this marked bias towards "white-collar" jobs has to some extent been modified in recent years has already been described in a previous chapter. The growing importance of science and technology in the outside world, and the wider range of opportunities available for grammar-school leavers in industry have encouraged larger numbers of pupils to seek work as scientists, technicians, or even craftsmen rather than as clerks or administrators. It has been pointed out how the proportion of leavers classified as "apprentices and technicians" has risen to about one-third of the total.

The new circumstances confronting the grammar schools as a consequence of these developments, particularly the need for a more technically biased curriculum in secondary schools, have not yet been as widely appreciated as they should, but already there are signs of mounting criticism of the traditional vocational role of the grammar and independent schools. This new approach can be seen in such events as the setting up of the Public Schools Appointments Bureau, which has the object, among other things, of attracting the best talent from independent schools directly into industry; in the creation of a new examining board for the General Certificate of Education primarily concerned with technical and practical subjects in the curriculum; in the publication by influential newspapers such as *The Times* and the *Manchester Guardian* of special supplements on careers in industry directed towards the grammar and public schools; and in many speeches by prominent politicians and industrialists emphasizing the need for closer links between grammar and technical schools. These speeches, which have been mainly a post-war phenomenon, are so numerous and so bluntly phrased that they can hardly be ignored. Some typical examples are given below.

A former Minister of Education, addressing the Conference of the Assistant Masters' Association in 1951 said:

Another factor in the changed attitude towards grammar schools is the increasing status, in terms of income and position, of the technical and manual worker as compared with the black-coated and white-collar worker. This change is removing one of the reasons which used to attract parents to the grammar school, and we should be foolish to ignore it. . . .[1]

A distinguished industrialist and educationist, Dr. P. Dunsheath, speaking at a recent conference on the grammar school stressed the

[1] George Tomlinson, M.P., at the Annual General Meeting of the A.M.A., January, 1951.

importance of the relations between grammar schools and industry. He said:

> Industry needed the better type of sixth form leaver who at present was inclined to think only in terms of the university and a professional career ... there was a constant call for more technologists and highly educated men, and women, in many branches of industry ... the demand for technicians and men of character and ability in industry was limitless.[1]

A famous aircraft manufacturer, Sir Frederick Handley Page, was even more forthright in his view on the necessity for a reorientation of grammar-school education and a closer relationship between grammar and technical schools. His words were so important that they are worth quoting at length.

Addressing the annual meeting of the Union of Lancashire and Cheshire Institutes at Chester on "The place of education in an Industrial Age", he said:

> The challenge to educationists was to resolve the false antithesis of technical education on the one hand, and an out-of-date view of liberal education on the other. A new society and an increasingly industrial age demand changes in our whole attitude to the content and method of education. The flow of technicians, applied scientists and technologists into industry needed to be much broader than at present. The universities, technical colleges, and schools must in future all make a greater contribution. Our educational system, like the Army fighting the next war with the weapons and lessons of the last in hand and mind, clung to its ancient forms and its snobbish interpretation of a liberal education as one devoted to the dead languages and the arts, and if the study of science was just respectable, technology was appropriate only to the second best.
>
> Many educationists were still out of step with the world as it was, and ostrich-like found educational value only in the traditional knowledge of the cultured country gentleman. In every walk of life, whether in the professions, the Civil Service, industry or commerce, science and technology were playing an increasing part. Our educational system must take cognizance of that and adapt itself to include the necessary training to fit the new conditions.

[1] Report of Conference on the Grammar School in English Education Today, pp. 18–19 (Institute of Education, London, July-August 1952).

That did not mean that our universities were to turn out streams of technicians and technologists and abandon their traditional subjects. It did demand, however, a complete and honest acceptance of the fact that if we were to live, let alone live more abundantly, we must secure the possibility of our living at all. The real problem was that of a complete revolution in our educational thinking. There was the superlatively difficult task of training the necessary flow of scientists, researchers, applied scientists and technologists, while preserving all that was worth while in our inherited culture.[1]

Need for Broader Approach

The fact that it is the politicians and industrialists, rather than educationists, who are calling so energetically for more technical education in secondary schools is significant. It confirms a previous conclusion that teachers and educational administrators may often fail fully to appreciate the way in which environmental influences may affect their schools, and that forms of school organization may become outdated by social and technological progress in the world outside. As suggested above, the blame for the failure of the grammar schools to move with the times, and the reason why research into broader philosophical, social, and vocational aspects of secondary-school curricula has been discouraged, undoubtedly mainly lies with the tripartite system and the way of thinking that supports it.

Not only has the division into modern, technical, and grammar schools tended to "freeze" the traditional school time-table into a rigid mould, but it has also made for stereotyped thinking, and an inflexible, or sometimes even prejudiced, approach to educational problems. Philosophically, there is still confusion and disagreement about the function of secondary schools in society, and no compromise has yet been reached between those who lay most stress on training an *élite* and those who emphasize the importance of secondary education for all. The sociological aspects of the curriculum have been virtually ignored, with the result that significant social changes, such as the development of the Welfare State or important advances in sciences and technology, have not yet been sufficiently reflected in the subjects taught at school. Very little investigation, for example, has been made into the problem of whether the grammar-school syllabus should be

[1] Reported in *The Times Educational Supplement*, Oct. 10, 1952.

174

adapted to make allowances for changes in child population or in class structure, or for the new technical needs of industry. Too often curriculum problems have been treated as though schools were isolated from their social environment, and children separated from their family background. The political and economic forces that have shaped curricula in the past are frequently regarded as though they were static, and not dynamic. The grammar schools especially are considered as though they had not changed with regard to organizational form or type of entrant since Morant's day.

That some authorities are aware, even if somewhat vaguely, of the need for a broader and more socially biased approach to the problem of curriculum is shown by certain official references to the question. The Spens Report, for example, says:

> The real root of the problem which confronts us today is probably to be found in the increasing complexity of the political, economic and social background of modern life and the rapid growth of knowledge which makes ever fresh demands on the schools and teachers.[1]

And a recent report by the National Union of Teachers says:

> We are living in a time of rapid change when it is difficult to distinguish clearly the essential elements of the common culture. Changes in the political, economic, and social forces which shape our life are so rapid that a lag occurs between the impact of these forces and the necessary modification of our thought and practice to meet them. Further, man's knowledge and skill have advanced more rapidly than the spiritual attributes and scale of values by which his control of natural forces is given purpose and direction. ... Consequently, an important task of the school today is to help the coming generation to apply its mental, spiritual and moral powers as effectively as possible to the complexities of modern life.[2]

But though they may increasingly agree about the importance of such environmental factors, the authorities have too often failed to face up to the difficulties confronting them, possibly because they are

[1] Report of the Consultative Committee on Secondary Education, p. 2 (H.M.S.O., 1938).

[2] "The Curriculum of the Secondary School", p. 2. A report by a Consultative Committee of the N.U.T., 1952.

175

N

too hidebound by routine and convention, but more probably because they are reluctant to face the political and social issues involved.

It is one of the great advantages of the comprehensive-school proposals that they should shake educationists out of their traditional grooves of thought, and stimulate new ideas about curricula in the three types of secondary school. The tripartite system has encouraged narrowness of outlook and routine thinking, and now that it is being challenged the opportunity arises for a revaluation of subjects taught in schools in all their manifold aspects—philosophical and sociological as well as cultural and psychological.

Chapter 7

THE GRAMMAR SCHOOL
IN A CHANGING SOCIETY

Secondary education must, for every individual, be a liberal education, ministering to three main types of interest—cultural interests for the enrichment of personal leisure, vocational interests in preparation for the successful gaining of a livelihood, and community interests leading to a responsible participation in the duties of citizenship.—Report of the L.C.C. Education Committee, July 19, 1944.

An education system based on a social class system would be contrary to the spirit of democracy; and democracy itself is naturally jealous of anything which even seems to suggest or resemble special treatment of a privileged class.—Report of the Board of Education, 1908–9, p. 44.

THE history of the London grammar schools during the last fifty years provides a remarkable example of the influence of environment upon education, and vice versa. School and society affected each other in so many subtle and important ways as to make it difficult, when estimating the various forces that shaped a particular idea or plan, to decide when the influence was primarily pedagogic, and when mainly social or political. At every stage in the development of its educational policy the London County Council was compelled to modify its theories—particularly in the organization of its secondary schools—by new economic and scientific trends that may appear, at first sight, to have had little to do with education. Similarly, the actual working of the secondary-school system powerfully influenced the type of society from which that system sprang. This was as true fifty years ago, when experiments in State-controlled grammar schools began, as it is today, when comprehensive schools are becoming a practical reality in certain parts of London.

When, in 1904, the London County Council assumed responsibility for the grammar schools within its area the facilities offered were totally inadequate to meet the growing needs of the population.

N*   177

Only about one child in twenty went to a secondary school, and out of that small number the great majority came from middle or lower middle-class homes. Working-class children, particularly the sons and daughters of very poor parents, were woefully under-represented in the grammar schools. Scholarships were few and unevenly distributed, and there was no comprehensive and centrally planned scheme whereby the intelligent children of parents unable to pay fees could proceed to higher education. The inadequacy of the scholarship provision could be measured by the fact that in 1890 there were less than 1,000 awards available for more than half a million children of secondary-school age living in London. Fifteen years later, only about one child in every seven attending aided secondary schools was a scholarship entrant. The position was worse in the independent schools.

Geographically, the schools were maldistributed because of the historical circumstances in which they had developed. Some areas in London, such as the City and Westminster, had more school places than were then needed, whereas areas near the County boundary were gravely short of places. Girls were particularly badly provided with opportunities for getting into secondary schools on account of the traditional prejudice against girls' education, which was only just beginning to be broken down at the end of the nineteenth century. The organization of the grammar schools was in a chaotic state because they still hung midway between the private enterprise and charity stage of the nineteenth, and the State aid and control stage of the twentieth century. There was an extraordinary variety of organizational forms and nomenclature in the schools, resulting in confusion as to their precise role and function. Generally, fees and endowments, which varied widely from school to school, were the main source of income. A small and unreliable trickle of money had been coming from various national and local-government sources, but it was quite insufficient to meet the rapidly growing demands being made upon it. Some higher grade schools were actually getting money illegally, as the Cockerton Judgment proved in 1899. This failure to provide proper State assistance resulted in out-of-date buildings, poor equipment, and badly paid staff. Finally, there was no provision for non-academic secondary schools, except for the higher grade levels of the elementary schools; and these were effectively killed by the Cockerton decision.

London at the turn of the century, therefore, though it was not, in this regard, much worse off than the rest of the country, lacked in practically every respect an efficient system of secondary schools.

L.C.C. Aid to Grammar Schools

After the passing of the 1902 Education Act, the old London School Board, which had been functioning for over thirty years, was abolished, and the London County Council became responsible for secondary as well as primary education. In 1904–5 the Council began preparing its long-term plans to introduce order and system where previously there had been confusion in the secondary schools. The basic principles adopted by the Council for the grammar schools were fairly clear from the beginning, and did not alter fundamentally until the Second World War.

The first task was to increase the number of grammar-school places as rapidly as possible by building new schools, and by giving substantial aid to old ones. An ultimate target of ten places per thousand population was agreed upon. It was proposed to remove the geographical anomalies, to give girls equal opportunities with boys, and to introduce a comprehensive and greatly enlarged scholarship scheme. Large sums of money were made available for improved buildings, better equipment, and higher pay for teachers. It was agreed that the curriculum in the new schools should remain liberal and academic in its bias, and that technical education should be conducted separately.

Lastly, the Council accepted by implication, even if it was not openly proclaimed, that the main role of the grammar school was to provide education for social status and a particular group of occupations. The new maintained schools were to imitate the old endowed schools in so far as they were socially or intellectually selective, and were to be kept distinct from whatever type of less privileged or more practically biased secondary schools that might develop later.

Gradually, over a period of years, these ambitious and far-reaching plans of the London County Council were put into effect. Between 1905 and 1927, for example, twenty-seven new grammar schools were opened or taken over by the Council. By obtaining substantial financial aid the endowed schools were enabled considerably to increase their number of places. During the period from 1905 to 1914, the number of grammar-school places rose from 15,000 to 18,000; by 1919 it had reached 29,000, and by 1938—34,000. In 1949 there were approximately 13,000 pupils attending twenty-seven maintained, and 22,000 pupils attending fifty-two aided grammar schools in London. During the same period the number of children aged from eleven to fifteen years

179

inclusive fell from about 500,000 to 216,000, and thus by the combined effect of a falling child population and a rising number of school places the original target of ten places per thousand population was reached, and indeed surpassed. This progress may be expressed in another way by stating that in 1900 about one London child in every thirty-four of the appropriate age-group went to a grammar school, in 1920 it was one in seventeen, in 1938 one in eight, and in 1950 one in five.[1]

A second major development in grammar-school policy was the "democratizing" of the schools. Fifty years ago the grammar schools were mainly the preserve of professional people, businessmen, shopkeepers, clerks, and other members of the well-to-do classes. At the beginning of the century, for example, it was estimated that the middle and lower middle classes comprised about one-sixth of the population of London, but supplied two-thirds of the grammar-school entrants. On the other hand, the skilled and semi-skilled workers, who comprised about one-half of the population, supplied less than one-third of the entrants. The position was even worse with the unskilled workers, who comprised one-third of the population, but supplied less than one-twentieth of the entrants. In 1906, out of approximately 15,000 children attending aided grammar schools less than 2,000 were scholarship winners; and most of the latter were children of artisans, clerks, shopkeepers, etc., and not the sons and daughters of the very poor, for whom the scholarships were, to a large degree, intended.

In 1905, however, the London County Council expanded its Junior County Scholarship scheme, which had first been developed on a small scale in the 1890s, and from then on an average of nearly 2,000 scholarships were awarded every year. Gradually, the proportion of fee-payers diminished, and by 1919 they had fallen to two-thirds of the total. By the outbreak of the Second World War the number had fallen to less than half, and eventually under the terms of the 1944 Education Act all fees in aided and maintained grammar schools were abolished completely—a revolutionary step that had hardly been envisaged by the pioneers of reform in the 1900s.

Simultaneously, there occurred a number of other social and educational changes that helped to speed the process of "democratizing" the schools. In the first place, the middle classes were moving out of many parts of central London, with the result that more and more areas were becoming proletarianized. At the same time the living

[1] See further discussion of this point in an article entitled "London Grammar Schools: Changes in Population", *The Times Educational Supplement*, Sept. 9, 1952.

standards of the working class were steadily rising as the Labour movement exerted pressure for higher wages, improved housing, better health services, more family allowances, and other benefits of the Welfare State. Economically, the poorer members of the community were no longer so depressed, and politically they exerted greater influence in national and local affairs. The primary schools, in which the vast majority of children were educated, improved sufficiently to enable poorer children to compete on more equal terms with their privately educated rivals. All these factors combined to bring about a transformation in the social structure of the grammar schools, so that by the 1950s they were taking a much larger proportion of working-class pupils into their ranks.

Culturally, the grammar schools spread knowledge and enlighten-ment through broad sections of the community that had previously had little opportunity to appreciate the riches of art, literature, and music. Vocationally, they served a most essential function in preparing large numbers of boys and girls for the rapidly growing "white-collar" occupations. Commerce, public administration, the professions, and science could not have expanded as they did in Britain during the last fifty years without the steady supply of trained and qualified fifth- and sixth-formers from the grammar schools.

Criticism of the Tripartite System

But, successful though the schools might be in their enlarged role of spreading "sweetness and light" where darkness had reigned before, or of increasing the supply of young men and women for the middle classes, nevertheless, as political and economic circumstances altered, they ceased to an increasing extent to fulfil the broader social and technical needs of society.

During the 1930s and the Second World War, it had already become apparent that the successful development of secondary education was hindered by the tripartite division into grammar, technical, and modern schools. The more far-sighted educationists had for long argued that it was undesirable (as well as impracticable) to try to separate the academic from the supposedly non-academic children at the early age of eleven. It was bad for the community, as well as definitely harmful to the children concerned, to divide pupils, as the Norwood Committee did, into grammar, technical, and modern types. The tripartite division

181

arose out of historical circumstances, and could not be justified on psychological grounds.[1] It was absurd for anyone, no matter how expert with measuring devices, to try to prophesy exactly how a child would develop in later life. The practical difficulties of selection and diagnosis at such an early age were enormous, and could never be overcome.

Furthermore, it was illogical to argue in favour of providing a separate education for an intellectual *élite*—which is the main theoretical vindication of the grammar school—when that *élite* varied so much in size from place to place, and at different periods of time. How could psychologists claim accurately to distinguish the grammar from the non-grammar type when one county took over 40 per cent. of its elementary pupils into the grammar schools, and another less than 10 per cent. Was it not official policy to fill all available grammar-school places, irrespective of changes in local child population? And did this policy not seriously invalidate the whole theory of selection?

Moreover, even after the selection process had been carried out, and the best pupils creamed off, the grammar schools were still not serving the community to the best possible advantage. The curriculum was criticized because it was too bookish and literary. It remained academic and liberal in its bias when the country wanted more applied scientists, technologists, and skilled craftsmen. The grammar school tried to maintain its traditional scholarly standards although a far higher proportion of the child population attended such schools; it kept its middle-class values at a time when ever larger numbers of working-class boys and girls were joining its ranks.

It was influenced too much by the requirements of the Certificate and university entrance examinations, although an appreciable number of pupils never sat (or alternatively failed to pass) the Certificate examination, and only a small minority went on to a university.

All these criticisms have been made with varying degrees of relevance and cogency during the last fifteen or twenty years. Since the Second World War the grammar schools have been further criticized on the grounds of their vocational function, in which respect their record has hitherto been considered by most educationists as irreproachable.

---

[1] "The tripartite arrangement of Grammar, Technical, and Modern schools must not be accepted as if it were the result of experiment; it is, of course, something of which we have experience, but which reflects the social origins of each type of school rather than any educational principle. It reflects, in fact, and tends to perpetuate, a social hierarchy." "The Comprehensive School", p. 7, a pamphlet published by the English New Education Fellowship.

Reference has already been made to the attack by industrialists on the conventional liberal curriculum and on the bias towards clerical and professional occupations in the grammar schools. Politicians, scientists, and others concerned with the economic future of the country have, in recent years, strongly developed this theme, claiming that too many pupils leave before the age of sixteen, thus wasting the public's money, and that too high a proportion of all leavers go into "white-collar" jobs, when in many cases they would have been better off both from their own and their country's point of view, going into manual or technical jobs.

The grammar schools, it is said, developed in more spacious political and economic circumstances, and grew out of the needs of a relatively cultured and leisured middle class. Their curriculum was designed more for the classical and literary tastes of country gentlemen or well-to-do professional people than for the technicians and applied scientists who are needed in the harsher economic atmosphere of today. Traditionally, the secondary schools were biased too much towards the parasitic administrative and distributive occupations, and this could no longer be afforded at a time when the best talent was needed in production.

It is revealing to see how two commentators—whose views about other aspects of education sharply diverge—are agreed as to the validity of this criticism (even to the extent of using the same phrase about "fat" years), The Right-wing *Times Educational Supplement* wrote:

> . . . liberal educational ideals found their most compelling form in an age when the conditions of life were very different from our own . . . the fat years are over, the lean are before us. It will be hard work keeping going at all on the British Isles in the later years of this century. . . . For the basis of our power we shall depend on our technical inventiveness and adaptability and our commercial skill; for our influence abroad we shall depend as much on the maintenance of our civilized culture, including our political institutions. It is to that appreciation of the situation that education should conform and contribute. The most obvious consequence of this view is that much more should be made of scientific and technical education.[1]

The Left-wing *New Statesman and Nation* commented as follows:

[1] *The Times Educational Supplement*, p. 1, Jan. 1, 1953.

... the pattern of our educational system was cut out for a social system that is fast disappearing. In the heyday of our Imperialistic success, we lived on the fat of Britain's lead in industry, met foreign competition by depressed wages, let our industrial technique stagnate, and built up an army of white-collar administrators. Our middle- and upper-class schools were designed as recruiting centres for that army; they continue to furnish an annual squad of recruits trained to non-creative functions. The result is an enervating frustration among the growing number of clerks, Civil Servants and other "parasitical" professions, in which a declining capitalism abounds. If Britain is to survive, it needs another economic revolution; it needs new industries and techniques; above all, it needs to place a majority of its working population in productive occupations. This cannot be done without a vast increase in technological education; but such a change must have a social dynamic.[1]

This theme was again strongly taken up by various speakers during a House of Commons debate on education. Speaking on behalf of the Labour Party, Mr. Chuter Ede, a former Parliamentary Secretary to the Minister of Education and one of the architects of the 1944 Education Act, said:

Unless we improve the quality of our technical education and the number of students who participate in it, and give it an appropriate place in the education firmament, this country is doomed. We have to live by the creative genius of our designers and by the skill of our craftsmen. Greek poems do not rank very high in the export market, and the man who wants to write Greek poems, if he wants to live in this country, will only do so because other men design, get, make and carry goods. There must be no doubt about that when we get down to the ultimate things of life, and for as long as we can foresee, it will be the success of our technical education that will determine our standard of life. . . . I want particularly to emphasize what (was said) . . . about technical instruction in grammar schools. It is quite wrong to think that in our great industries we want the second-best brains. Not merely in management but on the practical side of industry we want the best brains that can apply themselves to the practical problems that are involved in the carrying on and improvement of our historic industrial processes.[2]

[1] *New Statesman and Nation*, p. 26, Jan. 10, 1953.
[2] Speech by Mr. Chuter Ede in the House of Commons, July 26, 1954.

London Plan for Comprehensive Schools

The London County Council, which is responsible for nearly eighty grammar as well as some hundreds of other secondary schools working under difficult urban conditions, and which is also under the control of the Labour Party (which supports the comprehensive principle in secondary schools), has for long been aware of the difficulties arising out of the tripartite system of secondary education. It has also been aware of the complicated political, economic, and social factors involved. In 1943, therefore, after considering the Coalition Government's White Paper on Educational Reconstruction and the reports of the Fleming and Norwood Committees, the Council formally placed on record its opinion that the existing three types of secondary school had "emerged as a result of an educational system based far more on social and economic factors than the psychology of children".[1]

> The existing arrangement (of secondary education) in England has not come about as a result of purposeful and conscious planning, but is merely the inevitable outcome of our educational history,

said the Council.[2]

> By no means all children in the grammar and technical schools were the children selected for their native ability and promise . . . what are known as the "B" or "C" or "D" streams . . . do not consist of specially able pupils and the proportion of such children who leave early or who, even if they do not leave early, never get the modest standard represented by their presentation as candidates for the School Certificate examination has been a constant source of

[1] Report of the L.C.C. Education Committee, Dec. 1, 1943.

This viewpoint was not accepted by the Conservative minority party, and since that date there has been an open cleavage between the two political parties on the subject of comprehensive schools. The Conservatives attacked the latter mainly on the ground that they would destroy the grammar schools; and in this argument they have had the support of the Assistant Masters' Association, representing chiefly teachers in grammar and independent secondary schools. In 1954 the Conservative Minister of Education, Miss Florence Horsbrugh, intervened to prevent Eltham Hill School, a London County Council grammar school for girls, being incorporated in the new Kidbrooke comprehensive school. She also stopped another Council grammar school, Bec, from being similarly incorporated in a larger comprehensive unit.

[2] Report of the L.C.C. Education Committee, July 19, 1944, quoted on pp. 210–13, *London School Plan*, published by the L.C.C. in 1947.

disquiet to those concerned with education . . . the (tripartite) system has served the professions and administration rather than industry or commerce, and it cannot be said, that, as a whole, the educational system serves equally well all the activities of the community. . . . The curriculum followed in its general lines the subjects which had become conventional in the nineteenth century, and no great innovations or new conceptions have arisen during this otherwise very important period of expansion. . . . The Norwood Committee's vindication of the tripartite system on psychological grounds . . . was a piece of rationalization and does not profess to be an examination of the system objectively.

In consequence of these criticisms, the Council decided, when it came to prepare its plans for the post-war reorganization of education, to make a radical break with the past, and to introduce a number of comprehensive high schools that would combine the features of grammar, technical, and modern schools in one large unit. This proposal, which was first outlined in 1943, set out in further detail in the London School Plan of 1947, and begun to be put into effect in 1954,[1] had three main objects in view.

Firstly, there was the general philosophical aim of achieving what the White Paper on Educational Reconstruction described as a "more closely knit society". By avoiding sharp social or intellectual divisions in school at too early an age, it was hoped that boys and girls would be better prepared for the duties of citizenship in adult life. It would make for better human and social relations in community life and our industrial democracy if the "managerial class and operatives, the clerical and technical workers, and the skilled and unskilled artisans had a common school background at the secondary stage."[2] It was a matter of prime importance for modern society that "life in school should promote a feeling of social unity among adolescents of all kinds and degrees of ability."[3] There was a "certain corpus of knowledge and experience which all normal children, irrespective of their intelligence quotient or prospective occupation, should have; and one part of this is the knowledge and experience of children of different social

---

[1] Buildings for at least three comprehensive high schools were begun in London in 1953. The first of the new schools, Kidbrooke, was opened in the autumn of 1954.

[2] "The Comprehensive School", a pamphlet published by the English New Education Fellowship.

[3] "The Organization of Comprehensive Secondary Schools", p. 7, a pamphlet published by the L.C.C., 1953.

backgrounds, different aptitudes and interests, and different future vocations."[1]

Secondly, the comprehensive school should have the overwhelming advantage that it would avoid the iniquitous selection test at the age of ten or eleven years, which has for so long been the bane of secondary education. By making the entry truly all-embracing it would no longer be necessary to try to distinguish between different types of intelligence at such an early age, and late developers would be given a better chance to find their proper status in school. Eventually at the age of fourteen or fifteen, when the children's talents and aptitudes were more clearly discernible, a more sensible choice could be made about the pupils' future. Thus, at one stroke a major weakness of the tripartite system would be removed.

Moreover, inside the new school a wide variety of courses could be provided, with an abundance of staff, equipment, and general amenities, which would not be possible in smaller schools.[2] This would have the twofold advantage of ending the present artificial distinction between academic and technical education, and also enable teachers to link their pupils' interests in school more closely to their future occupations. As the English New Educational Fellowship put it:

> Secondary technical education in a Comprehensive School environment is well placed for making a special contribution to educational advance both in theory and practice, in that it should succeed in breaking down the false and mischievous dichotomy between vocational and cultural education. In an industrial society it is preposterous for the public in general, and educationists in particular, to deny cultural significance to the work upon which the life of society depends.[3]

Thirdly, the aim would be to educate and train pupils for the widest possible variety of occupations in industry, commerce, administration, and the professions. During the first three years every child would have a general education as well as physical training and instruction in music, art, and handicrafts. Later, as pupils developed specific talents

---

[1] "Some thoughts concerning the Comprehensive School", by Cyril Bibby, *L.C.C. Education Bulletin*, May 6, 1953.

[2] Comprehensive schools provide "flexibility of organization, varieties of the choice of the subjects which are the vehicles of education, and superior general amenities", (*London School Plan*, p. 221, L.C.C., 1947).

[3] "The Comprehensive School", p. 34 (English New Education Fellowship).

or preferences, there would be increased opportunity for specialization. Thus, from the age of about fourteen years, boys and girls contemplating unskilled manual work might follow a simpler and more practically biased curriculum. Potential manual workers would be given a general education as well as practice in handicrafts; those interested in commerce would be grounded in such subjects as English, geography, history, and mathematics and also have some training in accountancy and office methods; engineers and scientists would have a basic liberal education and then go on to specialized work in laboratories and workshops; possible entrants to the professions would take the traditional grammar-school course for five years, and then go on to the sixth form, and possibly a university. A variety of aptitudes would be encouraged and various skills inculcated. There would be no pigeon-holing of boys and girls for particular jobs at too early an age, and there would be no special vocational bias in the school as a whole, but, rather, differences of approach and emphasis in different departments. The object of the comprehensive school would be to produce artisans and clerks, doctors and labourers, as well as what the London School Plan described as "highly-skilled workers" and "broad-minded technologists".

Secondary Education and the Needs of Society

It is difficult to decide precisely to what extent the plans for comprehensive high schools arise out of the particular conditions of London and to what extent out of the wider social and educational needs of the country as a whole.

Undoubtedly, the London County Council has special problems, such as the shortage of building sites, that compel town planners and architects to think in terms of a few large rather than many smaller schools. The flight of the middle class into the suburbs and the decline in total child population has affected grammar-school intake in both quantity and quality, and there is the added difficulty of providing suitable education in a vast, amorphous community that too often lacks cohesion and civic pride. It is equally true, on the contrary, that demands for "adequate secondary education for all" and the trend to link liberal and technical education more closely together are nation-wide in their significance.

But, however strong the various influences involved (and opinions may differ in this regard), it should at least be clear how fundamentally important are social and environmental factors in the study of London education. The decision to modify such old and revered institutions as the grammar schools and to replace them with schools still largely untried and experimental has not come about, as some critics have suggested, as a result of an educational whim or temporary ideological prejudice, but has arisen inevitably out of the new political, economic, and technical circumstances of recent years. The reforms of half a century ago took place because the old endowed grammar schools were inadequate to serve the expanding needs of the time. Similarly, today in London and other parts of the country, new forms of secondary-school organization are necessary to meet the changing requirements of modern society.

Index